TWO NATIONS

ENDORS

Chaos. Carnage. Confusion. For many, that's the modern Middle East. But Tom Doyle gets it. Better yet, he can really explain it. With a pastor's heart, he clearly and concisely describes why God loves the Jews of Israel and her Muslim neighbors, and why we should, too. What's more, Tom reveals how powerfully God is moving in the modern Middle East, and how we can join Him. *Two Nations under God* is a must read—fascinating, insightful, and deeply thought-provoking. Get one for yourself, and another for your pastor.

JOEL C. ROSENBERG
New York Times best-selling author of
*Epicenter: Why the Current Rumblings in the
Middle East Will Change Your Future*

In *Two Nations under God*, Tom Doyle not only informs but inspires. Hope for the future is rare to find when it comes to the Middle East and Israel. Read this book and be informed not only about the history and political areas but of the witness of Jesus in the lives of people in the Bible lands. Tom helps us find ways to make a real difference and gives good news in troubled times. A must book for this day and time.

ARTHUR BLESSITT
The man who has carried the Cross into every nation of the world.
Guinness Book of World Records for world's longest walk.
Author of *Give Me a J!*

Tom Doyle knows no boundaries. He not only serves on the front line but on the spiritual front line in the Middle East, and has for many years. *Two Nations under God* is an extraordinary book! It looks into the political climate, turmoil, history, and future of the region. This is a must read for anyone hoping to understand why the Middle East is so volatile and what is driving this Holy War today. I am proud to call Tom Doyle a friend and brother in our Lord.

JASON ELAM
All-Pro Kicker for the Atlanta Falcons
Author of *Monday Night Jihad*

When searching for a word to describe the Middle East, most Americans would probably prefer *inscrutable*—"not readily investigated, interpreted, or understood; mysterious." Why is the struggle in the Middle East so hard to understand?

In *Two Nations under God*, Tom Doyle guides the reader through the Middle East maze. He "unscrews the inscrutable"—providing direction, balance, and sanity to an otherwise twisted pathway of claims and counterclaims. But this is no dusty tome. Tom populates the book with stories and illustrations from real people he has met in his travels. He ends by focusing on a profoundly relevant question for those of us living in the United States—"So what?" His call to action applies directly to every true Christian—and congregation—in our country today.

I can summarize the book in three words: *relevant*, *reliable*, and *readable*. This book will change the way you think about—and pray for—the Middle East!

DR. CHARLES DYER
Provost and Dean of Education
Moody Bible Institute

TWO NATIONS
UNDER GOD

TWO NATIONS UNDER GOD

Why You Should Care about Israel

TOM DOYLE

PUBLISHING GROUP

Nashville, Tennessee

ISBN: 978-0-8054-4771-2
B&H Publishing Group
Nashville, Tennessee
www.BHPublishingGroup.com

Dewey Decimal Classification: 956.94
Subject Heading: Israel—History /
Israel—Foreign Relations—United States

Printed in the USA
1 2 3 4 5   12 11 10 09 08

To JoAnn

You are the love of my life.
Thank you for believing in me. I love you!
"Many women do noble things, but you surpass them all."

To Shanna, Tommy, John-Mark, Lindsay, Joshua, and Sarah
You are worth more than treasure to your dad.
May your ultimate treasure in life always be Jesus.

TABLE OF CONTENTS

Section One

Why Should America Care?

Israel is the place, and the Jews are the people whom God promises to love unconditionally forever. But this produces an enormous amount of tension within the region. The nations of the world have been given an opportunity to bless or curse God's chosen covenant people. Their choice decides the health of the nation and determines its destiny. Though modern Israel's existence was off to a shaky start, America made a conscious effort to bless Israel and since that time has enjoyed the promised blessing of God. This has resulted in the United States soaring to the top of the most-favored nation list in all of recorded history.

Chapter 1
Extreme Spirituality

Jerusalem: The Spiritual Epicenter of the World

When measuring the magnitude of an earthquake's impact, the most extreme readings are generated from the focal point commonly known as the epicenter. The earth's underground jolting quickly makes its way up to the surface directly overhead, where the data readings are then evaluated and analyzed, both historically and geographically. If an earthquake is large enough, its seismic waves can be measured all around the globe.

The same kind of thing happens in the spiritual arena. From time to time, when religions clash and new holy wars begin, spiritual earthquakes occur. And without a doubt, the spiritual epicenter of the world is found in the tiny country of Israel—specifically, in the city of Jerusalem.

Out of all the great cities of the world, God chose Jerusalem to reside in and to place His name over forever. As a result, Jerusalem sends out enormous shock waves worldwide on a regular basis. It is and has always been the focal point of all spiritual history throughout the ages. No city has ever received so much attention. No city ever will.

The Anchor City of the Bible

Jerusalem, the capital city of Israel, is mentioned in the Scripture 881 times, and is given at least seventy different names and descriptions from cover to cover. God's love relationship with Jerusalem is seen in the tender words He often uses to address her: "My holy city," "My highest joy," "My holy mountain." Spiritual history has been cataloged here. In Jerusalem. This is where God met with humanity and one day will meet with us again. God is attached to this city—this Holy City—forever.

Notice how Yahweh feels about Jerusalem:

I have consecrated this temple you have built, to put My name there forever; My eyes and My heart will be there at all times. (1 Kings 9:3b)

The LORD loves the gates of Zion. (Ps. 87:2a)

For the LORD has chosen Zion; He has desired it for His home. (Ps. 132:13)

This was the city of the prophets, the home of the priests. Kings ruled here. Men and women of God served here. Abraham came here to sacrifice Isaac. Jesus came here to die—and continues to shock the world because He didn't stay dead here. And one day again in Jerusalem, He'll show the world that He's alive.

God's beautiful, eternal love for Jerusalem cannot be quenched. For more than a thousand years, His home address was here at the original "clean room" called the Holy of Holies on the Temple Mount, the very heartbeat of Israel's existence. And when eternity begins, the new Jerusalem will come down from heaven adorned like a bride on her wedding day.

When I first traveled to the city of God, the effect on me was like nothing I had ever experienced. The sheer spiritual intensity of the place gripped me and wouldn't let go. *What was happening to me?* I wondered. I couldn't get the ancient walled city out of my mind. I had already done a fair amount of world traveling, but I never once returned home and *dreamed* about Moscow, Buenos Aires, or even our own Washington, D.C. After being in Jerusalem, however, I often revisited the city in my dreams. Was I experiencing some kind of spiritual breakdown?

Actually, I found out that I was in very good company. After all, our Savior, the disciples, and selected prophets were all prone to emotionalism while in this majestic city. Jesus wept over it. The Twelve marveled at it. The prophets made it the focal point of their scathing messages to God's disobedient people.

Truly, the call of Jerusalem gets into people's blood—sometimes mystically and misguidedly so. Jesus predicted in Matthew 24 that many would proclaim to be the Messiah in the days to come. How true! Jerusalem has experienced this phenomenon for years. Today, I'm told that at least one person a week walks into Jerusalem and proclaims to be the true Messiah. A special wing in the city's famous Hadassah Hospital has a steady stream of delusional visitors. Some claim to be Jesus, others Elijah, John the Baptist, Moses, or one of the apostles.

But even those of us who are still of sound mind and body continue to sense its pull. And the majority of those who experience what is now called "Jerusalem syndrome" are American Christians! Jerusalem, it seems, has special powers over people unlike any other place.

The City That Just Can't Live Up to Its Name

Jerusalem is paradoxical by nature. Its name means the "city of peace," yet rarely does it ever experience any. The numbers are staggering! Throughout its history Jerusalem has:

- been leveled eighteen times
- been conquered thirty-seven times
- changed hands eighty-six times

International coverage of Jerusalem routinely highlights the fact that the city is the ultimate political minefield. A river of blood has flowed out of the city over the years, and the riverbed appears to be widening. As I write this, the day's top news story is a proposed plan that would divide Jerusalem between Jews and Palestinians. If this happens, Muslims will be rejoicing worldwide. Unfortunately, this would be a blatant disregard for history, since Islam has no valid claims to the city of Jerusalem whatsoever. Not only is history being ignored in this case but so is common sense. Islam makes no bones about it. They want all of Jerusalem minus the Jews.

One of the recent strategies designed to accomplish this aim is a phenomenon sweeping the world today called "Temple Denial." This attempt to revise history was originally stated by Yasser Arafat in December 2000 at Camp David meetings with then-President Bill Clinton and Israeli Prime Minister Ehud Barak. Clinton, desperate to leave behind something positive from his presidency after being impeached, was pushing hard for peace between the Jews and Palestinians. But in his plan, Israel had to sacrifice everything to get a "guarantee of peace" from the Palestinians.

This sacrifice included the Holy City of Jerusalem.

It is a vast understatement to say that Jewish concessions would have been catastrophic for Israel if they had accepted this peace plan. Here are the parameters for what Israel was expected to give up. The Palestinians would receive full control of:

- one half of Jerusalem;
- Israel's beloved Temple Mount;
- the Christian Quarter of Jerusalem;
- and all Palestinian suburbs.
- Israel would keep control of the Western Wall.

Sound fair? Again—in my view—Clinton was grasping at straws for something positive to leave behind in a presidential legacy marked by failure and scandal. In a selfish, sweeping move, he was prepared to give away Israel's holiest site. The Temple Mount is the heartbeat of Judaism. Likewise, the Church of the Holy Sepulchre is of major significance for Christians. True, the church is a turn off for most believers today because of the six warring denominations that fight over it continually, but it is central to our Christian history. Amazingly, Christians did not organize to protest the move.

Jews did.

On January 8, 2001, Jews gathered together and staged the largest protest in Israeli history. Four hundred thousand Jews rallied together just outside the Old City to vehemently oppose the plan that would divide their precious property.

On day nine at Camp David, Chairman Arafat had the ball in his court. The offer would never be better. Prince Bandar of Saudi Arabia, who attended the meetings, told Arafat that if he did not accept the peace plan, it was a "criminal act." This was an all-time no-brainer for Arafat.

That's when I believe God intervened. Arafat laid his cards on the table. He launched into a lecture claiming there was never a Jewish temple anyway, so why should he negotiate? He wanted all of Jerusalem. The talks were over.

Clinton had placed all of his eggs in one basket, and the basket had been thrown back into his face. True, the Palestinian chairman had been to the White House many more times than the prime minister of Israel during the Clinton administration, but all the cozying up to Arafat paid no returns for the outgoing president. It was over for Bill Clinton's hopes for Mideast peace under his watch.

I believe that God intervened because the results for Israel would have been tantamount to waving a white flag and giving their country in its entirety over to the Palestinians. Half of Jerusalem wouldn't have been enough—not when the Palestinian Authority mandate for existence is to drive the Jews into the Mediterranean Sea. A key component in eradicating the Jews from Israel is to prove that they never belonged there in the first place. This revision of history seems insane against the mountain of evidence both from inside and outside the Bible, but it is a movement that is gaining steam around the world. (We'll deal with "Temple Denial" in more detail later.)

Certainly, this had reared its head at a time in history when, in hindsight, other priorities may have been more pressing. Dore Gold, in his award winning book *The Fight for Jerusalem*, adds this insight from Clinton's last days in office: "Then there was the issue of terrorism. Outside of the peace team, some high-ranking U.S. government officials hoped that in his last months in office Clinton would attack Osama bin Laden and al-Qaeda. Richard Clarke of the National Security Council later recalled, 'Time was running out on the Clinton administration. There was going to be one last major national security initiative, and it was going to be a final try to achieve an Israeli-Palestinian agreement.' Thus, Clinton apparently chose to court Arafat instead of making the elimination of bin Laden his first priority."[1]

Interesting how attractive Jerusalem remains.

WHOSE CITY?

The three great religions of the world all collide in Jerusalem. Judaism, Islam, and Christianity are deeply entwined in the fabric of the Holy City.

For Jews, the glory days of their nation generated from Mt. Zion in Jerusalem. Israel soared to world prominence under David and Solomon before its spiritual implosion and subsequent captivities in later years. One of the main roads in Jerusalem is still called the Street of the Prophets. Jewish influence could never be extracted from the city. All of Israel's history is tethered there. The people and the city cannot be separated. Even in their many centuries away from Jerusalem, the hope of returning to her filled their hearts regardless of where they lived. Jews worldwide continued to have an eye on Jerusalem throughout the years.

For Christians, the church began in Jerusalem on Pentecost in AD 30. Although the first-century leaders were from the northern Galilee area, the dramatic events of Jesus' death, resurrection, and ascension all took place within the same general area. A short stroll today can cover all of these historic sites within minutes. The famous southern steps between the Temple Mount and the Mount of Olives are believed to be the very ones on which Jesus often taught the multitudes. Most pilgrimages give believers an opportunity to sit on the steps and read the words He spoke in that final week of His life. This experience is moving, to say the least. It's easy to see why Christians love Jerusalem so much. Some of the most significant events in Jesus' life unfolded there. From the Old City, the lights of Bethlehem are clearly seen at night only six miles away. Within those six miles, Jesus was born and died. Although the major part of His life was lived in northern Israel, specifically the Galilee area, His footprints are all over the city. The Mount of Olives, which now contains the largest graveyard in the world, will one day come alive with the return of Jesus Himself.

For Muslims, the historical attachment does not track as clearly as it does with the other two monotheistic faiths: Judaism and Christianity. Since Jerusalem is not mentioned in the Koran, the only Islamic link is the supposed tying of Muhammad's horse to the stone edifice that Jewish people affectionately call the Western Wall.

I realize my above statement carries very little weight with the Muslim community, since Jerusalem has become their ultimate battleground. On a recent trip to Iran this year, President Mahmoud Ahmadinejad again spoke openly about Iran's goal of wiping Israel off the map. Unfortunately, in the volatile Middle East, many Muslims resonate with this statement and see it as the ultimate goal of their religion

Islamic claims to the city, however, are fairly recent. After the Six Day War in 1967, Arab Muslims launched a campaign that named Jerusalem as its third holiest site. Formerly, Damascus, Baghdad, Cairo, and a host of other cities were all called the third holiest sites by various Muslim groups, ranking just behind Mecca and Medina. But now, the fervor for Jerusalem among Muslim extremists is seen all over the Middle East. Murals of the Temple Mount are painted all throughout the West Bank and in surrounding Islamic regimes, with the Palestinian flag flying proudly over it. For Muslims, the one goal that will bring their solidarity worldwide is the fight for Jerusalem. This will be the battle that finally unites Muslims, whether they are Arabs, Persians, Asians, Africans, Europeans, or (unfortunately) Americans. All ethnic divisions will evaporate between Muslims. Tribal differences and even fundamental fault lines between Sunnis and Shiites will disappear.

The Bible tells us that the coming battle for Jerusalem will be the bloodiest ever. It will involve many nations in the all-out fight, but as usual it will be a battle that is spiritual in nature rather than political. It is easy to see that the conflict described on the nightly news is misunderstood and severely underestimated.

It is not all about land; it is all about God.

Since we Christians believe Jesus will be the ultimate liberator of Jerusalem, we've left the fate of the Holy City in His hands. As Jesus taught us, we are to "turn the other cheek" and employ completely different weapons of warfare—weapons that will ultimately have greater impact. We use weapons that change lives and redirect the trajectory of destinies. They are spiritual in nature.

So there were no Christian suicide bombers in Israel the last time I checked! That knocks us out of the equation in the fight for Jerusalem. But for Jews and Muslims, the battle rages. After waiting nineteen centuries to return to Jerusalem, many Jews would have no trouble giving their lives to defend their spiritual home. They have waited so long to dwell in the city again. They have suffered so much in their long history to get back inside those Old City walls. This time it is for good, though they are a tiny group compared to the world's population. They are fierce in their desire to keep Jerusalem as their spiritual and political capital.

Muslims, however, see the taking of Jerusalem as validation of their Islamic beliefs. Some radical Muslims believe that becoming a suicide bomber and killing many innocent Israelis in the process would only bring more honor to their family. Jerusalem is the ultimate conquest for Islam. And since it is home to Jews now, Muslims covet it more than ever.

On May 14, 2008, Israel celebrated its sixtieth birthday. In recent years, protestors in Cairo marched in defiance of this historical date. One Muslim woman held a sign that summarized the statement of the day with these words: "Go to hell! Enemies Forever!" Can we really expect these deep-seeded feelings to ever leave?

Whose Land?

It is true that Jews and Arabs have struggled against each other for four millennia, but the stakes became significantly higher in the last century. The reason for this is easy to see by merely looking at a world map.

Before World War I, the Middle East was just a chunk of land in the middle of the Turkish Ottoman Empire. Since the Turks ultimately owned it all, the fights over land were minimal. But with the collapse of the Ottomans, the landscape began to go through radical surgery. Nations like Syria, Lebanon, Jordan, and Saudi Arabia were carved into existence, and land ownership became the name of the game. For centuries, the same land had been populated with area tribes. These people groups were a throwback to biblical days, not only in their dress but also in their nomadic lifestyle. All of a sudden, countries began springing to life in the 1930s and 1940s, and national identities emerged as the area was recreated.

What about the Jews?

The desire for Jews to return to their biblical heartland was not a recent one. Jewish families dreamed for centuries of a return to their home that the prophet Ezekiel had detailed in his famous "dry bones" prophecy of chapter 37. God had promised that He would gather the Jews from all the countries where they had been scattered and bring them back to their land for good. Despite the Jews' turning away from God and being displaced in the first place, these spiritual refugees would return in order that God's holy name would be exalted.

This process would involve two steps, as Old Testament Ezekiel prophesied in 36:24–25, "I will take you from the nations and gather you from all the countries, and will bring you into your own land. I will also sprinkle clean water on you, and you will be clean. I will cleanse you from all your impurities and all your idols."

First, Jewish immigrants would return to Israel from the four corners of the earth. Though this seemed improbable even sixty years ago, how quickly God moves when He seeks to fulfill His ancient promises. One former professor of mine, known for his particular interest and expertise in the area of prophecy, once said this: "Not all too long ago, it was laughable to most people when I talked about the enormous impact Israel would have on the world in the days to come." After all, before the Jews reinhabited it, Palestine was a barren strip of land that nobody wanted. What exactly would draw all the nations of the world to it with their armies in the future? Today, nobody questions how important Israel is to the world's overall stability.

So Israel did return to the land, and the results of this miracle are seen each and every day. The first step is completed—Israel is Israel again with a strong Jewish population right in the midst of strong regional hostility. The country's very existence forces the rest of the world to watch its every move. The first step in the miracle is "the return."

The second step of God's returning His covenant people to the land they love is "the cleansing." Israel is fragmented in its religious pursuits and for the most part is quite secular. Orthodox Jews wearing side curls and eastern European garb are what most people picture when they think of what a Jew from Israel looks like. But Orthodox Jews in Israel are only about 18 to 20 percent of the population. The rest are fairly modern and seem no different than the typical American—perhaps somewhat religious but certainly not to the degree of the bobbing Orthodox Rabbis deep in prayer in front of the Wailing Wall on a daily basis.

In short, Israel does not seem a whole lot more spiritual than most other nations. In the future, as we will see throughout this book, a future cleansing time of repentance is still in store for Israel—a time that will restore the people of Yahweh to Yahweh Himself. This certainly seems unlikely in our minds, but no more than their return to the land seemed unlikely only a few generations ago. For when God moves to fulfill His promises, what seems unlikely becomes reality in an instant.

As the smoke cleared from the Nazi death camp ovens in the 1940s, Jewish people began immigrating both legally and illegally back to what was then called Palestine. The British blocked much of it, and as a result, Jewish organizations like the Haganah, Palmach, and Mossad were born. Members risked their lives to transfer Jews who were making *aliyah* (immigration) to the land of their forefathers Abraham, Isaac, and Jacob. The Jews would not be stopped. Former Prime Minister Golda Meir wrote:

> When the war ended, when Jewish lives were no longer threatened with annihilation, the Mossad continued to operate and grow, not because of the rules of inertia but because the opportunity to fulfill its ultimate task was finally at hand. From 1945 to 1948, the Mossad continued to display the same determination that characterized it during the war. It exploited every device, every trick of wit, every possible channel to defy the British blockade against Jewish immigration to Palestine and bring the Jews out of the wreck of Europe to their own land. . . . Survival was no longer sufficient as an aim. The struggle now was not for Jewish lives but for Jewish souls—for the entire personality of Jewish people in the decades and centuries to come.[2]

As in biblical times, God used the holy and the unholy together for His glory. He miraculously gave back to the Jewish race its homeland in May 1948. And the Jewish people gave God a supreme effort in making sure they arrived there.

The United States became a major player in the effort to give the Jews a home after the war. President Harry Truman originally had wanted to stay out of all the madness in the explosive Middle East. Great Britain had already tried to stabilize the region for thirty years without success. Despite all its efforts, the British mandate period from 1917 to 1948 was in the end a no-win situation for England. It appeared to be political suicide for Truman, and initially he was lukewarm concerning the fate of the Jews.

But then God moved in his heart. Through a relationship with a former business partner, his viewpoint about a homeland for Jews changed in an instant.

Chaim Weizmann had a friend who had been in business with Truman a few years before their meeting. The bank they helped launch together in Kansas City failed miserably, yet a remarkable friendship began during those days that would ultimately lead to American support of the proposal sent to the United Nations that concerned partitioning part of the land of Israel for the Jews to return to. Truman was reluctant to visit with Weizmann, the chief architect of the push for Israeli statehood. Truman knew that Weizmann could only want one thing from the now most powerful man in the world. He wanted unconditional support for the Jews' return to Palestine. The small piece of land would be called Israel. Truman was right and Weizmann pleaded with him to step to the plate in this most historic hour of need for the Jews. In one meeting, Truman went from ambivalence to advocacy.

Realizing that the votes were going to come up short for Israel, President Truman strong-armed four nations to help swing the vote in favor of the Jews. Greece, Haiti, Liberia, and the Philippines all reversed their former position after Truman, several U.S. senators, and American businessmen applied economic and political pressure. Harvey Firestone of Firestone Tires, for example, told the president of Liberia that if it voted against partition for the Jews, he would have to consider moving his rubber plant to another country, costing thousands of jobs and revenue to the country. Instantly, Liberia changed its vote in favor of the Jews!

There were finally enough votes in favor of the partition. Truman had seen to it. Although our president's motives were hardly spiritual, God used all of it to magnify Himself and His ultimate purposes. Like other times in Israel's history, God used everything from a talking donkey to a bitter enemy to further His plans. God's ability to orchestrate the good, the bad, and the ugly for His desires worked once again. His moving in an American president's heart was the key to setting it all in motion. Harry Truman became a powerful instrument in the mighty hand of God.

With enormous tension in the air, United Nations delegates flooded into the assembly hall November 29, 1947, in Flushing Meadow, New York, to decide the future of God's chosen people. Had He completely forgotten them? After all, with normal annual population growth rates, the Jews should have totaled about 120 to 140 million worldwide. But with barely 12 million of them left on the face of the earth, Yahweh remembered His covenant people once more! The entire gathering of politicians, reporters, and spectators were now in place, and the auditorium fell silent. As the delegate from Guatemala rose to cast the first vote, a cry from a lone voice in the audience summarized Jewish feelings worldwide. In Hebrew, the words that filled the room were "Oh Lord, save us!" Within a short while, after tallying the votes, the short prayer that contained all of history was answered yes by God. Israel would indeed return, not to Palestine but to Israel.

As a young boy, my uncle told me that the greatest event in the twentieth century was not when the Allies defeated Nazi Germany and avoided world takeover. Rather, it was when God answered the aching prayer from Jewish hearts worldwide to return to their homeland after so many years.

On the very same day that the votes were cast, another miracle happened that was not coincidental. This one occurred far from New York, back in the biblical city of Jesus and King David in Bethlehem. While the votes were being read on the live radio broadcast around the world, Hebrew University professor Eleazar Sukenik took a six-mile bus ride from Jerusalem and bought the first installment of the famous Dead Sea Scrolls from Kando, the Arab broker of the precious parchments. Having been warned that if partition was approved his life would certainly be in danger in the mostly Arab village, Professor Sukenik ignored the advice and made the journey anyway. As all in Jerusalem were listening to the final vote being read, Eleazar opened the first scroll and read God's eternal Word from the prophet Isaiah that predicted the Jewish return centuries before.

In one miraculous day, Israel had its beloved land back—and the reassurance that God had indeed not forgotten them.

Home at Last!

Israel had truly experienced a miraculous rebirth. No people in history had ever come close to returning to their former homeland after a 1,900-year absence. The Jews had never fully assimilated into the more than 100 nations where they had been scattered. Their return to the land was always in some sense the fuel that kept the flame of their existence flickering. Now they were home. Their rebirth once considered impossible had become not just possible, but reality.

The Hebrew language was also revived, though having not been spoken for 2,500 years. Ever since Israel's Babylonian captivity, the language of the people had ceased being Hebrew. Rabbis and scholars had retained the ancient tongue, but the common folk had soon adopted Aramaic and Greek, dooming the Hebrew language to become a dead one. Even in Jesus' day, the people spoke Greek, and as a result it became the language of the New Testament.

Again, however, the God of the Hebrews made good on an ancient promise. In the book written by the minor prophet Zephaniah in about 640 BC, God had again promised something that appeared highly unlikely. He said this in 3:9: "I will then restore pure speech to the peoples so that all of them may call on the name of Yahweh and serve Him with a single purpose." What would this language be? Hebrew, of course! The ancient tongue of God's people.

But how could a dead language come to life again?

Eliezer Ben-Yehuda was the philologist who spent the majority of his days resurrecting the language, making it once again modern and spoken. Remarkably, Ben-Yehuda had to invent Hebrew words to match ordinary words that had come into being over the twenty-five centuries of Hebrew disuse. Words like "United States," "outer space," and "pizza" had to be formed into Hebrew. He used parts of Hebrew words to come up with a whole new vocabulary, devoting about fifty years of his life to the task. Never before in history had a dead language been revived. It could only happen to the people whose God had chosen them and had performed the impossible over and over throughout their entire existence. The turnaround was like a modern day exodus from Egypt.

Not everyone, however, was thrilled. The day after David Ben-Gurion, Israel's first prime minister, announced that Israel was officially a nation again— May 14, 1948—five Arab Nations attacked the one-day-old country. Yes, the Jews' zeal to return to their ancient land was greeted with outright and immediate rejection by their neighbors. Even today, many Arabs call the birth of Israel the *nackba*—the tragedy.

Since the nation's inception, it has experienced a major war every decade, and it looks as if another one may start soon. Yet Israel still perseveres through adversity. To emigrate from the United States or any other part of the world to Israel is not only admirable but certainly high-risk. Jews, however, keep coming—because no war, no strife, no threats can extinguish the flame in the heart of every Jew for their beloved Israel.

Islamic threats to Israel's existence are on the rise now that enemies like Osama bin Laden have risen to heroic proportions, just as Saddam Hussein and Yasser Arafat did before their recent deaths. When Hussein was in power, for example, he personally sent each suicide bomber's family a $25,000 check. The evil unleashed against Israel could hardly be more cruel and bloodthirsty, nor committed more enthusiastically. In the midst of such fierce animosity, how can peace be a plausible alternative? Samuel Smadja, who has lived his whole life in Jerusalem, often quotes former Israeli Prime Minister Golda Meir who, when asked a similar question, answered it this way: "When they love their children more than they hate ours."

The Goal—Jerusalem

When all is said and done, the reason for the battle is, of course, the ultimate prize—Jerusalem. In short, the spiritual epicenter of the world will always be right in the middle of a major fault line. Earthquakes will continue to reverberate from the Holy City of God until Jesus returns and creates one of His own.

As Christians, we have a permanent connection to Jerusalem. Our spiritual roots are buried deeply in Holy Land soil. We are grafted into Israel, as Romans 11 tells us. Roughly 85 percent of Scripture is about Israel. Our Messiah was Jewish, as were the prophets and the first church leaders. Sixty-four of the sixty-six books of the Bible were Jewish-authored, Luke being the only

Gentile author of Scripture, penning under the inspiration of the Holy Spirit the Gospel of Luke and the Acts of the Apostles. And, as we know, the kingdom of the future millennium will be established in Jerusalem, in Israel.

So how can we just sit by and watch this systematic unraveling of our spiritual capital city? True, the fate of the Holy City is in our Savior's powerful, loving hands, yet we can still be involved. What role does America play in all this? What role does the church play? Can we still make a difference? Yes, we can—and we should! The following chapters will help you see how.

Rami—The First Palestinian Christian Martyr

In the 1990s, a new phenomenon occurred in Israel that would often make the tiny Middle Eastern country the lead news story of the day. Suicide bombing became the most effective weapon that Yasser Arafat and the Palestinian Authority had ever used against Israel, though Arafat often denied that he had any connection to these killings.

Soon that would change.

When Israel attacked the chairman's compound in Ramallah in 2002, the evidence was all there. Israeli Defense Forces discovered in Arafat's personal office a list that contained the names of bombers, the places they would explode themselves, and the timing for when the mass murders would occur. All of this was carefully laid out in Arafat's own handwriting! Also found in his compound was a printing press where bogus money was printed at will. Some Palestinian families, it seems, were not even paid with real money after their son or daughter had blown themselves up.

Since Jews and Arabs mix freely in many areas within Israel, the "human bomb" tactic became (and has become) almost unstoppable. The chairman was indeed a clever planner. A bomber could be a young man dressed as a Jewish Rabbi, or a teenage boy, or a woman dressed in a burqa, shopping in Jerusalem. Israel was defenseless and back on its heels. No place was off-limits. The next target of detonation could be a pizza bar, coffee shop, Hebrew University, or a bus. Week after week the carnage mounted.

Adding to the savageness of these murderous acts, celebration parties were given in Palestinian areas in advance of the next bombing, with the mother of the suicide bomber being the honored guest. Presents were piled high. The parties were lavish, and a videotape of the culprit was left behind in an effort to make sure the killer was given honor for his "noble deed." In a few years, virtually every Israeli family would have a family member, relative, or friend who was dead from a suicide bomb. But in Gaza and the West Bank, some communities celebrated the announcement of the explosion, even though many good-hearted Palestinians wept over the senseless murders.

In 2001, Yasser Arafat claimed that Israel could expect a wave of one million suicide bombers. Impossible? Not with so much pressure at the borders, mingled with the frustration that Palestinians go through each day just to survive. Young men and women were joining the ranks in droves.

In the summer of 2007, Joseph Ginot, advisor to the last five prime ministers in Israel, observed two lines at a Palestinian college in the West Bank. One line was to sign up for classes; the other was to sign up for a militant terrorist group to become suicide bombers. "The line for the bombers was much longer than the line to register for classes," he reported.

For somewhere in the twisted logic of the Islamic leadership, suicide bombers became known as "martyrs." In the Gaza Strip and in the West Bank of Israel, pictures of *shaheed* (the Arabic name for "martyr") were found everywhere. Posters were hung in the city streets, and memorials to the "heroes" were everywhere. Young Palestinian boys began trading "martyr cards" that looked like American baseball cards.

The word "martyr," of course, is what we Christians use to describe those who have sacrificed their life for the cause of Jesus Christ. Stephen, whose death is recorded in Acts 8, was the first martyr in the history of the church. Because he would not compromise the message of salvation that Jewish ears needed to hear, he lost his life to a public stoning outside a city gate in Jerusalem. Rather than dealing with the veracity of his claims, the Jewish Sanhedrin responded with an immediate death sentence for this young believer.

For Christians, the stream of blood has never stopped flowing. Martyrdom has been growing ever since that first-century stoning. Throughout the history of Jesus' church, heroes of the faith have given their lives rather than deny their Master. In heaven, thousands upon thousands will one day be given the martyr's crown for paying the ultimate price for their commitment to Christ.

So for believers, the word "martyr" is connected to a rich tradition of those who gave their all and ended up losing their lives. Just like the Master who bought them with a price, these men and women voluntarily surrendered their lives rather than succumb to the fear of men. Martyrs are choice saints of the true God.

But in these days of moral equivalence, what is the difference between a Christian martyr and an Islamic one? Plenty! There is no comparison, actually. An Islamic martyr is a murderer. The suicide bomber tries to kill and maim as many innocent victims as he can. Men, women, and children are all targets, and since they are Jews, this brings pleasure to Allah. Christian martyrs, on the other hand, aren't the ones who do the killing. Their lives are given freely, taken from them because of their abiding love for Jesus Christ.

Rami Ayyad was one such martyr—the first Palestinian to lose his life for Christ.

On the afternoon of October 7, 2007, Rami left the Bible Society in Gaza City, locked the doors, and headed for home. He had been receiving a steady stream of threats for weeks, and had recently noticed that he was being followed. He sensed it. He knew it. In fact, the two men who had been following him were once again parked outside the Bible Society on this fateful day as Rami looked out the front door. Seeing them again, he phoned his wife and explained that if he was not home in two hours, he might not see her for quite awhile.

So with his killers waiting for him outside the downtown building, he stepped out into the street—and into eternity. One young Palestinian woman eloquently put it this way: "Rami's earthly home was a mere fifteen minutes away, yet he was on his way to his heavenly home."

The next morning at 2 a.m., his dead body was thrown from a car near the Bible Society, and the small Christian community went into shock. Pauline, Rami's sweet young wife, was overwhelmed with grief. Her sweetheart was gone. But he was now safe in his Savior's arms.

As Rami's friends looked back over his life, one thing stood out. Rami often talked about martyrdom. When three believers in Turkey had been brutally killed earlier in the year, Rami exhorted the believers in Gaza that one of them might be called upon to give his own life in the same way. With passion, he boldly challenged them to be faithful to the point of death no matter how much torture and persecution they might have to face. Rami lost his life because he knew the gospel has the power to radically transform people's lives. The gospel also has the power to radically transform radicals. For this reason, he was willing to risk everything. The Gaza Church is proof.

Rami was given the high privilege of becoming the first Palestinian to be a true martyr in every sense of the word. The body of Christ reached out to Rami's widow and family from all over the world. American believers gave generously to help the family, as did Arabic believers throughout the Middle East. Messianic congregations in Israel also gave to help the family of their fallen brother.

The coroner who performed the autopsy concluded that Rami died with no sign of any stress whatsoever. He was in perfect peace. Jesus was with him through the beatings and the torture. Like Stephen, he had been surrounded and killed by those who were afraid of the truth of his message, yet he bravely passed the test, and one day will receive a martyr's crown. Rami took the word "martyr" and gave it life again. No longer can it only be associated in the Middle East with demonized killers who live to kill. Rami was killed, but he lives—just like Stephen.

But Stephen, filled by the Holy Spirit, gazed into heaven. He saw God's glory, with Jesus standing at the right hand of God, and he said, "Look! I see the heavens opened and the Son of Man standing at the right hand of God!" (Acts 7:55–56)

Chapter 2
Endangered Species

Twenty-three nations throughout history have made the fatal mistake of cursing Israel by their words and actions and have paid the ultimate price—extinction. Is God's promise "to curse those who curse" Israel still valid today?

Forever Is a Long Time

Throughout the scope of human history, certain themes emerge consistently from generation to generation. These themes are often simple in nature. Here are a few:

- Empires come and empires go.
- Good rulers and evil rulers become powerful and then fall.
- Nations rise to prominence only to fall backward into mediocrity.

For a while, people groups and leaders appear invincible, yet time and mortality eventually level the playing field, and their greatness fades.

In his excellent work *Israel and the Nations*, F. F. Bruce explained Israel's remarkable stature among the Middle East nations:

Israel's national history was not lived out in isolation from other peoples. The Israelites were surrounded by nations greater and mightier than themselves, who impinged upon the life of Israel at innumerable points. It is in the varied response to the challenge presented by these other nations, Asian, African, and European, that Israelis' own nationhood acquires its special character."[1]

Bruce's point is well taken. The uniqueness of the nation of Israel is found in this fact: it is as relevant to the world's overall stability today as it was in Old Testament times. Bruce goes on to say:

What (is) so special about this one small nation of antiquity? Why should the story of Israel still be of interest and relevance to us in the late twentieth century and beyond? The answer to these questions can be found nowhere but in the distinctive features of Israel's religion. There was something about it that was unparalleled in the surrounding world. An Assyrian king once tried to discourage any resistance on the part of the Israelites by pointing to the uselessness of the gods of greater and more powerful states, which he had overthrown. "Where are the gods of Hamath and Arpad?" (2 Kings 18:34), he asked—a question which might well be repeated today. Where indeed are they? And how does it come about that the God of Israel continues to be worshipped by millions of people in every one of the earth's continents? The Israelites had their own explanation. As they considered their experience of the God of their fathers, they affirmed, "He has done this for no other nation" (Ps. 147:20). Their affirmation is vindicated by the course of their history.[2]

In biblical days, several nations living in Israel's backyard periodically exhibited as much swagger as an NBA superstar. Yet their pride ran its course, and soon they also lay among the fallen. Israel, however, remained. In some cases, these nations paid the ultimate price for their arrogance—extinction. They were wiped off world's map forever.

But why is it that twenty-three different nations mentioned in the Bible—once vibrant and powerful—no longer exist today?

In the animal kingdom, species come and go throughout time. The endangered species list garners world attention whenever another animal group tiptoes toward the edge of oblivion. Global efforts are launched to save the shrinking population of a particular species, and when carried out far enough in advance, they survive. There are failures, though. Many of them. Gone is the giant skink. The Cuban macaw will never return, no matter how much he is missed. The T. Rex likewise was erased from existence centuries before our lifetime, thankfully.

But what about people groups? What was it that these nations did to appear on the Bible's endangered species list? No matter how hard they tried, they eventually died out altogether.

First Things First

In Psalm 47:2, the sons of Korah remind us that God is the "great King over all the earth." From His holy throne, He reigns over the nations and owns the kings of the earth. The sons of Korah knew this all too well. When their family rebelled against Moses and Aaron in the desert, they faced an immediate execution when God sent an earthquake from below and fire from above to squelch their little protest.

To say the least, Korah and his 250-man opposition group were dealt with in seconds. Oh, God allowed a few of the descendants to survive, and for centuries their very presence among the Israelites made the people think long and hard before they opposed God or His current leader.

God's zero-tolerance stance on rebellion would eventually afflict several more of the unholy nations. His endangered species list would grow and grow quickly. Yet at other times, nations like Egypt rebelled against God and survived. Was God being unfair?

A Promise Is a Promise

In the first book of the Bible, God called a man from a pagan land and a pagan family. God's opening promise to him spelled out clearly the formula for the future survival of all nations. He promised Abram to:
- make him into a great nation
- bless him
- make his name great

- bless those who blessed him
- curse those who cursed him
- and bless all peoples through him

The promise that turned Abram into Abraham began a chain of events resulting in the birth of the nation of Israel and eventually the birth of the Messiah Himself. The entire world would be blessed by the coming Savior through Abraham's line. The entire world would be given the opportunity to bless or curse Abraham's line. God set it in stone. He repeated it several times. He then gave each nation the chance to "weigh in" in regard to this promise. Amazingly, the promise given in Genesis 12 was exactly one chapter after God Himself had scattered the nations of the world from the Tower of Babel. The die was cast. National survival was at stake. Many nations would *oppose* Israel throughout their history, but the ones that outrightly *cursed* God's nation authored their own personal death sentence.

Anyone Seen a Hittite Lately?

The list is long, hard-hitting, and comprehensive. The roll call of the annihilated has a familiar ring to it. Like an issue of "Whatever happened to . . ." from *People* magazine, the names are familiar; and their final days, when compared, are all similar.

The Hebrew word for curse, *haram*, means "to seclude from society." Therefore, when nations cursed Israel, they selected the Hebrews from society to be the focal point of their hatred. They "secluded" them from all others and fervently worked to destroy them. So since God had chosen Israel and determined to lavish them with His love and direct involvement, He had no choice but "to seclude from society" those particular nations and destroy them.

In short, if a nation cursed Israel, God cursed that nation.

No fudging with God. Not three strikes but one. Kingdoms and rulers would rise and fall. Israel would cycle through times of faithfulness and times of utter paganism. It didn't matter. God continued to keep score—the Hittites, the Jebusites, the Perezzites, the Ammonites. Empires came and went.

Leaders rose and fell. Nations ruled vast empires and then suddenly weren't major players anymore. God simply hit the delete key, and they were gone.

Several of God's leaders witnessed this phenomenon while serving as shepherds over Israel. Abraham, Moses, Joshua, the judges, and David all stood against mighty forces that were suddenly gone and then never a threat to them again. Like a great row of dominoes, each fell rather quickly, their cities and territories taken over by other civilizations—ruins built upon ruins. In some cases, the Bible was the only record of their existence. Later on, as archaeological mound sites called "tels" in Israel were excavated one by one, layers of history were peeled back. Archaeologists rediscovered lost people groups that had been so thoroughly destroyed that at one point Bible skeptics doubted they had ever truly existed at all.

The footprints of their existence were unmistakable. The people, however, had disappeared centuries ago—the Canaanites, the Amorites, the Hittites, the Amalekites.

Do not fear, you worm Jacob, you men of Israel: I will help you—the LORD's declaration. Your redeemer is the Holy One of Israel. (Isa. 41:14)

Remember, LORD, what the Edomites said that day at Jerusalem: "Destroy it! Destroy it down to its foundations!" Daughter Babylon, doomed to destruction, happy is the one who pays you back what you have done to us. (Ps. 137:7–8)

In that day—the LORD's declaration—will I not eliminate the wise ones of Edom and those who understand from the hill country of Esau? Teman, your warriors will be terrified so that everyone from the hill country of Esau will be destroyed by slaughter. You will be covered with shame and destroyed forever because of violence done to your brother Jacob. (Obad. 8–10)

Just as in the New Testament, the church is called to go to the nations where God's precious grace can be offered to each of them, Old Testament Israel was called to influence the nations of the world also. And what influence they wielded! The people of Edom were not the only people whose "forever" was radically changed.

Don't Mess with Israel

Striking out at God's chosen people was one thing. Cursing and calling for their destruction was another. When a nation went that far, God was sure to act.

These words, you see, were more than slander; they were an attack on God Himself. In his book *Israel: The Land and the People*, Wayne House correctly sums it all up with these words: "The land of Israel is not just dirt and rock. It is more than mountain and plain. The land of Israel is a promise of God. It is a promise so strongly held by Him that He stakes His promise concerning the land to His eternal character."[3]

If God is this zealous for His land, imagine how much He cares for the people who live in it.

In the future, the two will be united under the divine rule of God. As House wrote: "The land of Israel is where the people of God will enjoy the presence of God under the reign of God in the Kingdom of God. Ultimately, the land of Israel is the center of the planet, the focal point of the universe—for the outworking of the purposes of God Eretz Israel!* The land of Israel is the enduring physical place for the outworking of God's plan."[4]

The nations of the world would tread on holy ground when they entered the borders of Israel. They would be allowed to walk on the land but never to walk on God's people. Listen to God as He speaks of His beloved people Israel: "For the LORD's portion is his people, Jacob his allotted inheritance. In a desert he found him, in a barren and howling waste. He shielded him and cared for him; he guarded him as the apple of his eye" (Deut. 32:9–10 NIV). Five phrases in the passage vividly detail God's feelings about His chosen nation:

*Eretz is Hebrew for "land." Eretz Israel is the term for the "whole land of Israel" or "greater Israel."

"THE LORD'S PORTION"

The picture is one of food. God says Israel is all He needs to be satisfied. Later, in Psalm 119:57, the writer said, "The LORD is my portion." How beautiful to see God and His people wholly satisfied with each other. Like a dinner plate artistically arranged with the most delicious meal imaginable, God says Israel is all He needs to be filled up and content. He expects us to feel the same way about Him, as the psalmist did.

"HIS ALLOTTED INHERITANCE"

In biblical days, every family of Israel (except the Levites) had an inheritance in the land. These precious parcels of property were handed down through the generations and never traded or sold. The inheritance was each family's identity. So when asked where an Israelite was from, his answer also revealed who his family was. An inheritance of land not only told where he lived but who he was. God, by linking Himself to Israel, also defined where *He* would live and who *He* would call family. No other nation but Israel enjoyed this high privilege of living with God and being called His own.

"HE SHIELDED HIM"

If there was one thing Israel knew about, it was war. In the Israelites' history, they rarely experienced anything else. Even today, since becoming a nation in 1948, Israel has experienced six major wars and several conflicts. Along with the Gulf War, the intifada (the Palestinian uprising against Israel's occupation of the West Bank and Gaza Strip), and the constant barrage of terrorism, Israel can never rest. If God had not been shielding the Jews continually, they would have ceased to exist centuries ago. Frederick the Great once demanded an answer of one of his servants concerning the veracity of the Scriptures. He asked, "Why should I believe the Bible?" His servant replied, "I can answer that in one word: *Israel.*" Apart from God, there is no reason for Israel's continued existence. This is a people group that keeps coming back when given up for dead. Its survival depends on God's shield—daily.

"And cared for him"

With all its wars, captivities, anti-Semitic attacks, and attempted systematic killings (called *pogroms*), Israel has been bruised and bloodied for much of its existence. But shepherds have always roamed the Judean hills, and their firm, loving care for their sheep is an ongoing reminder of their Father's care for them. Throughout the years, Israel had God alone to care for them. More often than not, they have been at odds with the majority of nations. Today is no different. Even though they remain largely secular at present, there is a frequent SOS to God that goes out collectively from these battered and bruised people. God always answers their cry. He always will. He has shepherded them for over forty centuries.

"The apple of His eye"

This phrase may explain more about the phenomenon of Israel's continued existence than any other words in Scripture. Three times God calls Israel the apple of His eye. Since the apple refers to the pupil, four things are learned about God's personal connection to Israel:

1. *It is easily injured.* A mere eyelash, when stuck on the pupil, can bring instant pain that demands one's attention, pronto. God says every injury to His people is an injury to Him, and His pain is never unnoticed.

2. *It cannot be repaired.* Once the pupil is damaged, there is no medical procedure to repair it. Nations have brutally attacked Israel over the centuries. Egypt, Babylon, and Rome all did, and God experienced pain over each act of violence. They would all be dealt with in the future.

3. *It gives direction.* Israel was to be God's leader among the nations. The Jews' lives and their relationship with God were to be a light for the Gentiles to follow. Isaiah thundered, "'You are my witnesses,' declares the Lord!" (Isa. 43:10 niv). Israel was to be the eyes for all the nations in darkness—sight for the helpless, direction for the lost.

4. *It is protected.* As natural as it is for us to deflect anything headed for our eyes, so it is with God. He protects Israel as if He were protecting Himself. It's reflexive, natural, and done quickly. "For this is what the Lord

said to me: As a lion or young lion growls over its prey when a band of shepherds is called out against it, and is not terrified by their shouting or subdued by their noise, so the LORD of Hosts will come down to fight on Mount Zion and on its hill. Like hovering birds, so the LORD of Hosts will protect Jerusalem—by protecting it, He will rescue it, by sparing it, He will deliver it" (Isa. 31:4–5).

The tally continued: the Philistines, the Moabites, the Edomites, the Kerethites, the Pelethites, and the Hamathites. "In the year that King Ahaz died, this oracle came: Don't rejoice, all you in Philistia, because the rod of the one who struck you is broken. For the viper will come out of the root of a snake, and from its egg comes a flying serpent. Then the firstborn of the poor will be well fed, and the impoverished will lie down in safety, but I will kill your root with hunger, and your remnant will be slain. Wail, you gates! Cry out, city! Tremble with fear, all Philistia! For a cloud of dust is coming from the north, and there is no one missing from the invader's ranks. What answer will be given to the messengers from that nation? The LORD has founded Zion, and His afflicted people find refuge in her" (Isa. 14:28–32).

"An oracle against Moab: Ar in Moab is devastated, destroyed in a night. Kir in Moab is devastated, destroyed in a night. . . . For their cry echoes throughout the territory of Moab. Their wailing reaches Eglaim; their wailing reaches Beer-elim. The waters of Dibon are full of blood, but I will bring on Dibon even more than this—a lion for those who escape from Moab, and for the survivors in the land" (Isa. 15:1, 8–9).

Implicitly, Jews understood the enormous value of Jewish lives. Over time, they witnessed numerous attempts to ethnically cleanse them from the planet. If God was willing to wipe out entire people groups for their treatment of His chosen ones, then every life was important, even if just one were at stake. Ehud Avriel, who helped create Israel's famous underground spy network known as the Mossad, writes this in his book *Open the Gates!*—

In the summer of 1944, the Soviets advanced into Nazi-occupied Europe, and with unbelievable speed the liberating armies reached the borders of Rumania and Bulgaria. As they moved on, Jews in their communities and centers of deportation carefully dared to raise their heads and look around—the nightmare was over. Pessimists had always predicted that our rescue efforts could never save meaningful numbers of Jews, but we in Istanbul, and most Jews in Palestine, believed that the rescue of even a single life was to justify the greatest efforts, expenditures, and risks.[5]

Though it was undoubtedly one of the darkest periods in Jewish life—six million horrible deaths in Nazi concentration camps—the price of saving even one life was entirely worth it. If God wanted to protect His people so vigorously, then it's easy to see why Jews put such a premium on life itself. They were not disposable. There were no throw-away lives.

Admittedly, after the Holocaust, many Jews questioned whether God's desire was to still protect them at all. Perhaps this is the most serious stumbling block in Jewish evangelism. On a recent trip to Israel, I had the privilege of meeting a woman who is a Holocaust survivor. She was residing in a rehabilitation center in Tel Aviv because her age and painful journey through life had now caught up with her physically. Despite the tragedies she had witnessed, her nature was remarkably positive, upbeat, and happy. Her parents had died in the *Shoah* (Hebrew for Holocaust). Most of her family had died also. But I found this lovely lady a blessing merely to speak with. Her resilience was amazing. Life had not dealt her a bad card, in her estimation, and she believed that the God of Israel was still firmly in control of things. She even ventured to say that peace in Israel was on its way. How delightful she was! How rare!

For so many people, their understanding of God is shaped by their life experience. One of the most difficult tasks we have as humans is to avoid becoming "experiential theologians," those who derive their views of God solely from their experiences. Yet it is hard to fault Jews around the world who for the most part have become practical agnostics. I dare not point a finger at them. My ethnic group, the Irish, has not endured a fraction of what

Israel has undergone and continues to. That is why I believe Jewish outreach must be sensitive, respectful, and loving. These are a people whose existence has been far more difficult than any other's. No one comes close.

But the only one that possibly could have kept them going through time and history is God Himself. He fights for them. Always has. Always will. Many a Jew will say, "Where was God during the Holocaust?" One Jewish man from Tel Aviv remarked to me recently, "I thank God that we are His chosen people. I just wish He would choose someone else for a while." Most certainly, God has allowed Israel's endless pain and suffering for some reason. What is it?

Before you finish this chapter, you'll find out why.

Does God Still Wipe 'Em Out?

What about today? Nations appear to curse God's people and still survive. I haven't seen the fire of God myself. Is there some sort of plan B? For all that Nazi Germany did to the Jews of Europe, it would seem that they should be smoking ruins and nothing more. The Spanish Inquisition of the 1400s forced Jewish people to renounce their religious faith and become a *converso* or "convert" to Christianity. This was evangelism at one of its lowest moments. If Jews wouldn't convert, they were executed. Yet Spain still stands today.

Likewise, in the first century, Rome was the power broker of the world. To Rome, Israel was only an insignificant group of religious nuts who continually wasted the Romans' time and dominated their overextended military. After the Jewish revolt in AD 66, Rome had had enough. They moved into the Holy Land in full force under General Titus, and the results were disastrous for the Hebrews. The prolonged siege on Jerusalem was complete with ramparts to easily climb over the city walls and towers to shoot down at any resisters. The sacking of Jerusalem was complete. The second temple, built in 520 BC by Governor Jerubbabel, King David's descendant, and enlarged by Herod the Great five centuries later, was destroyed. One and a half million Jews were killed by the world's most powerful army. Many were burned alive or thrown off of the city walls to their deaths. All temple treasures, utensils, and holy articles were carried off to Rome. Even the gold on the inner temple walls was confiscated after the smoke cleared. In fact, the present day Western Wall where religious Jews pray so fervently is what's left of the retaining walls underneath the temple complex. The Romans proudly left it as a testimonial to their greatness. Their trophy was meant to point out that Rome prevailed over Israel as no other nation had.

In archaeological finds near the fallen city walls, some perplexing discoveries were unearthed. Major temple stones weighing several tons were hundreds of feet away from their obvious placements in the overall structure. Why would the Romans take the time to drag these monolithic heavyweights so far from the temple? Ronnie Cohen, a top tour guide in Israel, recently said that a plausible theory to explain the massive stone removals is that the Romans blew up the temple. *Blew up the temple?* After he explained it, though, it made sense. The Romans had no need to waste the time and manpower to move the stones so far away. So Cohen believes General Titus's army cut down olive trees—lots of them—from the Mount of Olives just across the Kidron Valley. Next, they placed the trees under the water channels and tunnels directly under the temple. Since the channels were filled with water, the constant burning of the trees over time caused the water to become so hot that eventually it boiled and finally erupted, causing an explosion that sent crafted boulders to their resting places far from the temple.

However the Romans leveled the temple, they did quite a job! Arrogantly, they carried their spoils back to Europe and boasted that the gods of Rome were more powerful than the God of Israel. Certainly the mighty empire would fall, but somehow one of Israel's worst enemies avoided a divine wiping out. Why them and not the Hittites? Why does Germany exist but not the Canaanites? Spaniards still reside in Spain. Why don't Edomites still dwell in Jordan?

What about the Promise to Curse Those Who Curse Israel?

Certainly a case is made for the fact that each of these nations after attacking Israel wielded considerably less influence. No one is worried about Italy becoming the next superpower and taking over the world. In its heyday, Spain became a world leader mainly through its conquests on the sea. In the tenth century, the Spaniards enjoyed a golden age of Jewish science, literature, and philosophy. Jews enjoyed more freedom in Spain than in any other European country. In some cases, they even held high offices within the government. Over the next few centuries, that would all change. By the time King Ferdinand and Queen Isabella reigned in the 1400s, Jews were openly called Marranos (swine), and the Spanish Inquisition was underway. A Jewish writer of the day penned these words, "One third of the Marranos have perished in the flames, another third wander homeless over the earth seeking where they may hide themselves, and the remainder live in perpetual terror of a trial."[6] At the height of hysteria, the king and queen gave Jews a four-month opportunity to leave or face execution. They fled to other countries like Russia, Turkey, and Eastern Europe, where later persecution continued. The location was new but the tactics were old, as over the years God's chosen people ran from one pogrom to another. Spain fell from its lofty position, going from superpower to also-ran, never returning to its prominence again. Somehow, though, it avoided the wrath of God's judgment.

Today, with six million Jews back in the biblical land of Israel, they are again in a familiar position—surrounded by their enemies! Outnumbered nearly a hundred to one, citizens of Israel are in the middle of the highest concentration of Jewish haters on the face of the earth. Islam teaches that no land under the control of Muslims can ever again be ruled by "infidels." The fact that Israel not only exists as a nation but thrives in such hostile surroundings is a major embarrassment to the Muslim world. That the land once conquered and controlled by the Islamic Ottoman Empire of Turkey for 400 years has now slipped through their hands is more than Muslim leaders can stomach. That the land was lost and is now in the hands of Jews makes it ten times worse for any Koran-believing Muslim. In some cases, Israel's existence is ignored by them altogether. Weather maps and geography books in many Muslim countries show the location of the land of Israel yet fail to even put a name on the territory.

Yet the law of diminishing influence is certainly visible in today's Muslim empire. Recent statistics from the United Nations reveal that Islamic countries rank the lowest of the low in national literacy and abject poverty. Mighty empires of the past like Egypt continue to wallow well behind the majority of the world, all the time watching Israel grow and prosper. If it weren't for their vast oil reserves, they would be as insignificant as the underdeveloped countries in Africa.

What's amazing to realize is that Arab people truly have one of the most beautiful cultures in the world. Their warmth, passion for life, and hospitality can hardly be rivaled. What's sad about Middle Eastern Arab culture, however, is that it experienced a hostile takeover at the hands of the Muslim religion. As Jews rejected Islam and as the Arabs embraced it, a poisonous hatred permeated the region. Hatred of Israel came to be the unifying theme of Middle Eastern Islamic countries.

I have to say at this point, most Arabs and also most Muslims do not experience a latent desire for the state of Israel to be driven into the sea. Yet because Islam is only compatible with governmental dictatorships, somewhat like the Mafia, the worst and the cruelest often rise to the top positions of power. One exception was Jordan. The late King Hussein, though thoroughly Muslim and a supposed descendant of Muhammad, appreciated Israel and conducted secret meetings with former Prime Minister Golda Meir.

At best, Islamic nations of the region tolerate the existence of Israel. At worst, other Islamic nations look for, pray for, and find their national identity in an outright destruction of Israel.

A reporter in Egypt recently questioned why so many Islamic nations were in financial chaos and plagued by illiteracy. He concluded that the best way for them to advance themselves was to give up one thing and one thing only—a hatred of Israel. Truly, Islamic nations have an obsession with Israel that holds them back from progressing. It also keeps their leadership from taking responsibility for their own failures. But within a day of his article being published in Cairo, threats to the newspaper began immediately, calling for his death. Arab nations sadly will remain in a virtual "dark age" until the death grip of Islam is released and the true beauty of Arabs emerges again. Until then, their influence is diminished.

When God Comes Through

What do all of Israel's enemies throughout the centuries have in common? Each one of them has a coming appointment with God. It can't be rescheduled or skipped, and no one will be late. An audience with the King of kings is going to be held in the future, and all the nations will be in attendance.

The book of Joel gives us a glimpse of the Gentile judgment in chapter 3, starting in verse 1. What's so significant about this time is that the nations have not been assembled like this since their meeting on the plain of Shinar at the Tower of Babel. Because the people would not listen to God's command to fill the earth, He forced it on them. By creating a multitude of languages, the people stumbled away in confusion, and the nations of the world began. The last meeting was one they called. This one, God calls.

The scene from Joel's prophecy takes place in the Kidron Valley just east of the Temple Mount in Jerusalem. God first "restores" the fortunes of Judah and Jerusalem. They are then firmly planted in the land with no more talk of displacing them or conquering them. God then says to all the nations gathered in the famed Valley of Jehosaphat, "I will enter into judgment with them there because of My people, My inheritance Israel" (Joel 3:2b). Matthew tells us in chapter 25 of his Gospel that nations will be divided into two groups—sheep and goats. The goats on the left will receive God's holy wrath due them for their treatment of His chosen people Israel. The sheep on the right, the place of honor in the presence of God, will receive the ultimate favored-nation status and will be spared eternal devastation.

God will come through. Though present-day nations seem to pick on Israel endlessly and get away with it, this won't last forever. God will honor the unconditional promises of the Abrahamic covenant and finally curse those who curse the patriarch's line. He's keeping score even now. When God's promise comes full circle and collides with eternal judgment, the Holocaust, the Spanish Inquisition, and the Crusades will appear minor in scope. We are talking about large segments of the Gentile world being lost at one time. Apparently, with Israel's endless supply of enemies down through history, the goats far outnumber the sheep. I would imagine that the sheep count is a remnant, while the goat count is enormous.

Words will be replayed:

- Hitler calling the Jews "filthy vermin."
- Bin Laden calling the Jews "monkeys."
- The Grand Mufti of Jerusalem in 1948: "We must make the Jews live in hell."
- Anti-Semitic slogans: "Kill the dirty Jews!"
- Saddam Hussein's cash award to Jewish murderers falsely labeled as *shaheed* or martyrs.
- Mahmoud Ahmadinejad's "Iran will wipe Israel off the map!"

The fight for Jerusalem, the city God chose to reside in, will be remembered. Yasser Arafat delivered these words in a South African mosque on May 10, 1994: "The jihad will continue. . . . You have to understand our main battle is Jerusalem. . . . You have to come and fight a jihad to liberate Jerusalem, your precious shrine. . . . No, it is not their capital. It is our capital." Premier Aleksei Kosygin of the Soviet Union in 1967 called Israel "fascists" filled with "atrocities and violence" after they reclaimed their Holy City on the final day of the Six-Day War.

The present-day intifada will be seen for what it is as suicide bombers pay dearly for their demonic zeal to kill Jews on city buses and in crowded marketplaces. Men and women who wired themselves with dynamite measured in pounds will be exposed as cold-blooded killers of God's people.

On a recent visit to Israel, we visited a rehabilitation center in Tel Aviv.

Seeing soldiers and civilians who will spend their remaining days in hospital beds was an emotional experience for our mission team. A blinded twenty-year-old engaged soldier, a man without his legs, a woman with a horribly burned face. The gruesome side of the endless news stories about another bus explosion brought to light the sad reality of this new holy war. Until Israel built the much disputed wall between Palestinian areas and Jewish areas, the numbers flew by us almost nightly: ten dead, thirty-four wounded; fourteen dead, twenty-eight wounded. But these are real people, with lives that will never recover from the newest way to get rid of more Jews.

In April 2002, while preparing to worship at the Garden Tomb in Jerusalem, my prayer partner Allen Reedall and I heard a deafening explosion that sounded like it was just across the street. We were wrong. Nearly a mile away, all were deeply saddened to hear that a young Palestinian woman had just detonated twenty pounds of dynamite strapped around her waist, neatly hidden under her baggy burqa. Her killing spot was carefully chosen—the crowded Jewish marketplace on Mahane Yehuda Street where Jews were busy buying last-minute items before sundown officially began another Sabbath. Ironically, Colin Powell was a few blocks away from the blast on another diplomatic quest for the elusive peace that once again was evaporating in Israel. Unfortunately, this misguided Muslim woman believed she would be met at heaven's gate by Allah and his prophet Muhammad to receive a reward for her "courageous act." She, too, will have an appointment with the King of kings in the Kidron Valley and receive her just reward—eternal punishment.

To say "turnabout is fair play" during God's judgment one day in Jerusalem is to put it mildly.

At Last . . . Deliverance!

In the early years of Israel's spiritual formation, God swiftly and completely judged the nations who cursed His people. During their establishment in the land, people groups that mocked God soon were recorded on God's endangered species list and then died out. After Israel experienced a spiritual defection and went the way of the pagans into wholehearted idolatry, God sent a nation to take them out of their beloved homeland into captivity. The sentence was carried out by the wicked Babylonians, whose prison was located in the ancient homeland of Abraham. Yes, the place where the promise had been given to a future people was ironically the place where God chose to discipline them seriously. A major shift had occurred, and one must wonder if Israel, while sitting on the banks of the Euphrates River, fully grasped the turnaround. It was so simple:

- God used Israel to punish the nations who had rejected Him and His people.
- God was now using the nations to punish Israel, who rejected Him while being His people.

As far as history goes, the extermination of nations ceased. The Israelites, through their rank disobedience, was no longer any different in lifestyle from the people living all around them. But God kept score. He always does. The Babylonians punished Israel, and then God punished them by collapsing their kingdom. The Medes and the Persians overran the people from the area of present-day Iraq. But their capital city fell, and the influence of all these groups became a feeble whimper from the past.

The law of diminishing influence had begun to take effect.

And so presently, God does not "smite" the nations as He once did. That's not to say that He couldn't or won't again. But compared to all the smiting that God did in Israel's early days, times have changed. His weapon of choice today appears to be one that slowly removes a nation from prominence to mediocrity over time. While cursing Israel today, a nation may encounter a type of slow leak that reduces the people group in scope and world stature.

Muslim nations are marginalized economically. The former Soviet Union collapsed after a century filled with anti-Semitism as a core value. Even Great Britain, which once boasted that "the sun never sets on the British Empire" when describing its world influence, has ceased to be the power it once was only decades ago. The sun does indeed set on the British Empire now. Could this be yet another case of how one nation turned its back on Israel and paid dearly for it?

Great Britain ended up fighting against the very state they hoped to help create one day. From 1917 to 1948, the English ruled then-Palestine and severely restricted the flow of Jewish immigrants to Israel through its famous series of white papers. The six documents spelled certain death for Europe's Jews by blocking them from mass immigration and allowing them only to trickle back to Israel in small groups. Otherwise, thousands could have avoided the gas ovens that were already warming up for them throughout the growing Nazi regime. Heavy stuff to say the least, but a promise is a promise, especially when God makes the promise. "He comes to sift the nations in a sieve of destruction" (Isa. 30:28b).

Okay, enough cursing, smiting, annihilation, and removing of world powers! Has anyone experienced blessing because of blessing God's people Israel? I'm glad you asked! We'll look at that in chapter 3.

Jasmine—An Iranian Woman of Great Faith

Living for Christ is dangerous in Iran. Living for Christ in Iran as a woman is even worse. Living for Christ in Iran as a woman and a convert from Islam is impossible. Or is it?

Jasmine had a good life in Tehran. She was married to a husband who provided well for her, and they had a two-year-old daughter. Jasmine's in-laws adored her. Life was great. But her life was about to change—over-night—when Jasmine began to question Islam and the validity of the Koran. This is a religion that allows no questions. The Koran makes it very clear: if you ask questions, you are considered an infidel.

But her questions would not go away.

Jasmine soon met some believers in Iran. They had to be careful as they reached out to her because Iran is crawling with secret police whose job is to root out the underground church and destroy it. But the believers could tell that God was bringing conviction to Jasmine. Her quest to personally know God was real.

Women have few rights in Islam. This stems from Muhammad's belief that women are inferior to men. In the Hadith, which is the commentary on the Koran, Muhammad spells it out. "The prophet said I looked at Paradise and found poor people forming the majority of the inhabitants; and I looked at Hell and saw that a majority of its inhabitants were women" (Hadith 4.54.464). Yet in the Bible, Jesus elevated women and gave them a sense of dignity. When believers shared this with Jasmine, she was amazed to discover that Jesus gave two women the high honor of discovering He had been raised from the dead. The disciples were not there, but two women were.

One day, Jasmine repented of her sins and received Jesus as Savior. She was instantly transformed in Christ and was at peace with God, a joy which radiated all over her face. But she would need His strength in the coming trials, for not everyone was excited about her new faith. Her husband, Mahmoud, realized something had changed in Jasmine and he didn't like it. She was happy and loving and seemed secure—less dependent on her husband. Mahmoud became filled with jealousy, and the confrontation arrived.

One day in front of his family, Mahmoud angrily asked, "Are you still a Muslim?" Jasmine took a deep breath and answered, "No, I am following Jesus now."

That was all it took. Within a few days, Jasmine was standing in court in Tehran, and Mahmoud was demanding a divorce. *Why would he go to court?* she wondered. In Islam, all that was required was to say "I divorce you" three times and it was over. But Mahmoud wanted to ensure that the court enforced the anti-conversion laws in order to make Jasmine's life miserable.

He would not be disappointed.

The trial was quick, and the divorce was granted immediately. Next the judge ordered Jasmine to stand. "You have two choices," he ordered. "You can reject Christianity, return to Islam, and all will be forgiven. But if you reject this offer and remain a Christian, you will be deported from Iran, and you will never see your daughter again. The court demands an answer right now!"

With the composure of a seasoned believer, Jasmine rose and faced her husband, the judge, and the all-male court. "I have only known Jesus for a short time," she said, "and He has given me so much already. What you are asking a mother to do is the most difficult thing imaginable because I love my daughter so much, but . . . I choose Jesus!" With those words Jasmine was handcuffed, taken to the Tehran airport, and flown to another country in the Middle East. She would never return to Iran.

Today, Jasmine's smile lights up the room when she enters. The perfect peace that Jesus has given her is evident for all to see. She has devoted her life to training young women who are going into missions. And their destination when they finish Bible college? Iran!

Jasmine is a heroine of the church in the Middle East. Her testimony is known throughout the region. One day I asked, "Jasmine, how could you have the strength as a young believer to stand up for Jesus when it meant leaving your four-year-old daughter for good?" Jasmine smiled and said, "You know, Tom, you have to come to the place in your life where you trust Jesus with everything, even your children. I cannot be there to raise my daughter, but I know Jesus is faithful to take care of her, and He will give her the love that she needs even without her mommy being there. He is good, and I trust Him with my daughter."

Jasmine smiled and walked back into her classroom. Her students were waiting for her. They want to reach Iran for Christ.

But when they hand you over, don't worry about how or what you should speak. For you will be given what to say at that hour, because you are not speaking, but the Spirit of your Father is speaking through you. (Matt. 10:19–20)

Chapter 3
A Promise That Shaped America

God's road map for a nation's security is found in the first book of the Bible. It's no coincidence that America soared to its prominent world position after its all-out support of Israel becoming a nation again in 1948.

Road Map to Prosperity

Vacations for the Doyle family have always been a mixed blessing. On one hand, it's wonderful getting away from it all, but with six children and two adults in one car, I often feel like I need some kind of counseling afterward. Driving for a day with teenage hormones and brother/sister rivalries while crammed in an overstuffed minivan is major combat duty. Our number-one goal, of course, is to get wherever we're going by setting a new land speed record. The quicker we get there, the less chance there is of an all-out mutiny.

One vacation a few years ago, though, was admittedly over the top. We tried to make it from Colorado to Florida in two days. Two days! That's about fourteen hours of driving, two days in a row. On our way back to Colorado, my wife, JoAnn, was driving. Let me first say this. JoAnn is my beautiful little Italian bride. She has many wonderful qualities and numerous spiritual gifts. She does, however, struggle with a directional disorder caused by an inability to decipher north from south and east from west.

While cruising through West Texas toward New Mexico, I decided to get a little shut-eye. I was exhausted from two 3:00 a.m. starts, and I told my sweet wife I probably wouldn't fall asleep but just rest. Wrong! Before I faded out, though, I told JoAnn what to do after we hit the big cities of Dumas and Dalhart. "Just go west on 87 into New Mexico, honey."

After sleeping for nearly three hours, I awoke and immediately had a funny feeling as I looked outside at our surroundings. They didn't look familiar. As I saw the next mileage sign, we were nearly in Boise City, which meant we were really making good time. The only problem was that we weren't going to Boise City. Boise City is in Oklahoma. Boy, were we lost! After the whole car broke into prolonged laughter, we grabbed the map and found our way back toward the Rocky Mountains and headed out of Sooner land. Getting lost can sure leave you feeling mentally exhausted.

It was the same way in Old Testament days. In the first book of the Bible, God purposefully laid out a clear road map which, when followed, would lead any nation along a path that resulted in abundance, blessing, and prosperity. Throughout the centuries, nations that followed the map and stayed on course experienced everything God said they would.

A modern-day example of God's all-out blessing is the United States of America. The course of our country was dramatically altered in the last century when American leadership decided to take the plunge and support the reforming nation of Israel. It was risky and decisive for the U.S., but with strong leaders and a national Judeo-Christian thrust at the time, we followed God's map, stayed on the path, and have never looked back. I believe this is the main reason for our rise to the top spot on the world powers list. In about sixty years, America has soared to prominence never experienced by another nation in history. In short, we are number one in influence, power, and prosperity. The road map took us exactly where it promised—to the place of blessing. America has faithfully been a blessing to Israel over six decades now, and God has in turn generously poured out His blessings on us.

Following God's road map has not been without conflict, however. There has always been a fight over which road map we would follow. Significant groups of people have wanted to throw away God's road map, claiming it's outdated and that its benefits are few, if any. Failing to see the power of God's unconditional Abrahamic covenant, they attribute American prominence to intellect alone. We are just smarter than all of the other nations, they think.

This argument is easily shot down when we compare ourselves to the Asian nations that routinely outscore us in academic testing. Why is China not experiencing more prosperity than we are? Admittedly, things are changing in China with its ability to field an extremely cheap labor force. Yet with its failure to bless Israel, China is light years behind us in world influence, economic prosperity, and basic living conditions. We are not smarter than everyone else, but our blessing of Israel overcomes even intellectual shortcomings. God blesses us as a nation because we support Israel, not because of our national IQ.

Anti-Semitism in America

Unfortunately, the other suggested road maps often reeked of anti-Semitism. Their paths called for us to distance ourselves from Israel or to reject her altogether. The battle was birthed during the chaotic first half of the twentieth century. Two world wars were fought during that time, and intertwined in each conflict was the sticky problem of European Jews and their growing desire to reinhabit the biblical land of Israel.

America was in the midst of an upsurge in immigration due to European instability. Irish, Italians, Germans, Poles, and Jews were streaming into Ellis Island in search of the American dream and to escape the economic uncertainty of their native lands. The United States offered jobs—plenty of them. The modern industrialization of the nation was built on the back of a seemingly never-ending labor force that arrived by the shiploads.

But instead of New York City becoming a melting pot, in time it became "little Europe" with the various ethnic groups living together. Other American cities experienced similar growth patterns, with little homogenization of cultures. Rather than cultures blending together, the majority of people groups occupied a certain turf within their respective cities. As a result of this, many of the old prejudices from Europe traveled with the immigrants and became as strong as they were in the old country.

During the 1800s in America, Jewish immigrants had experienced little or no discrimination. National issues were not particularly applicable to Jews at the time. With the Civil War dominating the century, Jewish immigrants were ignored and for the most part irrelevant. By the 1880s, however, a wave of German Jews immigrated to America. And when the turn of the century arrived, the seeds of anti-Semitism had already been planted. Things were changing rapidly for the American Jew.

By the 1920s, Jews were the fastest growing ethnic group in the United States. Henry James reflected the mood of the times with his book *The American Scene*, published in 1907, as Jewish families were filling up New York City's lower east side. "Jewry that had burst all bounds . . . the children swarmed above all—here was multiplication with a vengeance. . . . There is no swarming like that of Israel, when once Israel has got a start."[1] Jews were streaming in; and to many, New York resembled a twentieth-century promised land.

Not many were applauding their arrivals, however. Oscar Handlin wrote, "A great number of Americans became obsessed with the fear of Jews."[2] Within years, Jews were not looked on with favor as hard-working, blue-collar types. They were seen instead as a threat to America, suspicious at best. The garment industry had been home to a large Jewish labor force, and many Americans desired for them to remain there with little chance to move up the social ladder or to explore other employment avenues. This is one of the reasons why so many Jews started their own businesses and eventually became entrepreneurs. What happened to change how American Jews were perceived in the land of the free?

The Power of Print

Anti-Semitism in modern days has deep roots in the soil of Europe and in the nation of Germany in particular. Germany launched repeated attacks on the Hebrew race in the second decade of the twentieth century. The heat was turned up to a boil in America, as well, following the widespread distribution of three publications.

The Protocols of the Elders of Zion was authored in Russia and translated into English in 1920. The translation proved to be a spurious one, but this fact was revealed only after it had made its way into full circulation, and by then the damage had been done. The book falsely accused Jews of just about everything under the sun.

Another book followed in the same vein. *The Cause of World Unrest* claimed that the Bolshevik Revolution was Jewish in nature, and the real reason behind it was a massive underground effort to destroy Christendom worldwide. Europe's problems were all being hung around Jewish necks, and the masses were duped into believing laughable assumptions: Jews were dangerous, and hostile takeovers were probable wherever they lived.

Interestingly enough, in the current Israeli-Palestinian conflict, the video version of *The Protocols of the Elders of Zion* has been continuously shown in Muslin-dominated countries such as Egypt. The movie, which has three episodes, was shown over three-week periods. It was accepted hook, line, and sinker with no verifiable evidence to support any of the film's outrageous claims by Arabs all over the Middle East region. The propaganda has proven quite effective again by making the Jewish race a scapegoat again for everything that has gone wrong in Arab culture itself.

As if these two books weren't enough to fuel an uproar and pervert public opinion, a third came along to fan the flame into a wildfire.

Did Ford Have a Better Idea?

With Americans becoming obsessed with Judaiphobia, the country's most important piece of anti-Semitic literature was yet to come, authored by an American icon named Henry Ford. *The International Jew* was written by the automobile-manufacturing guru and legendary businessman during the tide of rising anti-Semitism of the 1920s. With a well-known figure like Ford selling a book that capitalized on anti-Jewish fears, the work sold in the millions in a few short years. Again, the book was based on bogus claims that Jews had a calculated plan to take over the world through finance. America's true enemy, Ford claimed, was the influential Jewish culture that was growing by leaps and bounds and soon to dominate the United States. Jewish immigration had grown to 2.5 million between 1880 and 1925, and it seemed to sound a national alarm across America.

Even Mark Twain, who was normally sympathetic to the plight of the people without a land, got into the act. He quipped this concerning Jews in America: "When I read in the *Encyclopedia Britannica* that the Jewish population of the United States was 250,000, I wrote the editor and explained to him that I was personally acquainted with more Jews than that in my country, and that his figures were without a doubt a misprint for 25 million."[3]

The International Jew swayed a significant portion of Americans to believe that Jews were multiplying out of control and that all would soon be lost to the race that bore the guilt of single-handedly wrecking the continent of Europe.

Henry Ford was finally forced to stop printing the book in 1927. Today, however, you can see a copy of it in Jerusalem's Yad Vashem Holocaust Museum in the section titled "Pre-Nazi Anti-Semitism." Again, the damage had been done, as Ford was one of the chief architects behind American anti-Semitism.

Ford was not deterred one bit by the book ban. He quickly began printing a newspaper called *The Dearborn Independent*. This insightful slant on American news routinely ripped American Jews, and all Ford automobile dealerships nationally were ordered to carry the newspaper.

Recently while at lunch, I heard a commercial about Ford Motors and how Henry Ford was the first American businessman to pay his workers five dollars a day. In those days, that was a huge step forward in American plants and was hailed as a major breakthrough for our labor force. Ford was well loved for this and became known as a leader among leaders. That's why his relentless hatred of Jews proved to be so damaging, since it was launched by an American hero.

H.L. Mencken, writing for the Michigan-based paper, summarized the publication's intentions with these words, "The case against the Jews is long and damning. . . . It would justify 10,000 times as many pogroms as now go on in the world."[4] It seems unbelievable that words like Mencken's would emanate from the United States instead of Russia, Germany, or the Muslim-dominated Middle East.

This was serious. Americans were being hit hard with anti-Semitism. What the Jews had encountered throughout history, such as their enslavement at the hands of an Egyptian pharaoh during the days of Moses, was exactly what they deserved, according to their racist accusers. They had it coming, and more was on the way. All of this was being spread throughout the United States, the nation born out of a quest for religious freedom.

Jews were now going it alone in many ways. Wall Street and Ivy League schools began to deny Jews jobs that formerly were open to them. So they began migrating in growing numbers to the West Coast, where they were less suspicious to the older institutions that existed on the East Coast. And because Jewish Americans displayed a natural talent for business, they eventually became the primary movers and shakers in the growing movie industry developing in southern California.

America Follows Suit

With all the propaganda creating national panic, something had to be done. So legislation began to emerge in an effort to put a very short leash on American Jews.

The Johnson Act of 1924 restricted immigration and began to establish quotas on the less-desired races. At the top of the restriction list, of course, were Jews. Racially-motivated intellectuals led by Henry Cabot Lodge of Massachusetts along with southerners Madison Grant and Prescott F. Hall believed that the northern and western Europeans were superior to Mediterraneans, Slavs, Orientals, and especially Jews. English, Irish, German, and Scandinavian people were not restricted in the immigration process; only the undesirables were held back.

The anti-Semitic trend jumped tracks quickly into the business world. Large insurance companies, banks, retail chains, and law firms generally did not hire Jews. So by the 1930s, with American Jews wanting to venture out of the garment industry and into new lines of work, they found that they were virtually shut out from every possibility.

Like a brush fire, discrimination against Jews was spreading everywhere. College teaching jobs and university faculty positions were almost always off limits to Jews. Private colleges and universities began to establish quotas to limit Jewish admissions. Institutions of higher learning fell into the grip of racism. It was most difficult for Jewish students to be accepted at medical schools. This forced many Jews to study abroad. Harvard, the cornerstone of the Ivy League founded on Christian principles, pushed to implement Jewish limits through the quota system. The plan was voted down by the faculty, but President Lawrence Lowell allowed it anyway, thereby bypassing the vote.[5]

Charles "Lucky" Lindbergh, the legendary American aviator who successfully flew the first flight over the Atlantic Ocean, hated the Jews. He actually liked Adolf Hitler. He portrayed him as a nonthreatening leader after meeting with him in Berlin before World War II. He joined the chorus claiming that Jews were the most dangerous group in America, boldly predicting that any U.S. involvement in war would be directly linked to a Jewish push toward it. At an America First rally, he attacked American Jewry.

Truly, the ranks were swelling. By 1944, 24 percent of polled Americans regarded Jewish people as "a menace."

But in an ironic twist, 85 to 90 percent of Jewish voters backed Franklin D. Roosevelt in presidential elections and openly embraced the New Deal. Some claimed that behind the scenes the New Deal was really the "Jew Deal," but Roosevelt quickly dispelled those rumors with an overt attempt to distance his administration from Jewish Democrats.

In 1939, a low point occurred in the FDR presidency with America's treatment of Jews. Joshua Brandt explained: "The story of the *St. Louis* is an ignominious and often overlooked chapter in the history of the Holocaust and World War II. The ship departed from Hamburg, Germany, in the spring of 1939 and set sail for Cuba. After various anti-Jewish rallies prevented the refugees from settling in Cuba, the ship sailed for the United States. There, too, the ship was turned despite the State Department's awareness of the severity of the situation. The ship later disembarked in four European ports after a month at sea. More than 300 of the passengers eventually perished in the Holocaust."[6]

Over time, America has had to come to grips with what the government allowed to happen to the Jews on that ship. Many of them ended up going to Auschwitz concentration camp. Michael Barak of the United States lost his father as a result of the American president's refusal to do anything about the *St. Louis.* He immigrated to Israel years ago and holds the United States responsible for the death of his father.

What perhaps is more shocking to learn from America's failure during World War II is that FDR's administration knew what was going on in Nazi Germany to the defenseless Jews and did nothing. Poland sent a secret envoy to inform the president about the mounting Jewish carnage, and still nothing changed. Even U.S. Jewish Supreme Court Justice Felix Frankfurter, who was Jewish, heard the same evidence about the Holocaust and remained silent. Perhaps the American leadership did not believe the reports, which must have seemed outrageous. To have heard of thousands of Jews being gassed in several European camps and remaining neutral seems unfathomable.

But perhaps saddest of all during the Jewish onslaught, an old front began to emerge again in open Jewish attacks. The church stood in line next, awaiting their turn to bash the descendants of Abraham.

Anti-Semitism in the Church

Irish Catholics, who previously had been recipients of widespread discrimination themselves, joined the chorus of boos leveled at Jewish immigrants. Father Charles E. Coughlin, a very influential Roman Catholic priest, led the way. This new Irish Catholic version of anti-Semitism became the Christian front for the United States.

The Jews were now getting it from all major sectors of society. And

Father Coughlin's weekly radio program, which was broadcast into millions of homes across the country, was filled with Jewish slander and vicious attacks. For Jews wanting to enjoy religious freedom without persecution that had been so prevalent in Russia and Europe, this seemed like the same song, second verse. But what was a new kind of assault for American Jews was unfortunately an old one worldwide for Judaism itself. Centuries earlier, the church had positioned itself as a bitter enemy of the Jewish race.

OFF TO A BAD START

In the first century, Jesus' church was in its spiritual formation stage, and several key questions were decided over the next few hundred years. Doctrines of highest importance were debated for decades and then finally formulated. Some of the earliest questions turned into enormous battlegrounds that the church had to maneuver its way through and then define. Questions like:

- Is it proper to fight in a war?
- Was Jesus truly God while at the same time truly man?
- Is Scripture to be read literally, or figuratively?
- Was Mary the mother of God?
- Is the Holy Spirit God?

At the same time, the church had questions about Jewish people in general. Even though their Messiah was Jewish, as were the apostles, what was the church to do with Jews? Unfortunately, the church fell into a theological trapdoor that set the stage for its checkered history. That trapdoor is unmarked, and many Christians fall for it yet today. Its name is "replacement theology," wherein the church replaces Israel, and the Abrahamic covenantal promises become void due to Israel's disobedience and outright rejection of the Messiah.

PROMISES, PROMISES

Yes, even though the church was birthed within Judaism, many Israelites did reject Jesus as Messiah altogether. The Jews had been confronted with the messianic claims of Jesus of Galilee centuries before and had passed Him off as a deranged rabbi gone astray. Their rejection of Him was thorough, branding Him a "blasphemer," torturing Him, murdering Him. God had visited the people that He chose out of all the nations of the world to offer them forgiveness of sins, and they had led the way in putting Him to death. No plunge into iniquity has ever been any deeper.

Obviously, this was an enormous sin, and it set the stage for the next several centuries of the Jews' tragic history. In Luke 19:44b, Jesus Himself predicted a coming Jerusalem catastrophe because of Jewish rejection of Him: "And they will not leave one stone on another in you, because you did not recognize the time of your visitation." The lowest point in Jewish history is not the Holocaust, although six million Jews dying needlessly is certainly nothing to make light of. The lowest point in Jewish history was their rejection of the Messiah.

The question is whether or not this cancels out the promises of Genesis 12. If the covenant was based on Israel's ability to obey, then replacement theology would be our only option. But even with the most casual reading of the verses, it is clear that the burden of fulfillment is on God and not His people.

In Genesis 12, God promised it. In Genesis 15, after Abraham had cut the series of animals and birds in half, it was God whose holy presence walked between them to confirm the covenant and personally guarantee it. Abraham had no responsibilities in the covenant. He did not participate in it since he was sleeping and viewed it through a vision. Every part of it was based on Yahweh and rested squarely on His shoulders. The covenant had no conditions. No ifs, no buts.

In other instances, our holy God promised blessing if the recipient remained in good stead with Him. The classic biblical example of a conditional covenant like this is the one made to Israel's third royal monarch, King Solomon. The setting for this promise was during an all-time high point for Israel. Solomon was God's man carefully selected to build the first permanent structure that God would reside in. The previous place God had dwelt in was a portable tent called the tabernacle, which was moved several times during Israel's years of wandering in the desert. But those days were over now, and God desired His house to be the heartbeat of His people's existence. King Solomon was given the sacred honor of constructing Israel's first temple. The breathtaking centerpiece of the Holy City would be much more than a place of worship. The temple would define Israel's very existence.

Upon completion of this massive task, God appeared to Solomon for the second time in his life:

> The LORD said to him: I have heard your prayer and petition you have made before Me. I have consecrated this temple you have built, to put My name there forever; My eyes and My heart will be there at all times. As for you, if you walk before Me as your father David walked, with integrity of heart and uprightness, doing everything I have commanded you, and if you keep My statutes and ordinances, I will establish your royal throne over Israel forever, as I promised your father David: You will never fail to have a man on the throne of Israel.
>
> If you or your sons turn away from following Me and do not keep My commands—My statutes that I have set before you—and if you go and serve other gods and worship them, I will cut off Israel from the land I gave them, and I will reject the temple I have sanctified for my name. Israel will become an object of scorn and ridicule among all the peoples. Though this temple is now exalted, every passerby will be appalled and will hiss. They will say: Why did the LORD do this to this land and this temple? Then they will say: Because they abandoned the LORD their God who brought their ancestors out of the land of Egypt. They clung to other gods and worshiped and served them. Because of this, the LORD brought all this ruin on them. (1 Kings 9:3-9)

Clearly, two major ifs were embedded in this promise. *If Solomon walked with God*, his lineage would have a continuous ruler on Israel's throne, *but if he or his sons turned from God*, then Israel's days in the Promised Land would be numbered.

Solomon did turn from God. In a selfish attempt to gain power no matter the cost, he married foreign wives in an effort to expand his burgeoning kingdom. An ancient Middle Eastern expression had found its way into Solomon's thinking: "trade follows the bride" worked well in the king's life. The more he married foreign princesses, the more his kingdom grew. Solomon forged alliances with all the important kings around him by simply marrying their daughters. This "all in the family" approach to doing business lavished wealth and prestige on the nation of Israel. The glory days were here, Solomon's strategic economic formula made him the fair-haired king of the known world, and Israel enjoyed being the lead nation of the world.

But it wouldn't last long, and its prosperity came with a price they were unprepared to pay. The Israelites were rejected by God, and their kingdom eventually disintegrated as they were carried away into two forced captivities. Solomon succeeded in opening up trade routes virtually everywhere through his multiple marriages. But the trade routes that traveled to pagan nations were also conduits to export idolatry back into Israel. Satan carefully crafted a spirit of religious tolerance in Israel, and God's holy nation finally crumbled.

God had specifically guaranteed that if Solomon went too far, everything promised was off. And when Solomon did, Israel's crash proved to be complete as Jerusalem was sacked and the people were carted off to live in the pagan capitol of Babylon. That's a conditional covenant.

God's promise to Abraham, however, had no strings, escape clauses, or conditions. Since it was based on God's unchanging nature—His immutability—it could not be reversed.

The prophet Jeremiah wrote the longest book of the Bible during the days just before Israel's Babylonian captivity. His prophecy dealt with the coming judgment on Israel, but in some places, he provided Israel with hope for the future. Through the Holy Spirit, God gave Israel concrete evidence they would have a future. That evidence is still in effect today. In Jeremiah 31:35–37 (NIV), the weeping prophet writes:

> This is what the LORD says, he who appoints the sun to shine by day, who decrees the moon and stars to shine by night, who stirs up the sea so that its waves roar—the LORD Almighty is his name. "Only if these decrees vanish from my sight," declares the LORD, "will the descendants of Israel ever cease to be a nation before me." This is what the LORD says: "Only if the heavens above can be measured and the foundations of the earth below be searched out will I reject all the descendants of Israel because of all they have done," declares the LORD.

THE EARLY CHURCH'S ANTI-SEMITISM

But somehow, the unconditional covenant with Abraham was rationalized and quickly forgotten by the early church. Church fathers that helped forge direction and shape doctrine led their followers into fully embracing anti-Semitism. Some of their thoughts on Jews are chilling to say the least:

- Justin: "Kill the Jews."
- Chrysostom: "Kill the pigs."
- Origen: "The synagogue is a brothel."

How sad the heart of God must have been! The church is to be the best friend Israel has. Paul in Romans 10 said that Jesus' church was to be the instrument God used to bring Jews to God. The Jews were to marvel at our living relationship with God, becoming envious and then turning to Him in repentance. Paul went on to drive the point home in Romans 11:1 with this question for us, the church: "I ask then: Did God reject his people? By no means" (NIV). The words "by no means" are an excellent translation of the Greek word *meganointa* which answers the question of a possible Jewish rejection with "never!"

Apparently, however, God's emphasis on His plan for the Jewish people fell on deaf ears. Over time, church leaders continued to use heavy artillery in dealing with Jews worldwide. The term "vermin" did not originate with Adolf Hitler but shockingly with the great leader of the Reformation movement, Martin Luther.

So when Father Coughlin in the 1930s began slandering American Jewish immigrants, it was nothing new. He merely was following an unholy church tradition of tearing down God's chosen people. *Encyclopedia Judaica* concurs that Coughlin's words were every bit as convincing and persuasive as Henry Ford's were.

WWII—Dark Days for Jews, Dark Days for the Church

The central figure that set the pace for an outright rejection of the Jews was seated in Rome, and he was unmoved by the desperate cries for help. His name was Eugenio Pacelli, Pope Pius XII. As leader of the Catholic Church from 1939–1958, he not only failed to speak out about Hitler's Final Solution; he formed an alliance with the century's most evil figure that ensured the fate of European Jews.

In *Hitler's Pope*, author John Cornwell catalogued the tragic reign of one of the Catholic Church's leaders. In the days before his papal rule, Pacelli was a lawyer who played a major role in Catholic theology and politics. In the 1920s, he served as papal nuncio in Berlin (a high-ranking Vatican official who acts much like a foreign ambassador to a particular country) and became quite familiar with Nazi ideology. Eventually, he came into a strategic association with the rising Adolf Hitler. Their relationship was a warm one, evidenced by the fact that Germany contributed more money to the Vatican than any other nation. In fact, "Germany had donated more funds to the Holy See than all other nations of the world put together."[7]

This startling fact led to an agreement between Germany and the Vatican that would deliver economic prosperity to the Catholic Church. The deal was advantageous for Germany as it clearly spelled out that the Nazis would rise unopposed by the most powerful Catholic community in the world. In 1933, then serving as a cardinal, Pacelli negotiated the *Reich Con-*

cordat with Hitler. Cornwell drew his information from Vatican and Jesuit archives that clearly outline the agreement. Privately, Hitler claimed that when the Catholic Church rolled over in compliance with the Nazis, the die was cast for Jewish eradication.

The case can easily be made by Protestants that Pope Pius XII did not represent the majority of Christians. Unfortunately, this objection matters very little to Jews who collectively lost one-third of their race in the Holocaust. Not only does it matter very little to Jews, but historically it doesn't hold up either. Certainly, it is easy for us to distance ourselves from the pope, but did evangelicals stand up en masse against the demonically infested empire of the Third Reich? No, again.

These are some of the most painful issues we as Christians can ever face. We can try to explain it away, but reasonable explanations fail. Evil flourished in the midst of church apathy toward the horrendous plight of God's chosen people. Years of pain, suffering, and murder passed by unopposed as we, the church, watched it all unfold. It is very easy for us in hindsight to point fingers and lay blame on others. But in my heart I know that I must ask myself, "Would I have done anything?"

While speaking to the Hadassah Jewish Women's Group of Albuquerque in 2002, I decided to face history head-on and ask the largely Jewish audience to forgive us as Christians for one of the worst examples of passivity ever. We will make strides in Jewish outreach only when we show a change of heart in dealing with anti-Semitism in the future. It will arise again. It is already on the horizon. A global hatred for Jews will culminate one day on Jerusalem's doorstep with the hopes of Jewish annihilation forever. The Lord Jesus will intervene at that time, and anti-Semitism will be eradicated forever.

But for now, back to World War II.

In *Hitler's Cross*, pastor Erwin Lutzer took us deep inside the church during the height of Nazi Germany. Seeing himself as some sort of Aryan savior, Hitler substituted the government of Germany for the church. The lines of distinction between the church and the Third Reich during these days blurred until they were nearly invisible. Lutzer reluctantly writes these condemning words: "Hatred for the Jews, I'm sorry to say, also flourished within the churches."[8] It's much more pleasant for evangelical leaders to remember heroes like Dietrich Bonhoeffer, Corrie ten Boom, and Martin Niemoller. Bonhoeffer, a pastor and Nazi resister whose classic book *The Cost of Discipleship* is still inspiring Christians, was executed on Hitler's gallows. Corrie ten Boom, who with her family helped innocent Jews escape via their secret hiding place, spent several years in Ravensbruck concentration camp. Martin Niemoller, another pastor, was sentenced to Dachau concentration camp until he was set free by Allied troops at the end of World War II.

These stories are exceptions, though, as by and large the German church was completely deceived. In Lutzer's book, the chapter "The Church is Dismembered" delineates how organized opposition to Hitler was all but impossible. Germany had now rebounded from its humiliating World War I defeat. The economy was exceptionally strong. German national pride was at an all-time high. Dr. Werner, Hitler's deputy for church relations, sent a letter to all German pastors in 1938, calling them to swear absolute allegiance to the Fuhrer. Later that year, the *Chicago Tribune* ran an article titled "Bible Twisted to Nazi Creed." The story uncovered Reich Bishop Ludwig Miller's rewrite of the Sermon on the Mount and the entire gospel of John to make it more favorable to the mood of the day. "The words *sin* and *grace* were deleted from the texts, and the Golden Rule was rewritten to apply only to relationships between Nazi comrades. All references to Old Testament prophets, from Moses to Abraham, were also deleted. Everlasting life was defined as 'true life.'"[9]

The pressure on the church was enormous, and the German body of Christ imploded. Crosses were now being replaced by swastikas on most churches. During Holy Week 1938, one bishop sent an enthusiastic telegram to Hitler with news that a great historic time had arrived. All the pastors in his district had obeyed a command and "have with joyful hearts taken an oath of loyalty to Fuhrer and Reich. . . . One God, One obedience to the faith. Hail my Fuhrer!"[10]

With church and state now walking hand in hand, anti-Semitism was the official stance of Germans whether they were Christians or not. During the "Night of Broken Glass" (*Kristallnacht*), when 177 synagogues were destroyed and 20,000 Jews arrested, the church fell silent. No outrage was expressed. Muted into oblivion, the church of Germany was marginalized during its greatest hour of need. Jews would be seized and taken off to die by the millions, and the church sadly sat by and watched.

In one church during worship each Sunday, parishioners clearly heard screams from trains filled with Jews headed for death camps. Week after week, the hideous sound interrupted the church service. Finally, the pastor had the people sing loudly during the exact time the train would pass the church, drowning out the cries of Jewish victims on the way to the slaughter. How sad! How indicting! Would we have joined the few resisters, or would we have just sung louder to avoid dealing with it all?

The head of the Gestapo described the church this way: "The situation in the churches is characterized by weariness with struggle, by uncertainty of purpose, and by lack of courage."[11] Lutzer's closing words pierce the heart of every follower of Jesus Christ: "If only the church had seen that when the Jews were persecuted, it was the Lord Jesus who was suffering."[12] Even more so, those who stood against the Nazis and faced imprisonment or death are to be remembered with honor. Their awards await them in heaven.

D-Day—The Real One

Knowing how widespread anti-Semitism was during the first half of the twentieth century and how Germans, Americans, Catholics, and Protestants got caught up in it, the conviction that U.S. President Harry Truman demonstrated in helping Jews establish Israel as their homeland is all the more remarkable. Certainly there was sentiment after the Jewish devastation of World War II to help them find a home and end their wandering after nineteen centuries. Yet with so many American lives lost during the conflict, the mood could just as easily have been to blame the Jews for it all.

The American failures were becoming obvious, as the photographs of living skeletons liberated from the death camps began shocking the world, making the rumors of what was going on under the Nazi regime pale in comparison to real life. The collective guilt that people of conscience felt left many Americans wondering what to do with the decimated house of David.

President Roosevelt died in April 1945, and the Jews—who seem to be able to forgive and forgive again—mourned the death of the four-term president. It would be decades before the truth was revealed about the extent of the president's knowledge of the Holocaust while it was in full swing. Would the next American president do anything to change the nation's course?

Indeed he would! Harry Truman turned out to be the man who would single-handedly change the direction of America. President Truman was the first American leader to risk his political livelihood by answering the call to lend a hand in helping Jewish survivors return to their biblical homeland as the reconstituted nation of Israel. As mentioned in chapter 1, the United Nations' proposed resolution for a Jewish homeland was so hotly contested that Truman had to use his influence to garner the last few votes needed to pass the historic vote in 1947. This was an American president's finest hour. In chapter 1, we looked at the political pressure Truman placed on Greece, Haiti, Liberia, and the Philippines in order to convince them to vote for the new Jewish state in November of 1947. In the book *O Jerusalem* we learn:

> The United States, again acting on the instigation of the White House, threw the full impact of its tremendous prestige behind the Jewish cause. Two justices of the United States Supreme Court personally cabled Philippine President Carlos Rojas warning that "the Philippines will isolate millions and millions of American friends if they continue in their efforts to vote against partition." Twenty-six senators cabled Rojas and urged him to change his nation's vote. The Philippine ambassador was summoned to a blunt but intensive briefing at the White House. Finally, Rojas ordered his delegation "in the higher national interest" to switch its vote from "against" to "for" partition.[13]

A Thanksgiving recess for the United Nations began the Wednesday before the official vote on November 29, 1947. This allowed time for more pressure and more communication with the nations that were needed to swing the vote Israel's way. A two-thirds majority was needed to pass the proposal—twenty-two votes—and President Truman turned up the heat even more with intense political pressure. O *Jerusalem* continues: "By direct order of the White House, the United States had exerted every form of pressure available to it on those nations in the United Nations opposed to partition or hesitant in their support of it. President Truman had personally warned the United States delegate to the United Nations, Herschel Johnson, to 'd--- well deliver the partition vote or there will be hell to pay.' His advisor Bernard Baruch had shocked France's United Nations delegate Alexandre Parodi with a blunt threat to cut United States aid if France opposed partition."[14]

Truman was in rare form! The pressure was working, and Israel was voted a nation again by the United Nations by twenty-three in favor, thirteen against, and ten abstentions. The vote to divide Palestine and give a portion of it back to its ancient inhabitants, Israel, was now a reality.

Chaim Weizmann, who had been the leader of the Zionist movement for decades and had been the one to persuade President Truman to support the Jewish state, was not able to attend. The severity of the moment complete with its historical significance leveled him with emotion. He was not able to leave his hotel room and attend the reading of the votes. He sat alone with his radio, sobbing uncontrollably.

Golda Meir, the future prime minister of Israel, sat in Jerusalem with a notepad in her lap, keeping a tally of the votes. At one point, her tears had so flooded the notepad that she was no longer able to read her own writing.

The reaction of the Syrian delegate to the United Nations was quite the opposite, of course. With chilling accuracy, he boldly proclaimed that the holy places of Jerusalem would now become a place of war. He also rightly predicted that peace would be absent from the area for generations.

Put Your Money Where Your Mouth Is

It is clear that God was moving powerfully throughout the earth during the 1940s. The war was over; and now that the Nazi war machine was destroyed, the question of a Jewish homeland had to be addressed. Several waves of *aliyah* (immigration) had already brought thousands of Jews back to what was then called Palestine. But alternative sites were also being suggested as a homeland for the Jews in an effort to avoid confronting the ultimate political nightmare.

At one point, Uganda had been offered by Great Britain as a possible new promised land for the Zionists. But Israel was the only place ever considered by the Jewish leadership. Israel was the land of the Hebrew nation. Jewish roots were deeply buried in the soil of Israel 3,400 years before. And try as they might, the nations of the world could not extract them. A Jew belonged in Israel. For centuries, the phrase "next year in Jerusalem" filled Jewish hearts with hope to keep their belief alive that one day they would return home.

President Harry Truman halted the tidal wave of anti-Semitism in America and, in so doing, changed the course of the United States. By blessing Israel, he impacted America more than he could have ever known, setting it on a trajectory for its meteoric rise to prominence among the nations of the world. On May 14, 1948, Israel became a nation again—brought back from the dead, and our American president was the first world leader to officially recognize Israel as a state. On the following page is a copy of the actual note from President Truman about the historical event.

This Government has been informed that a Jewish state has been proclaimed in Palestine, and recognition has been requested by the *provisional* Government thereof.

The United States recognizes the provisional government as the de facto authority of the new *State of* ~~Jewish~~ ~~state.~~ *ISRAEL.*

Harry Truman

Approved,
May 14, 1948.

6:11

But although this radically changed the course of history for Jews and Americans alike, it was obviously very unpopular with Arabs worldwide. America had oil interests in the Middle East, and its partnership with the Arabian American Oil Company (ARAMCO) was threatened with the rebirth of the Jewish nation. Amazingly, one of history's bastions of anti-Semitism, the Soviet Union, actually voted for the Jewish state. In retrospect, the Soviets probably thought that Israel would either be Socialist or even Communist since kibbutz life is based on principles of shared community. Not long after the founding of the state of Israel, the Soviets dumped their support and sided with the oil-rich Arab nations of the region.

The hand of God was evident in bringing Jewish people back in throngs to their beloved Israel. On May 14, 1948, the rebirth of the nation of Israel officially began. It was 4:00 p.m. in Tel Aviv when David Ben-Gurion, soon to be Israel's first prime minister, read these words that reverberated around the world: "In the land of Israel, the Jewish people came into being. In this land was shaped their spiritual, religious, and national character. Here they lived in sovereign independence. Here they created a culture of national and universal import and gave to the world the eternal Book of Books." The bones of Ezekiel 37 were no longer dead and dry; Jewish life was being breathed into the ancient land of Israel again.

America has for the most part been true to Israel ever since its rebirth in 1948. While the United Nations has frequently opposed the tiniest Middle East nation in a majority of its rulings, the United States has supported Israel. Over the years, America has helped Israel develop technology to defend itself. Like a big brother, the United States has at times been Israel's sole backer. Billions of dollars are sent from the U.S. Treasury to Israel each year to help the Israelis finance the enormous cost of being the area's only democracy while existing and thriving in the midst of so many hostile nations. Islamic-dominated countries are not the only ones ganging up on Israel. Many other powerful groups also speak out routinely against Israel: the Vatican, the World Council of Churches, the United Nations, the European Union, the Arab League, China, Russia, American Islamic groups.

Yet during the decades of faithful blessing of Israel, the United States has become the world's superpower. God's gifts have given America status that it never could have enjoyed had it failed to support Israel. The billions we have invested in God's chosen people have been much like a tithe to God. The more we have invested in Israel, the more God has blessed us.

In Malachi 3:10b, God says, "See if I will not open the floodgates of heaven and pour out a blessing for you without measure." This premier passage on tithing sounds very much like the results of our continual blessing of God's people, Israel. The promise found way back in the first book of the Bible to Abraham is the foundation by which our American nation has been shaped. Israel and America over the last sixty years truly have become two nations under God.

Jamal—Son of Thunder

Jamal is a work of art. This Arab believer is a ball of fire if there ever was one. His sense of humor is nonstop. He has an infectious smile. He loves Jesus with all his "heart, soul, and strength." He is one of those rare people in life who uses laughter like a spiritual gift. In the midst of danger, threats, and constant scrutiny, Jamal's smile is always present. He has been aptly described as an Arabic version of Jonathan Winters, the comedic "teddy bear" of the sixties and seventies. When Jamal is holding court, the jokes are clean and really funny. Then he turns to spiritual issues, and his wisdom and experience really begin to pour out.

Jamal is a veteran of the spiritual war that has been waged in the Middle East throughout his life. He lives in the trenches. He fights the good fight that is all around him. He knows all the right people throughout the Arabic world. He even shared the gospel with Yasser Arafat once! Onlookers say the Palestinian chairman had tears in his eyes as Jamal shared with him. Jamal has also told Jordanian officials about Christ and his life-transforming ability. He backs down to no one. The "backing down" component just doesn't fit within his spiritual nature.

Certain people in life are thoroughly committed to Christ and accomplish much for Him. Jamal is that and more. He is not only a high achiever but an influencer as well. To spend time with him means doing a spiritual self-examination at the end of the day. It just naturally happens while ministering with him. Christian leaders of the region look up to him. He achieves much for the kingdom of God and influences so many in the region.

For the Middle East world, he's perfect. As he often says, "If you want to serve Jesus faithfully in the Middle East, you must be a little crazy!"

Jamal grew up in Nazareth, an Israeli/Arab town. Much different from the desperate state that other Palestinians find themselves in, Nazareth's Arab citizens have a solidly middle-to-upper middle-class living situation.

Since they chose to accept Israel and also accepted citizenship, they hardly resemble their Palestinian relatives who struggle to survive. Most Arabs of Nazareth have good jobs and find themselves isolated from the ongoing conflict that blazes only a few miles away in the West Bank. Yet although Jamal was comfortable in Nazareth, he wanted to join the battle, to be enlisted on the front lines.

That's when God began to burden Jamal for the lost in Jordan.

Jamal certainly knew what he was up against. He knew that so many Muslims think they know what Christianity is all about, not realizing that their prejudice against Jesus and the Bible stems from the erroneous presentation of both by Muslim leaders who claim that:

- Christians worship three Gods.
- Jews corrupted the Old Testament.
- Jews hate Muslims because they themselves have been rejected by God, and Muslims have been accepted by God.
- Miriam, Moses' sister, was the mother of Jesus.
- Jesus did not rise from the dead.
- Jesus will convert to Islam.
- Christians took prophecies of Muhammad out of the New Testament.

Jordan is the gateway to the world of Islam. It is respected by other Muslim countries. The king is supposedly a descendant of Muhammad. It borders three strategic Islamic nations—Syria to the north, Iraq to the east, and Saudi Arabia to the south. On the western side is Israel. Jordan is definitely placed in the heart of the conflict, a hub for evangelism among Muslims. With Jordan's relatively easy access into surrounding countries, Jamal is able to travel freely and encourage believers in ministry all around the Middle East. He gives of himself tirelessly and often gets only four hours of sleep a night, his wife says.

Since Jamal lives on the edge and encourages others to do so, he has been arrested many times, as has his leadership team. He is hauled in for questioning. He is followed. He knows at all church services there are "listening ears." Jamal has written ninety Iraqi praise songs. Ninety! They are beautiful expressions of praise and worship to the God who is over all, even Jordan.

More than one Christian leader has told me that Jamal is a hero for Jesus Christ in the Middle East. He is intense yet lighthearted all at the same time—not only a pastor but a regional head for a parachurch ministry with forty staff members under him. He leads evangelistic campaigns and who disciples many men. He has a wonderful marriage and beautiful children.

One night, we met a man in his forties who had lived a very worldly life in Jordan. Don said that he smoked four to five packs a day of cigarettes a day and drank hard liquor in large quantities. As a songwriter and a nightclub singer, he had developed a self-serving lifestyle that robbed him of his health and wrecked his marriage. He wanted to kill himself—and almost did. Until Jamal reached him. After sensitively sharing Jesus with this nonreligious Muslim, Jamal knew he was ready. When confronted with his sinful problems and the need for forgiveness, Don fell on the floor and began to weep. He stayed there for an hour and a half. He embraced Jesus and was set free from sin and death.

Don now shares Christ effectively and daily. He is also writing Jordanian praise songs. He just recorded his first CD. He sings and plays the biblical lute instrument. Gone is the depression that once darkened his soul. He has a continual smile. He laughs constantly.

Jamal is discipling Don.

And what you have heard from me in the presence of many witnesses, commit to faithful men who will be able to teach others also. Share in suffering as a good soldier of Christ Jesus. (2 Tim. 2:2–3)

Section Two

Sorting Out the Middle East Maze

The solution to the Middle East powder keg is the church of Jesus Christ. Only He can transform the hearts of Arabs and Jews. No peace treaties or extra amounts of international pressure will change a thing. Only Jesus can save His homeland.

Chapter 4
Dangerous Alliances

Nations are currently realigning, forming new partnerships that will end in a regional Arab-Israeli war. This disaster will destabilize the world and spark a new holy war.

Deep Wounds

We Americans have relatively short memories. In our history as a nation, we quickly normalize relations with former enemies only a few years after being at war with them. During the birth of our nation, Great Britain, of course, was the feared evil empire of the day. The British invasion originally had nothing to do with the Beatles, the Rolling Stones, or the Dave Clark 5, but with England's famous redcoat army that fought us in one of our nation's bloodiest conflicts. "The British are coming" were the feared words of that period in history. Today, however, Great Britain is one of our most trusted allies worldwide. Our war wounds have healed, and relatively little animosity exists between the two nations.

During World War II, Germany and Japan fought against us and claimed thousands of U.S. lives in Europe and in the South Pacific. From Normandy to Pearl Harbor, American soldiers were killed and wounded defending our freedom from tyrannical world leaders who tried in vain to defeat us. My father served in the United States Army Air Corps, flying in B-17s as a radioman while America made its way into Europe through France. The lives lost fighting the Axis powers were not sacrificed in vain. Both Hitler and the Japanese invasion were stopped as America and its allies successfully defended democracy on two fronts in the turbulent 1940s.

Today, however, Germany and Japan are both forgiven and have become important allies for the United States. The regimes that drove them into a global conflict are long gone, and both nations that formerly despised us have firmly adopted our democratic ways. Apart from the recent war with Iraq, Germany has been a strong ally for years, and so has Japan. World War II is long gone. The wounds have healed. Forgiveness exists.

In the Middle East, however, forgiveness is rare. Wounds run deeper. Wars that concluded thousands of years ago still carry latent hostilities that are as strong today as ever.

While traveling to the Middle East for the first time, I quickly found out that a major stumbling block in Arab Muslim evangelism was a period in Christian history called the Crusades. Beginning in 1095, fueled by Pope Urban II's desire to establish Jerusalem as a Christian city, various "church armies" made their way to the Middle East. Their goal was to recover the Holy Land from the Muslims. Three waves of crusaders all coming from Europe extended the war from 1095 to 1291.

This dark chapter of church history was an abysmal failure. Thousands of Muslims, Jews, and Christians died needlessly as the church lowered itself, trading salvation by grace for salvation by force. The Crusades backfired on all fronts. And in the end, the church appeared to be no different from Islam in its approach to world evangelization.

The last battle was fought in 1291 in the coastal town of Acre. But Christian domination and control of Jerusalem ended when Saladin, the great Islamic general from Turkey, defeated the Christian army near the Sea of Galilee at the Hattin in 1187.

Other attempts were made over the next century. The famous Richard the Lionhearted of England fought and regained some ground but not Jerusalem itself. "The Crusades joined together two themes which were developing strongly in eleventh-century Europe: the Holy War or military expedition blessed by the church, and the pilgrimage to a holy place. The journey of a Christian army to recover the Holy Land from the Muslims fulfilled both of these."[1]

Shockingly, it is common to meet Muslims in the Middle East who still hold the Crusades against Christians as if they were fought last week rather than 800 years ago. The unforgiveness will not seem to go away. Like a bad cup of Turkish coffee, the Crusades left an awful taste in the mouths of millions of Muslims worldwide. And it remains this way today in Israel and the Middle East, where bitterness permeates an unsteady history.

Today's political commentators often try to settle the Middle East maze of conflict without allowing any room for the enormous religious and historical roots that run all the way back to the first book of the Bible, some 4,100 years ago. Old scores continue to be settled in this region over and over again. And speaking of old scores, some followers of Islam have plenty of them in their eyes to settle with both Christians and Jews. When it comes to Christians, Saladin still fights the Crusaders. When it comes to Jews, Ishmael still fights Isaac.

Islamic Agenda

Yet despite the incredible odds in their favor, Israel's surrounding nations—the descendants of Ishmael—have failed to achieve solidarity, and have not only hated the Jews but have hated each other. Truly, the deepest wounds Islam has experienced in the last century have been self-inflicted. And because of the differing interests among them, a comprehensive plan has yet to emerge from the region's Islamic nations. They lack two things as of yet: a common goal and a unifying leader.

But the common goal has started to become clear from Cairo all the way to Baghdad in the last few years. The goal is to take Jerusalem under Islamic control. The phrase "final status" is all about Jerusalem and what will ultimately happen to the city itself. This is the common goal that will unify Muslims not only in the Middle East but worldwide.

To Islam, control is everything. The advancement of the Islamic empire globally has been a textbook example of systematic seize-and-control land acquisitions. But no piece of earth yet to be taken is even close in importance to the city of Jerusalem. It is the ultimate test of the power of Islam, the one thing that would prove the superiority of the faith of all Muslims. For how can Islam call Jerusalem its third holiest city and fail to have complete control over it?

All that Israel has accomplished during its brief existence is galling to followers of Islam. Since the Jews' return, the achievements are quite remarkable. Here is a partial list:

The Desert Has Bloomed

For 400 years under Islamic Turkish rule, Israel was a treeless wasteland. Gone was the land of milk and honey that God promised to the Jewish slaves of Egypt in Exodus. Yet the land is a good land that God gave to His covenant people Israel. "The land of milk and honey" speaks of the inherent beauty and its subsequent crops that would burst forth with productivity.

During the time when Israel was in its dispersion and Muslims ruled the land, swamps emerged and the trees were cut down. But with Israel back, more than 100 million trees have been planted, the swamps are long gone, and the harvests are again lush and abundant. The malaria-infested area of northern Israel is now beautiful again. "A swampland until the twentieth century, the Jezreel Valley was drained in the 1920s by Zionist pioneers and now is one of Israel's major agricultural breadbaskets."[2]

The "green line" that marks Israeli territory is green because plants are growing on the Israeli side. In most areas, they are not growing on the Arab side. The reason for all the green within Israel is because Judaism values it; Islam does not. Oh, that God would liberate the beautiful Arab culture from Islam's life-squelching choke hold! Israel is only one of three countries worldwide that is self-sufficient and has no need to import anything to feed its growing population. Israel is a slice of paradise in the midst of the Middle East's sweltering sand.

Israel Has Brains

I don't know of any other way to put it. Israel is one of the most productive nations in the world. Their ingenuity is off the charts. This tiny nation is the third most technologically advanced nation in the world. The United States and Japan are numbers one and two. Here are some of their accomplishments:

- The cell phone was developed in Israel by Israelis working for Motorola.
- Voice mail technology was developed in Israel by Israelis working for Microsoft and Cisco.
- Instant Messenger for America Online was developed in 1996 by four young Israelis.
- Israel has the largest number of NASDAQ listed companies outside the United States and Canada.
- Israel has the highest number of scientists and technicians per capita in the workforce. 145 out of every 10,000 Israelis are employed in these technical professions.
- Israel is the only country to enter the twenty-first century with a net gain of trees.
- Israel ranks number two in the world with the second highest per capita of new books.
- Israel has the world's best airline flight security.
- Israel also has the largest number of biotech start-ups per capita.
- And this one is just flat-out mind-blowing—of the 750 Nobel Peace Prize winners between 1901 and 2006, Jews have accounted for 158! Twelve million Jews account for 22 percent of all Nobel winners.

ARABS HAVE RIGHTS

Since Israel is a democracy, Arabs who remained in the land and became citizens enjoy life more than in any other country of the region. Israel was the first country in the Middle East where Arabs could vote. Did you catch the full impact of that statement? Arab Israelis who have applied for citizenship vote in all elections!

Every Palestinian for years had the option to become a citizen of Israel and enjoy full privileges. And today, they are well represented within the Knesset. They even receive free health care. About one-fifth of Israel is Arab, and these citizens retain the same rights and privileges as its Jewish citizens do.

In East Jerusalem, where Arab residents share fears of a coming corrupt Palestinian state, many Arabs have applied for Israeli citizenship. I find this amazing in light of the fact that the Grand Mufti of Jerusalem has threatened death to anyone who makes application. (In fact, so many Palestinians have applied for Israeli citizenship in the past few years, the government has now closed that window of opportunity. Israel feared that within a decade their state would have an Arab majority.)

Arab citizens of Israel have it made compared to Arab citizens of all other Middle East countries. Arabs who live in Palestinian-controlled areas of Israel have no rights whatsoever. Arab-Israeli Muslims, on the other hand, experience the rarest lifestyle found in the Middle East—one of freedom and democracy.

REFUGEES ARE ASSIMILATED

When nations began to form in the Middle East during the 1930s and 1940s, the culture of each and every country changed drastically. The Jews left. Every Arab nation became hostile to its Jewish population. A great refugee problem was therefore birthed. More than 900,000 Jews were forced to leave the countries where they had lived for generations. With Jews returning to Israel, they were no longer welcome in Syria, Iraq, Jordan, and all the other Islamic countries. Israel opened its arms and gladly welcomed all Jewish refugees without hesitation.

WEALTH IS FOR ALL

Israel has developed a thriving economy even while being preoccupied with defending itself against the surrounding hostile nations. Though the Israelis possess no oil, they have become world leaders in technology, farming, tourism, and education. Israel, for example, is the world leader in diamond production—amazing, since diamonds are not even unearthed in Israel but are rather imported from Africa. The "princess cut" was invented in Israel along with a computerized method of cutting diamonds perfectly. This industry has become the number-one moneymaker in Israel today. Jobs are plentiful as the tiny nation puts to work its endless flow of immigrants who arrive on a daily basis. What a contrast to the oil-wealthy Muslim states that purposefully keep their citizens economically destitute while a privileged few hoard the billions of dollars that flow through their oil pipelines.

Of course, the ultimate goal of Islam is to dominate not only the Middle East but the entire world. Islamic leaders make no attempt to camouflage this. One of the modern jihad promoters of Islam is Mawlana Abul Ala Mawdudi of Pakistan, considered a scholar and a leader throughout the Islamic world. He summarizes Islam this way: "Islam is not a normal religion like the other religions in the world, and Muslim nations are not like normal nations. Muslim nations are very special because they have a command from Allah to rule the entire world and to be over every nation of the world." He went on to say:

> Islam is a revolutionary faith that comes to destroy any government made by man. Islam doesn't look for a nation to be in better condition than another nation. Islam doesn't care about the land or who owns the land. The goal of Islam is to rule the entire world and submit all of mankind to the faith of Islam. Any nation or power in this world that tries to get in the way of that goal, Islam will fight and destroy. In order for Islam to fulfill that goal, Islam can use every power available every way it can be used to bring worldwide revolution. This is jihad.[3]

No rules are brought to the table when it comes to Islam and jihad. This is the ultimate end-justifies-the-means religion. The name of the game is conquest.

Fundamentalist Islam projects a takeover of America by the year 2020, according to Islamic expert Dr. Robert Morey. One month after September 11, 2001, in a message titled "Christianity's Response to Islam," Dr. Morey shared this in a La Mesa, California, church. The formula is a simple one—a birthrate that exceeds everyone else's. Muslim's traditionally have very large families. In areas like Western Europe that promote small families and have liberalized abortion laws, it is easy to see why Muslim population growth skyrockets while the rest of Europe inches along slowly. In Russia, the numbers are staggering, as many Russians have one child while Muslims may have as many as ten.

The great success story of the Middle East, however, is not Islam but Israel. Muslim states privately seethe at Israel's golden touch. Without their oil, they would be insignificant third-world countries. This is not a result of Arab culture but of the Islamic religion. Islam enslaves, controls, and seeks to squash any democratic possibilities. Therefore, it has failed to advance its culture since its inception in the eighth century.

But the Muslim nations of the Middle East have enough oil to turn the table and level the playing field no matter how prosperous Israel becomes. In their eyes, they hold the ultimate trump card.

Oil, Oil, Oil

The discovery of oil has produced numerous rags-to-riches stories worldwide. Saudi Arabia is perhaps the most classic picture of this. This country is a huge desert, home to some of the hottest recorded temperatures on earth. It is also home to Islam's two most holy cities—Mecca and Medina. Saudi Arabia is the world's largest oil producer. Its oil influence dominates our globe, and its primary dependents are found in the West. East truly does meet West when it comes to oil deals.

Though Saudi Arabia has a small army and has yet to enter a war with Israel, it provides financial backing to the nations that do take on the Zionist enemy. The house of Saud has a wise strategy when it comes to dealing with Israel. The Saudis routinely help arm countries like Syria and Iraq with their vast wealth that pours into other countries' banks day after day.

The Saudis' generosity toward American universities, meanwhile, has catapulted them into the "major player" network. In recent years, the universities of Georgetown, Harvard, and Arkansas all received twenty million dollar gifts from Saudi Arabia. All three gifts came with strings attached. Prince Alwaleed bin Talal designated the money for Islamic studies. For Georgetown University, the check from the prince was the second largest throughout its long history. The University of Arkansas contribution from the late King Fahd was designated to a Middle East center in his name. Could there be a better way to turn America against Israel than to buy off American universities that are responsible for educating our next generation?

Saudi Arabia can buy the most sophisticated weapons available anywhere. And it does. Since it is a power broker in the financial world, the nation appears on the surface to be preoccupied with economic growth and not fighting a holy war. Yet as September 11 taught us, Saudi Arabia was where most of the terrorists were from, and anti-American sentiments are high there. Business is still business, but the Saudis are the major influence in the entire Middle East region whether or not they ever fire one shot at Israel.

Dave Dolan wrote, "With petrol dollars inundating Saudi coffers, the government went on a military buying spree in the mid-1970s. Over 63 billion dollars were spent in just the seven years before the preliminary Oslo accord was signed in 1993. The Saudis also doled out a couple billion dollars for Iraqi military purchases before the Gulf War and financed weapons for Syria before and after the conflict. Among other things, Saudi aid has been used in Damascus to purchase North Korean-made Scud missiles. The desert kingdom also helped finance the PLO, especially before Saddam Hussein's invasion of Kuwait."[4] Yet because of their business sense, the Saudis seem to be friends of the United States. Pictures of sheiks driving their latest Mercedes or BMW give the appearance that the Saudi kingdom is a desert version of Beverly Hills.

The financial strength of the country puts it at the top of the list in the Middle East in terms of worldwide clout and influence. Saudi Arabia is revered and honored by one billion Muslims worldwide as the birthplace of Muhammad and Islam. Mecca and Medina are the "twin cities" of Islam and are woven into the fabric of the religion itself. These holy cities receive millions of observant Muslims every year making their spiritual pilgrimage. But Mecca is a forbidden city for any non-Muslim. Christians, Jews, or nonreligious people cannot set foot in Mecca and are considered infidels. To violate this law would guarantee a death sentence.

Anti-American feelings are strong in Saudi for two major reasons:

1. *Our support of Israel.* Saudis believe the United States gives Israel everything it wants and that our support signifies a hatred of Arabs and Islam. The fact that we give billions in financial aid yearly to Egypt, Jordan, and even the Palestinian Authority is overlooked.

2. *Our supposed desecration of Saudi Arabia.* During the Gulf War, American soldiers were on Saudi soil. To be sure, Mecca and Medina were not "defiled," yet the sight of America launching a war with an Arab Islamic nation was more than religious Muslims could stomach. Osama bin Laden used this as the very reason for his vicious attack on America.

Saudi Arabia, then, has two powerful forces cooperating together in its midst—money and religious fanaticism. The Saudis must strike a delicate balancing act to keep the economic river flowing into their kingdom while at the same time appeasing fanatical Muslims who hate America and Israel with a passion.

But which side will win is easy to see, as it has been reported that the kingdom will run out of oil in the next fifty years. This seems unrealistic at first when we take into consideration that Saudi Arabia produces eight million barrels of oil a day and contains one-fourth of the world's oil reserves. But at our current oil usage rate, those reserves will run dry in a few decades, and Saudi Arabia will cease to be the world's biggest supplier. Religious fanaticism in Saudi Arabia, however, will never evaporate.

Saudi Minister of Interior Prince Nayef Ibn Abd-Al-Az, referring to the tragic events of September 11, 2001, in New York and Washington, D.C., said this: "I think the Zionists are behind these events. It is impossible that 19 youths, including 15 Saudis, carried out the operation of September 11th."[5] The prince went on to describe how he believes Zionist-controlled media in the United States manipulated the events and turned world opinion against Arabs and Islam.

I remember hearing about this fabricated story that was being circulated throughout the Middle East concerning the attack on America, and I seriously thought the Arabs would not believe it. How could they? The facts could not have been any clearer, and the motivation behind it was also well-known. But while ministering in the Gaza Strip, I met people who believed it without question. Obviously, the terrorist strike was a major embarrassment to Muslims and especially to Saudi Arabia, the origin of most of the terrorists. But what better group to hang the dirty deed on than the Jews, which is exactly what was pushed forward by a public relations campaign launched in the Muslim world to counter all negative publicity.

The roots of Islamic hatred toward Jews stem from Islam's very beginning in Saudi Arabia. In fact, because of how Islam was birthed, it will forever make despising Jews worldwide a positive virtue.

Down with Israel

When talking with Americans about the complexities of the Middle East situation, they eventually voice solutions having to do with the superficials behind the problems. To many it seems that Israel should give the Palestinians a state. If only Israel would pull troops out of the West Bank. If only Israel would remove the settlers from the Gaza Strip.

But when Israel did this under Ariel Sharon, it proved to be a disaster not only for Israel but for Palestinians, too. It seems so easy—until you travel there and receive your personal crash course on Middle Eastern religions. Herein lies the real problem. The wars, the intifadas, the suicide bombings, and the endless conflict have much more to do with religion than politics.

In his excellent work *Islam and the Jews*, author Mark Gabriel chronicles why Islam and Judaism got off on the wrong foot. Although it seems impossible now, at one time Mecca and Medina each had a sizable Jewish population. Jewish merchants residing there filled Arab markets. Orthodox Jews lived out their faith with no serious problems or interference for the most part. Arabs and Jews, the ancient cousins of the region, lived and worked side by side before Islam was established and the Jews were forced out.

Muhammad took the claims of the fledgling religion to Jews and Christians alike, believing that Islam was the logical fulfillment of both religions. He expected Jews to welcome him with open arms and embrace him as the latest in a long line of prophets from God. But Jewish residents thoroughly rejected Muhammad and the new religion of Islam. They not only rejected him; they laughed at him. In early chapters of the Koran, Jews are respected and honored for their religious zeal and for being "people of the Book." But that changes suddenly in Islam's holy book, as Allah supposedly gives Muhammad "further revelation" and proclaims judgment and condemnation on the Jews. At one point, they are even called "monkeys." When Osama bin Laden gave the hated Zionists this label, he was merely quoting from the Prophet Muhammad in the Koran, Surah (chapter) 7:166 and 5:60.

Also in the Koran, Surah 2:65, Gabriel quotes, "And indeed you knew those amongst you [children of Israel] who transgressed in the matter of the Sabbath (i.e., Saturday). We said to them: 'Be you monkeys, despised and rejected.'" In his own words, Gabriel concludes that "Muslims interpret this to mean that Jews were literally turned into animals. But there is no information in the Quran (Koran) or in the Islamic history to answer the basic questions: 1) When did Allah transform Jews into monkeys and pigs? 2) Where did Allah transform Jews into monkeys and pigs? 3) Did Allah do that to the whole Jewish nation or just some of them? I never found any evidence that something like this happened to the Jewish people during their history. *The earlier revelations said the Jews were Allah's chosen people*" (Surah 2:37).[6]

(Incidentally, Gabriel earned his doctorate from the famed Al Ahzar University in Cairo, Egypt—the most prestigious university for Islamic studies—and became a believer in the midst of teaching Islam there. He has since his conversion changed his name and moved out of the dangerous Middle East to the United States.)

Not only does Islam have anti-Semitism as one of its core values; it also loathes the fact that Israel is back in the land and growing in all areas. To be fair, I have met numerous Muslims during my Middle East travels who do not hate Jews. Many of them see the issue differently than one would expect. How can this be? Simple. As there are many Christians who do not take the Bible literally, so it is with Muslims. It is as easy for a Muslim to "spiritualize" his Koran as it is for a Christian to do so with his Bible. To some followers of Muhammad, the holy Koran is an historical account of the life and struggles of Islam. To others, it is spiritual teaching good for their soul. In short, if a Muslim fails to take the Koran at face value and believe it word for word, he may not show animosity toward Jews. Rather, the Muslim Jewish struggle may be relegated to ancient tribal skirmishes that have no bearing on today's world.

Unfortunately, though, Muslims who fall along these lines fail to ever be in any leadership positions. Leaders of the movement do take the Koran literally, and that is the reason no comprehensive peace will ever be forged in the region. To take away Jewish hatred would be to rob Islam of its soul. There will be land-for-peace attempts and peace treaties drawn up and re-drawn. But the fundamental problem that Islam has with the Jews is their nagging existence. For Islam, it seems the Jews are here to stay. Recent statistics out of Israel report that Israel's population stands at 6.7 million people. The country's Jewish population is now 5.4 million. This is staggering for Muslims to comprehend that 38 percent of the world's Jewry now live in Israel.

Despite the current intifada, countless suicide bombings, and the daily threat of all-out war, the population in Israel continues to grow, with more new immigrants arriving every year. The campaign to intimidate Israelis and discourage Jews from immigrating has backfired. Israel's population has grown more than eight times since it became a nation in 1948. People are flocking to Tel Aviv and to Jerusalem. They aren't flocking to Amman, Damascus, or Riyadh.

The War on Terrorism

In the last few years, we as Americans have learned what it's like to be Jewish and to be living in the nation of Israel. With terrorism alerts and reports of fundamentalist Muslims roaming freely about America, our sense of security seems like something only experienced long ago. When President Bush correctly and courageously declared a war on terrorism, he drew a line in the sand that ultimately pitted America against Islam.

His administration worked long and hard to differentiate between peaceful Muslims and hostile Muslims. He even talked about how Muslim extremist terrorists had *hijacked* the religion. I believe he is absolutely right. Sure, the Koran glorifies persecution of Jews and Christians. But most Muslims don't have any intention of fulfilling that call or of becoming terrorists. Most are no different from Americans who want to raise their children in peace, feed them well, and provide them with a good education. The majority of Muslims are truly peace-loving. Yet the leadership of the typical mosque continuously calls Allah's followers to join the battle and get in step with jihad so Islam can eventually take over the world. The messages are nonstop. To radical Muslims, our war on terrorism is only a convenient excuse for America to keep Islam from spreading around the globe. It also is perceived as an excuse for us to unconditionally support Israel and its fight against Palestinians in Gaza and the West Bank.

But bear in mind—in thinking through the justifications for war in Iraq—that Saddam Hussein not only encouraged all-out war with America and Israel; he rewarded suicide bombers for killing innocent people all over Israel. The $25,000 he offered to the family of each "martyr" helped inspire deceived Palestinian young people to blow themselves up and kill as many Jews as possible. A disco filled with teenagers, families pushing baby strollers after attending evening worship, and shopping malls filled with women and children were all popular targets. Palestinian terrorist groups elevated suicide to a religious calling. The results of these suicide bombings were and are as despicable as anything ever recorded in history. And Saddam Hussein personally wrote the big checks to families of the murderers. Even Adolph Hitler didn't think of this one! By any measure of reckoning, the reign of the "Butcher of Baghdad" was one of the most evil periods in Middle Eastern history.

The Middle East Bullies

Yet for all the American troops in the region, a major menace still exists. Iran. The Islamic Republic of Iran has barrels of money and thousands of committed terrorist Hezbollah soldiers to fight against Israel, threatening to level it. And with Iran's nuclear development during the last few years, they are now close to a confrontation. With at least thirty-nine sites in Iran working on nuclear development, Israel has a major challenge if they hope to stop Iran before it is too late.

The Ayatollah and his Islamic regime have gained friends all around the globe with their continual promises of impending doom for Israel. Even though President Mahmoud Ahmadinejad is a mere puppet in the hands of the Ayatollah, he has somewhat of a cult-following with his tough talk against America and his steady stream of anti-Semitism. Right now, Iran has missiles capable of hitting Rome and London. They are currently working on one that will be able to strike New York City. Iran has catapulted over major hurdles—both ethnic and religious—to become the new face of Islam.

For example, since Iranians are Persian in ethnicity, they have been at odds with the Arabic Islamic leadership of the Middle East for centuries. On top of that, 85 percent of Islam is from the Sunni branch; Iranians are Shiite Muslim. The Iran-Iraq war had at the core of its conflict a Sunni-Shiite showdown. But in Islam, centuries of war and hatred can be overlooked when the common enemy turns out to be the hated Jews of Israel.

Even if Iran never fires a nuclear warhead at Israel, they still can cause the country great damage. Iran has a weapon in their arsenal that keeps Israel on alert each and every day. Their weapon is Syria. Syria is a strong Iranian ally and has an army just miles away from Israel's famed Golan Heights, also known as Bashan from biblical days. David Dolan again underscored the serious threat of Israel's northern neighbor:

> A new Mideast war is almost inconceivable without Syrian partici-
> pation. Damascus has an arsenal of weapons that nearly matches all
> of the other listed nations combined (Saudi Arabia, Jordan, Leba-
> non, Iraq, and the Palestinian Authority). Syria's standing army is
> estimated to be about three times the size of Israel's. Its tank and
> artillery forces, while substantially older than Israel's, are numeri-
> cally much larger. In recent decades, Syria has acquired advanced
> warplanes and anti-aircraft missile systems from Moscow. But the
> main threat posed by Damascus is its substantial ballistic missile
> capability. Israel analysts estimate that the country can deploy up
> to 1,000 independently targeted warheads. North Korean-built mis-
> siles have poured into Damascus airport; and the rogue Commu-
> nist State has even licensed local production of Scud-L missiles,
> an improved version of the ones shot at Tel Aviv by Saddam Hus-
> sein. The prospect of such weapons striking Israeli targets is made
> more gruesome by the likelihood that they would carry chemical
> payloads. Syria is known to be producing VX nerve gas, one of the
> deadliest chemical agents on earth."[7]

Syria means business when it comes to dealing with Israel. Their military is ready and able. And their relationship has never been stronger with
Iran than it is now.

In the end, I believe Iran and Syria's military prowess combined with
Saudi Arabia's money and guardianship of Islam's religious capital cities will
eventually be one of the strongest coalitions ever assembled when it comes
to fighting against Israel. Other Islamic nations will certainly have to follow
along with the tidal wave movement to battle Israel.

When Saudi Crown Prince Abdullah proposed a peace proposal and an
initiative to normalize relations with Israel, it was Syrian President Bashar
Assad who pressed the Saudis to backtrack from the proposal. Assad him-

self arrived in Saudi Arabia and pressed hard for fundamental changes that would keep the process from going any farther in March 2002. After the dictator's visit to Riyadh, the Saudis dropped the term "full normalization" of their relationship, and Syria's state-run news agency declared that Syria and Saudi Arabia had identical views on the matter. Saudi Arabia was clearly thinking about business growth around the world that would result with a softer treatment of Israel, while Syria was thinking of maintaining the ongoing war of Islam versus Judaism. But in the end, religion won out.

In the Middle East, it always does.

Next time, Iran, Syria and Saudi Arabia will most likely move forward together when dealing with Israel. As the three nations team up, the Middle East and the world will feel the effects of their money, military strength, and religious fanaticism that brings it all together under the banner of Islam.

And there is no question about the prize radical Islam covets most: Jerusalem. The Muslims lost it once to Christians. They lost it again to Jews. Islam demands control of Jerusalem. Muhammad taught that Judaism came first, Christianity came second, and now Islam is the fulfillment and culmination of the three great faiths. As a result, it is imperative for Islam to flex its muscle and to control the Holy City of Jerusalem.

On the Horizon

What appears to be on the horizon? Dangerous alliances are coming together throughout the Islamic world. Iran, Syria, Saudi Arabia, and Palestinians in Gaza and the West Bank literally have Israel surrounded. Hamas, the terrorist group that now controls Gaza, has intensified talks with Tehran and many are now referring to the Gaza Strip as "Hamastan." Northern Africa is almost exclusively Muslim now and has its own special brand of violent Islam. The ranks of Muslims are well spread globally.

Here are some startling statistics: "Listed below are the fifty-three countries of the world that have at least 50 percent Muslim population or a Muslim plurality. The total population of these countries is more than 1 billion people, more than 78 percent of all the Muslims of the world. The countries are listed according to the actual size of their Muslim populations, not their total population."[8]

Country	%	Population	Country	%	Population
Indonesia	80.3	165,550,000	Libya	96.5	5,018,000
Pakistan	96.1	139,316,000	Jordan	96.2	5,002,000
Bangladesh	85.6	114,316,000	Chad*	55.0	4,785,000
Turkey	99.6	66,061,000	Kyrgyzstan	78.1	3,904,000
Iran	99.0	65,452,000	Sierre Leone*	70.0	3,780,000
Egypt	86.5	60,391,000	Palestine	86.6	2,856,000
Nigeria*	41.0	51,906,000	Mauritania	99.8	2,696,000
Algeria	96.7	29,971,000	Lebanon	59.7	2,570,000
Morocco	99.9	29,156,000	Oman	92.7	2,224,000
Afghanistan	97.9	26,235,000	United Arab		
Iraq	96.9	22,857,000	Emirates*	65.5	2,160,000
Uzbekistan	83.5	20,959,000	Eritrea	47.9	2,063,000
Sudan	65.0	20,670,000	Bosnia-		
Saudi Arabia	92.8	19,587,000	Herzegovina*	60.1	2,042,000
Yemen	99.9	17,989,000	Kuwait	87.4	2,011,000
Syria	90.3	15,445,000	Albania*	38.8	1,319,000
Malaysia	58.0	13,166,000	Gambia	88.8	1,243,000
Niger	97.6	10,149,000	Burkina Faso	50.0	615,000
Tunisia	99.7	9,667,000	Comoros	98.1	588,000
Mali	87.0	9,570,000	Bahrain	82.3	576,000
Kazakstan*	60.5	8,954,000	Djibouti	93.9	563,000
Senegal	92.1	8,931,000	Guinea-Bissau	43.0	516,000
Somalia	99.9	7,496,000	Qatar	79.4	477,000
Azerbaijan	83.7	6,777,000	Western Sahara	100.0	300,000
Guinea	85.4	5,549,000	Maldives	99.4	298,000
Turkmenistan	91.8	5,051,000	Brunei	64.4	193,000
			Benin	20.0	132,000

*Countries that have either a Muslim plurality or control of the government

These figures are from 2001 and have grown significantly since then. One-quarter of the world is now Muslim, approximately 1.3 billion people.

This sheer strength of numbers, influence, and wealth, along with the control of Arab culture and strong European Islamic backing, appears to be catastrophic for Israel in the future. Dangerous alliances worldwide are Muslim-influenced, anti-Semitic, and contain the belief that one day Jerusalem will be taken out of Jewish hands altogether. A phrase being thrown around today is "international city," through which a group would seize control of Jerusalem and give it a United Nations form of government. But this would fail to appease Islam, which wants complete sovereignty in Jerusalem. In the future, I look for surrounding nations to enter a regional war for Jerusalem and Israel itself. How can Islam rest with Zionists in control of their "new" Holy City?

Samad and Shiraz—Escape from Iran

Samad and Shiraz had a good life in Iran. Samar was well paid at his job, and his wife Shiraz was a very sweet and good mother to their son and daughter. They were the typical Iranian family. Their home was filled with lots of love, great food, and a large extended family. They were proud of their Persian heritage.

Samad and Shiraz were in love. Who could ask for anything more?

Yet Samad and Shiraz were restless. They both had a large spiritual void in their lives. Islam was not satisfying them. How could this be? This was the faith of their family, the faith of their nation. Iran is 98 percent Muslim, and as a family they had gone through the Islamic Revolution and welcomed it. Iran was going to get rid of the Shah and all the secular Western influences. The nation would become a strict Islamic state. Surely the glory days would return to the Persian people. The Ayatollah promised that the people of Iran would be a worldwide model for the rest of Islam to follow. The families would be more secure, and the nation of Iran would soar to new heights as a worldwide spiritual giant for the glory of Allah. The Revolution would set the people free. The prophet Muhammad would be studied and followed by every Iranian, and this revolution would sweep the world with an Islamic revival.

But none of these promises were fulfilled. Within years, a national depression settled into Iran. Hopelessness was seen everywhere. Iran soared to the top as a nation with the highest drug addiction percentage in the world. Jobs were scarce. College graduates had nothing to look forward to after completing school. At the same time, the strict Islamic regime was enforcing its new standards through Sharia law, carrying out the edicts of the Ayatollah with an iron fist—intimidation, persecution, even execution,

The people were dislodged from their normal lives, and great fear gripped them. Freedom of thought and expression exited the country. Books were banned unless they were government propaganda pieces. Women feared public places since the secret police were always present and watching to see if their hair was completely covered. If even an inch of hair was showing, they could be taken in "for questioning" and then beaten. Men had to display support of the Ayatollah and his regime or their job might be lost. Next, isolation from the West occurred.

This was especially difficult, since the average Iranian loves America and probably has a cousin living in Los Angeles or Detroit. Many Iranians jokingly referred to L.A. as Tehran-geles—a quarter million Iranians lived there. All together, two million Iranians living in America watched as freedoms their families had once enjoyed evaporated. Young Iranian men could not return to their country to visit relatives or they would be immediately forced into the Iranian military. On my second visit to Iran, I was shocked to hear many college students talk openly about threatening suicide if they were not able to leave the country after graduation. To many, death seemed the only possible escape.

Samad and Shiraz, however, planned another way out. Samad applied for a work visa from the government. He had located a job in a secular Muslim country, and miraculously it was granted. In reality, Samad and Shiraz knew deep in their hearts why they were leaving Iran. They were on a journey to find God. "We know that we could never have a personal relationship with God in Iran. Our spiritual life consisted of rules, obligations, and threats if we didn't fulfill them to the letter of the law. We tried all of those things. We kept all the rules, yet a personal relationship with God was nowhere to be found in Islam. So we gave up everything and went on a spiritual quest to find Him."

They would not be disappointed. Though their hope first turned into desperation after arriving in Turkey and finding no place to live or a job to support the family, both of them came into contact with Christians who helped them with food and clothing.

Samad and Shiraz felt their hearts warmed by the message of love and hope that radiated off the pages of the Bible. This was new to them, as the god of Islam was so harsh, judgmental, and distant. Samad and Shiraz both knew that they were on the right track, but they had to know for sure. How could Jesus prove Himself once and for all to them? If He really loved them, they needed something tangible. They needed proof.

One day, out of need and desperation, it came to them. Since they were out of money and had no place to live, Samad cried out to Jesus: "Show us that You are real and that You love us? Today, I ask that You find a good paying job for me so I can feed my family. I must start working today. Also, we need a place to live. We have no money for a deposit. If You are God, let us sleep in our own apartment tonight."

Did God care for them? Would He come through?

Within a few hours, both requests were answered! A friend suggested they look at an apartment in a different part of town. The friendly apartment manager said, "Samad, you can move in today. I need to get this apartment filled, so I don't even need a deposit! Will this work for you?" Samad was in shock! He could hardly get the word "yes!" out. God cared about them! He had answered one of the prayers.

When they were moving, one of the neighbors stopped by to meet them. He said, "Samad, I don't suppose you need a job do you? I am looking for someone, and I'm really desperate. You could start today." Samad and Shiraz both stopped dead in their tracks. At that point in time, they both had the same thought go through their minds: "How powerful this Jesus is!" Samad blurted out, "Yes, I need a job and I accept your offer! Thank you!"

They accepted Jesus' offer too. How could they not? They reached out to Jesus, and He reached out to them.

Later that day, Samad and Shiraz knelt together in their new home, repented of their sins, and committed their lives to Jesus. The children joined their parents. "From that day on, Jesus took over—and we saw one miracle after another!"

Perhaps the most amazing miracle was that Samad was asked to give his testimony of God's faithfulness on a Christian television program. The program was carried all through the Middle East. The program was aired live, and Samad was naturally nervous, but God spoke through him. Samad had no idea that at that very moment, his own mother in Iran was flipping through the television channels. (Christian television is forbidden in Iran, but the government has not been able to figure a way to control the airwaves yet.) To her amazement, she came across the Christian station and saw her son on the program.

She was shocked! Anger arose within her as she came to the horrible realization that her son who had been raised as an observant Muslim had defected and left his faith. She felt hurt, betrayed, and increasingly angry. But as her emotions began to calm down, she noticed Samad was serene and had a joyful countenance—a joy she had never seen on his face. After sharing in detail his encounter with Jesus Christ and the love that His Savior had extended to Samad and his family, Samad got on his knees and prayed for God to reach the people of Iran. He then led the television audience in the sinner's prayer.

Samad would find out later that his mother was on her knees, too, as she joined her son in prayer, weeping and rejoicing, as her own son led her to faith in Jesus Christ.

Blessed are those who hunger and thirst for righteousness, because they will be filled. (Matt. 5:6)

Chapter 5
Heroes of Our Faith

Despite the Middle East powder keg, the church is experiencing an outpouring of God's power when it comes to salvation among Arabs and Jews. Meet the believers who are the leaders of this great revival. Their stories will inspire you with their "live every day as if it's the last one" mind-set.

The Globalization of Sin

In his best-selling book *Jihad vs McWorld*, Benjamin Barber wrote about democracy and its current global struggle with terrorism. Despite his obvious distaste for the church, he made a strong case for the reason Western culture is being rejected in places where jihad is prized. "McWorld in tandem with the global market economy has globalized many of our vices and almost none of our virtues. We have globalized crime, the rogue weapons trade, and drugs; we have globalized prostitution and pornography, and the trade in women and children made by porn tourism."[1]

His point is well taken. One thing Muslims and Christians agree on is this: Western culture is depraved and decadent. Certainly there is much good in our freedoms, yet the inherent danger is that we will become a people of no restraint. Freedom without personal restraint leads a culture into a spiritual free fall. Barber quoted James Wolfensohn, president of the World Bank, with these words: "Two billion people live on less than two dollars a day. We live in a world that gradually is getting worse and worse and worse. It is not hopeless, but we must do something about it now."[2]

I agree that our world has entered into a new period of desperation. Poverty is on the rise. More wars are on the horizon. Terrorism is just getting started. Money won't solve our problems. Globalization won't solve our problems. Neither will democracy. In fact, democracy comes with a built-in trapdoor: the bad guy can get elected.

In the Gaza Strip, Hamas, the worst terrorist group in Israel, did just that. It got elected. As Americans, that puts us in an uncomfortable position. Do we question the results? Do we say the election was no good? No. After the votes are counted, it's over. So although democracy in most cases will improve people's lives and set people free, it is the church that must pick up the slack and deal with the spiritual vacuum left behind once an evil regime is removed. Iraq, for example, cries out for revival, not for Western culture. Democracy is a blessing to any nation, but if the church is not strong, vibrant, and able to influence within the democracy, heathenism will likely result.

The Church Is the Answer

How disturbing it was to watch CNN when Afghanistan was being liberated from Taliban rule. I was thrilled, of course, to see that a certain amount of religious reform would now be allowed. Good! The fear gripping millions of Afghans that is always a by-product of fundamentalist Islam was receding. This also was good. Women would no longer be squelched and would now be free to receive an education. Another good thing. American soldiers entered into an extremely difficult war and served faithfully and valiantly with effectiveness. Osama bin Laden may have eluded our special forces in the endless caves of Afghanistan, but since he was on the run, he was marginalized, at least for a time. America has not been attacked by him directly since. All of these things are good.

What disturbed me, however, was to watch CNN broadcast videotape to the world of Afghan men holding *Playboy* magazines up to the cameras with big smiles. My heart sank! After all, that was what Muslims of the Middle East say we Americans are all about anyway. We are portrayed as a nation of addicts—addicted to pornography, alcohol, overeating, immorality, and violence. Where in the world would Afghans get an idea like that? By what they see and hear about us in American movies and television, of course. Our culture is infamous worldwide. Our personal excesses and extremism are what we are known for globally. America is a fast-growing mission field.

But what Afghanistan needs is a big dose of Jesus. Western culture will leave Afghans feeling as empty as they were before. Maybe their lifestyle will improve, but without Christ they will still die in their sin and go straight to hell. Jesus' message of real freedom is what is needed—in a hurry. The pure gospel that sets us free from our personal sin is the only thing that will revolutionize Afghanistan. McDonald's won't.

Don't get me wrong. I love a Big Mac, but the church is the one with all the answers. Western culture without Jesus Christ in the middle of it will not deliver what it promises. Americans can testify to this.

So can Israel.

A Wrong Turn for Israel

Becoming a state recognized by the United Nations in 1948 presented Jews and Arabs with a unique set of problems. Jews from Eastern Europe and Russia, for example, were used to a communist form of government. Some of these tenets were adopted into kibbutz life throughout Israel. Jewish families together bought land and farmed. The kibbutzim of Israel were small villages that provided a certain amount of protection to its many residents. The profits were split evenly no matter the job or the production level, just as they had been in the Soviet Union. But Israel would certainly not adopt communism as a form of national government, would it? Apparently the Soviet Union thought it might, and actually voted for Israel's reconstitution as a nation in the 1947 United Nations vote.

At the other end of the spectrum were Orthodox Jews from many countries who longed to return to Israel's form of government they enjoyed in Old Testament days. We know from the Bible that before Israel demanded a king like the other nations had, it was a theocracy—literally, a nation "ruled by God." Unfortunately, Old Testament Israel wanted a monarchial system which would provide the Hebrews with a king. Their leaders previously had been prophets and judges that Yahweh handpicked to serve directly under Him. But the prophet Samuel's sons did not walk after God as Samuel did, and the spiritual void left the leaders of God's nation feeling insecure and vulnerable. They wanted to redo Israel's system of government, which ended up being the colossal failure of the Old Testament. Recorded in 1 Samuel 8:4–7 is their reasoning:

All the elders of Israel gathered together and went to Samuel at Ramah. They said to him, "Look, you are old, and your sons do not follow your example. Therefore, appoint a king to judge us the same as all the other nations have." When they said, "Give us a king to judge us," Samuel considered their demand sinful, so he prayed to the LORD. But the LORD told him, "Listen to the people and everything they say to you. They have not rejected you; they have rejected Me as their King."

To be sure, there were some high points with King Solomon and his father King David. But this governmental model—borrowed from the surrounding pagan nations—was all wrong to begin with, and it ended up causing Israel to unravel at the seams and fall apart completely, doomed from the start. God had laid out clear rules and responsibilities in the Pentateuch along with spiritual ones, and He was quite capable of managing His holy nation Himself, thank you very much! Yet God granted the peoples' request, and Israel never recovered. Orthodox Jews in Israel certainly didn't want to repeat that error again. They desired a theocracy—the only pure form of government.

As it turned out, Israel opted to become a democratic republic like America, which backed the new nation throughout the whole process. This form of government was replete with voting privileges, freedom of religion, and a free enterprise system that soared upon takeoff.

These freedoms were new for many of Israel's residents. For Arabs, they were no longer under Turkish Ottoman rule. The British mandate period was also over, and Arabs who became citizens of Israel finally lived within the boundaries of a free society. A friend of mine in Nazareth whose family has lived in Jesus' hometown for a few centuries sings the praises of how his life and very existence changed for the good when Israel was reestablished in the land.

For Jews, freedom was just as sweet! Fresh from Nazi death camps and European oppression, Jews were finally free. No wonder early films of Israeli citizens so often showed them dancing in a circle with joy! Everyone had rights, and Jews would no longer be under the cruel dictatorships they had been subject to in the past. There was good—so much good.

But just as with other democracies of the world, when the church is weak and ineffective, there is great potential for problems. Israel was enjoying life within the world of the free. The church, however, was traditional in form and for the most part devoid of anyone having a born-again experience. Jerusalem, the birthplace of Jesus' church, was a far cry from first-century days when the apostle Peter spoke to the masses at Solomon's Colonnade and 5,000 Jews were saved. Now that Israel had become a nation again, salvation experiences were almost nonexistent. One longtime Jerusalem resident who moved to the city in 1960 remembers only four believers in all of Israel that he knew of.

Lots of religion—not much Jesus.

Over the years, religion did grow in Israel. But since it was for the most part without Jesus, so did worldliness—a condition that religion alone can never fend off. Only Jesus living and residing in people's lives and hearts will turn a culture away from the false claims of the world and toward God Himself. Israel would have been a miracle merely by hanging on after each decade's major war. The Israelites not only hung on; they prospered. They became world leaders in medicine, technology, and agriculture. God's hand of blessing clearly was guiding the nation once again.

The church, however, was miniscule. And over time, Israel has gotten caught up in a level of worldliness that is shocking to see on one's arrival in

Tel Aviv. The city named the "hill of the spring" prides itself in its modernity and liberal nature. It's like a San Francisco in the Holy Land. If Jerusalem is the old Holy City, then Tel Aviv is the new secular city. The place where David Ben-Gurion read his opening words to the new nation of Israel recently was voted the "Gay Capital of the World." Somehow it's hard to believe that this is what the nation's forefathers had in mind during the rebirth of Israel in May 1948.

It also is interesting to note the rise of Kabbalah, which is the current rage in Israel and throughout the world. Kabbalah is a sort of New Age form of Judaism whose capital city, Safed, is just north of the Sea of Galilee. With heavy marketing and superstar appeal, Kabbalah is Judaism without all the confining rules. Terms like "negative energy," "creative guidance," and "rays of light" permeate the hip, growing Hebrew splinter group. Madonna, Barbara Streisand, Jeff Goldblum, Mick Jagger, Elton John, Demi Moore, and Elizabeth Taylor have all turned to Kabbalah.

Today, Israel is still free. Jews are free! So are Arabs who become citizens of the state of Israel. Democracy and freedom are blessings that stand out in the midst of oppressive dictatorships all around. But freedom without the restraining power of the Holy Spirit is resulting in a wave of modern iniquity. Israel finds itself wanting to be like other nations again, primarily in the West, that are rapidly turning away from God.

Just Say No to Jesus

Colorado Springs contains about 150 ministry headquarters within the city. Some of the most notable are Compassion International, the International Bible Society, Focus on the Family, and the Navigators. With so many ministries in town, the area is often in the midst of Christian initiatives sweeping the country. One of these campaigns was the WWJD movement. Youth all over the United States were wearing the wristbands with the letters WWJD, which stood for "What Would Jesus Do?" It was a physical reminder for believers to live as Jesus would in any situation. I can assure you, Colorado Springs was knee-deep in WWJD bracelets. They were all over the place!

One day, a young local girl who was wearing her bracelet encountered some resistance from a group of young people known within school as Satan worshippers. (Unfortunately, yes, *these* are in Colorado Springs, as well.) One of the rough-looking kids approached her in a crowded hall and said, "I like your WWJD bracelet. I think it's cool." He baited her. "I wear mine upside down. It means to me 'We want Jesus dead!'"

The hall fell silent as the sweet young Christian replied very calmly, "We want Jesus dead, huh?"

"Yeah," he said.

With a burst of confidence, she answered, "Well, they already tried that once, and it didn't work!" The hall full of kids laughed hard as the pure facts of the gospel quite nicely turned back his arrogance.

So it is in Israel. Pictures of Jesus are everywhere, often pictured on the cross. That's where many people want Him to stay. Jesus still makes as many waves in Jerusalem as He did 2,000 years ago. There is not much difference. In fact, Israel's unofficial "Just Say No to Jesus" campaign in the last few years has been evident in a variety of places. Here are some of the places the campaign to squelch Jesus has been found:

IN THE POLITICAL REALM

During Prime Minister Netanyahu's administration, Orthodox rabbis pushed a bill all the way to the Knesset that would have forbidden all forms of evangelism within Israel. This was obviously aimed straight at Christian evangelicals. It was perceived in America as a big slap in the face to Christians who are for the most part supportive of Israel. This anti-missionary law in Israel was ultimately too difficult to pass. Since Israel is a democracy, this would have clearly cut at the right to religious freedom. Netanyahu's office was besieged with protest faxes, mainly from America. This shows how sensitive the issue of conversion is in Israel—so hot that some wanted the nation to undo some of its core values in order to put an end to it. Thankfully, the resolution failed.

On Television

Only a few years ago, an important television program aired live in Israel. Gathered in the studio were religious leaders from every spectrum of Judaism. The topic was "What is a Jew?" Various spokesmen each had their allotted time, waxing eloquent about their respective movements within Judaism. Orthodox, Conservative, and Reformed Jews all spoke with passion about their slice of the ancient religion. There were also atheistic Hebrews present at the television show—environmentalists who worshipped nature and found no room in their theology for a personal God whatsoever. Messianic believers were present, as well. The religious groups represented were quite diverse.

At the end of the program, "What is a Jew?" was answered finally, and the conclusions drawn were predictable. A Jew could come in all sorts of flavors, from Orthodox to atheistic. All were acceptable in Israel. You could take the Tanach (the Old Testament) literally and be a good Jew, or you could not take it literally—be a tree hugger, for instance—and still be a good Jew. The only thing that disqualified you whatsoever from Hebraic roots was believing that Jesus was the Messiah. If you were a messianic Jew, you were no longer considered Jewish. Despite the protest of the messianic participant, the entire panel agreed with this conclusion. Judaism had no room for followers of Yeshua. Amazing! Atheists were welcome. Messianics were not.

In the News

About eight years ago, the *Jerusalem Post* ran an article, "The Problem of Messianic Judaism," which talked about Jews converting to Christianity in Israel. They considered this a real threat. More Jews had converted to Christianity in the last nineteen years than in the last nineteen centuries, they reported, and the Orthodox rabbinate was concerned about the thinning ranks of traditional Judaism. The leaders were now offering a seminar on how to defeat the claims of Christianity and its supposed negative effects on Jewish culture. No wonder Jesus wept over Jerusalem! *What* negative effects on Jewish culture? Jesus is the fulfillment of the Abrahamic covenant that will bring blessing to all the nations. It was amazing to me that messianics were considered dangerous. After all, this is a country that is stocked with plenty of suicide bombers.

A New Work of the Spirit

In no way can the miracle of Israel's return, preservation, and prosperity in the land be minimized. The hostility encircling Israel could be all-consuming. Yet Israel continues to develop and soar to new heights economically. Lifestyles are good in Israel. There is absolutely no comparison anywhere in the region. God's covenant to bless Israel is the only way to explain all of this. We have witnessed a miracle in our lifetime that is on par with any act of God in Old Testament days.

Yet the people thirst for a *personal* work of God in their hearts. In the last few years while visiting Israel, I have seen an openness like never before. Jews and Arabs are finding Jesus. It appears that God is using the three-year intifada to bring about a mood of desperation. Both groups of people are wrestling with the endless struggle and are searching for some kind of hope. The operative word here is *desperation*. God works in desperation. He moves in the midst of it. It is fertile ground for the gospel. It is the best spiritual climate for the church to advance within.

A few years ago while attending a worship service in Tel Aviv, the messianic pastor spoke of the fear pervading the city. Suicide bombers were dressing up as Hasidic Jews and infiltrating heavily populated Jewish areas before detonating their bombs. Women were now blowing themselves up. The attacks were steady, deadly, and devastating. The mood of the normally upbeat youth was understandably oppressive and gloomy. People avoided coffee shops and clubs. Terrorism was winning as people's lives were becoming severely affected.

This spiritual leader asked for a show of hands to a revealing question: "How many of you have had a relative or a close friend involved in a suicide bombing?" With great sadness, every hand went up. It was a clean sweep. Terrorism had affected every Tel Aviv resident within the church. The pastor skillfully reminded the believers of God's words written by King David in Psalm 27:1: "The LORD is my light and my salvation—whom should I fear? The LORD is the stronghold of my life—of whom should I be afraid." The words couldn't have been more timely. These Israelis live in a country where no place is safe because such everyday, high-traffic venues as schools, city buses, synagogues, and holy sites are often targeted. Yet God is using all of the pain to drive His people back to Him. The body of believers in Israel is growing faster than ever.

Today in Israel, there are between 120 and 200 messianic congregations. The promulgation of the gospel has been slow among Israelis for decades, but it appears the spiritual logjam is now breaking up. In a new magazine called *Kivun*, which means "direction" in Hebrew, Messianics are finding connection, and the growth of the movement is impressive. The first issue of *Kivun* said:

> Gone are the days when Israeli Messianic Jews were a small se-
> cluded group. The changes in recent years have created the need
> for a Hebrew language magazine that meets the unique needs of its
> readership. Not the least of these changes is the impressive growth
> in the number of Messianic Jews, especially over the past two de-
> cades. We're not speaking of a few dozen here and there, but of
> thousands who express their loyalty to the God of Israel by their
> lifestyle. The increase in numbers has birthed a heightened sense
> of confidence on both an individual and congregational level. This
> confidence translates to a growing willingness to be exposed to the
> general public, an exposure dictated by reality and consistent with
> the philosophy of messianic Judaism."[3]

What a big step forward for messianic believers! Formerly, if a Jew ac-
cepted Jesus as the Jewish Messiah, the temptation was to keep it as quiet as possible. Jobs were lost, families were ripped apart, and public scorn was intense whenever a Jew "defected" to Christianity. Nothing could have been

considered worse for a Jew than embracing Jesus as Messiah within the borders of Israel.

The church that Jesus founded in Israel was one that exuded power, abounding grace, and contagious love. Yet the bride of Christ over the centuries had become weak and institutionalized. Life was missing in the very place where Jesus conquered death. But that life has returned! Only a few years ago, there were four messianic congregations. Now there are dozens of life-giving congregations bringing living water to the spiritually thirsty.

Creative Evangelism

Outreach to Jews in Israel can be tricky. Residents are very familiar with what we Christians believe and what the New Testament says about Jesus, the Jewish Messiah. The apostle Paul experienced a burden in his heart for his Jewish brethren. His emotional outpouring about Jewish outreach is detailed masterfully in Romans 9–11. As the apostle began, his heart was breaking for his Jewish kinsmen who are separated from Christ. In Romans 9:3, he said: "For I could wish that I myself were cursed and cut off from the Messiah for the benefit of my brothers, my countrymen by physical descent." He was saying, "If I could take their place and go to hell on their behalf, I would do it." Powerful words. The height of sacrifice.

So it is with those who labor with Jewish lost people. They are so close, but through their own heart's hardness, they are missing out on the pinnacle of their spiritual heritage. Paul rolls out their vast spiritual wealth in verse 4 and 5: "They are Israelites, and to them belong the adoption, the glory, the covenants, the giving of the law, the temple service, and the promises. The forefathers are theirs, and from them, by physical descent, came the Messiah, who is God over all, blessed forever. Amen."

Jews, God's chosen people, could not have been more spiritually advantaged. God's revelation. God's spokesmen. God's miracles. All of these are forever contained in their spiritual history. That's why it's so heartbreaking. The missing centerpiece of their spiritual puzzle is right before their eyes. Yet now Jewish eyes are beginning to open. Let's look at a few recent examples of this.

A BOMBED-OUT SHOP

After a suicide bombing in Jerusalem on Ben Yehuda Street a few years ago, an American tour group decided to get involved. A pastor and several parishioners went to pray at the site of this attack on innocent Jewish lives. As they were walking through the area, they spotted a Jewish man sitting in his souvenir shop. Since it was close to where the bomb had exploded, the man's shop was in shambles. He sat in a chair and wept.

The pastor, sensing the man desperately needed an encouraging friend, entered the shop that was now a burned disaster area. He asked, "Could I please buy a Menorah?"

The shopkeeper never looked up, but said, "Fifty percent off."

The pastor said, "I don't want to buy it for 50 percent off."

"Okay, 60 percent off."

The wise minister then shocked the Jewish merchant by saying, "No, I want to pay full price!" The rest of the group then lined up behind the pastor and likewise each bought a Jewish lampstand at full price. It was an amazing gesture. *No one* pays full price in Israel! It is the Middle East home for "let's make a deal!"

Moved by their goodwill, the elderly Jewish man asked, "Who are you?" The pastor told the man that they were Christians from America, and they were visiting to show their solidarity with Israel. The old shop owner went on to tell the group that it was the Christians from America who were keeping the Israeli economy from collapsing. He said Christians were coming to Israel in the midst of the intifada, which amazed him, since Jews were no longer visiting. Hardly any Jewish bar mitzvahs were being done any longer at Jerusalem's Western Wall. But Christians were still arriving daily. The man said to the group, "Tell me about Jesus again. Maybe I need to give Him a second look."

The apostle Paul would have been smiling. Now *that* is the way to reach out to Abraham's descendants! We cannot give them any more information. They have heard it all before. But they can be reached by our love. They resent Christian know-it-alls, but they are moved by humility. They are touched by our friendship. Put yourself in Jewish shoes for a minute. They are surrounded by enemies everywhere they look. Imagine the impact of only one group consistently reaching out to them with genuine love in their hearts. The Christians. I believe Jesus is calling His church to step forward right now and love Israel back to Him. We can do it. We must!

An Orthodox Rabbi's Son

Traditional Orthodox Judaism is struggling to reach today's generation. Orthodox parents have a battle on their hands with the overt worldliness that is so prevalent in the land. Since Judaism is steeped in legalism, it often is a real turnoff to the young people of Israel. In some ways, the traditionally garbed Jews are seen as outdated and irrelevant. Like the Amish of Lancaster, Pennsylvania, the Orthodox Jews stand out in modern Israel. Many families have lost their young people to the enticements of the world.

At the Dugit Coffee Shop of Tel Aviv, an Orthodox rabbi's young son was disenchanted with religion. Avi engaged him in a conversation and asked the man why he hadn't considered Jesus in his life search. The young man was unfamiliar with any evidence from Scripture, so Avi gladly gave him prophetical verses about the Messiah from the Old Testament.

After a week or so, the young man returned for a cup of coffee. Avi was there. They reconnected. The rabbi's son said he thought Jesus might be the Messiah spoken about by the prophets of Israel. Avi pressed further: "What would Jesus have to do to prove to you that He is the Messiah?" The young man said, without hesitation, "If Jesus could get me a job, I'd believe He was the Messiah. I haven't had one in about six months."

Avi never missed a beat. "Let's pray that He does that for you!" Avi put his arm around the man and prayed a prayer of faith, "Lord Jesus, show this young man that You alone are God and that You want to save him from his sins. Please get him a job, Lord Jesus!"

As they were praying, the man's cell phone began to ring. He looked at Avi, and his Jewish face turned white. He answered the phone, and he was offered a job right then and there—starting the next day! Avi reminded him of his challenge to Jesus, and how He had more than met that challenge. Now it was up to him. The Orthodox rabbi's son lowered his head and received Jesus Christ as his Messiah.

As you can imagine, this set a spiritual bomb off at his parents' house, and they ceased all contact and communication with him. They said their son had died. But his new church family welcomed him with open arms, and he is walking with Jesus Christ, his Savior. God loves to answer prayers of faith like that.

HOSPITAL AND REHAB OUTREACH

Zeke and Carrie Bristol had a dream to start a different type of ministry in Israel. As the tragedies mounted, they decided to do something. People were being killed throughout Israel by suicide bombers on a regular basis. The numbers of the wounded in the attacks were staggering, and these people were often overlooked. In May 2003, the intifada was thirty months old, and 5,157 people had already been wounded. Almost nightly on the news, the body count was growing, and many of the wounded were being doomed to remain in hospitals or rehabilitation centers for the rest of their lives.

The Bristols, along with other local believers, now host a weekly event at one of the rehab centers. Patients stream into the cafeteria every Thursday night, some in wheelchairs, others in hospital beds. They are greeted with soft drinks, chips, and lots of desserts. A messianic group sings praise songs, and believers mingle with the patients. The mood is light and happy, and everyone is having a great time.

The best part is definitely the wheelchair dancing. We've been there to see it. The people go away knowing they are loved and not forgotten. This is practical outreach at its best. As Jesus reached out to the sick and the hurting and prayed for them, His church is following His lead and doing the same for the neediest people of the land today.

Jewish outreach is being carried out by messianic believers and dynamic churches all throughout Israel. There are several effective parachurch groups, as well. The gospel is moving freely throughout Israel once again.

The Cross vs. the Crescent Moon

The news from Palestinian areas and among Israeli Arabs is even better. Arab churches are growing rapidly, and their goal to reach Muslims and nominal Christians is contagious.

Caught in between Muslims and Jews, the Arab church is in one of the most difficult situations anywhere in the world. These dynamic believers operate on the front lines of the ongoing Arab-Israeli conflict. They often are caught in the middle. The situation in the Gaza Strip and in the West Bank is deplorable. Refugee camps have housed frustrated Palestinians for sixty years now.

At this point, I must clarify a few things. My heart goes out to Arabs in Israel, especially Palestinians. So far we have looked at Israel's history and the great moving of God to preserve them in this hostile land. I believe it is Israel's historical and biblical right to possess the land. When I shared this on a radio program this year, a local caller accused me of hating Palestinians. I said, "Absolutely not!" Ninety percent of our ministry right now is with Arab believers. We love them, and my wife and I are so drawn to the Arab culture. They are the most hospitable people we have ever met!

But we are talking two different issues here. Israel has a right to the land, and Israelis have proven over the decades that they are willing to share it with the Palestinians. Most Palestinians want peace with Israel. Palestinian leadership, however, has often proven that it does not. So although the Palestinian church leadership is top-notch—some of the finest, most dedicated, humble servants of God anywhere—they are forced to minister within a cauldron of hate.

The Gaza Miracle

Brother Andrew is one of my heroes. He is the Christian version of Indiana Jones. His exploits for the kingdom of God are legendary.

In his 1996 book *The Calling*, Andrew talked about the Muslim world as the final frontier for the gospel. Like most of us, he was surprised to hear of kingdom expansion that was occurring in the midst of Middle East Islam. The work being done by Jesus' church is remarkable. Andrew correctly drew the battle lines for us:

I have come to believe that Islam possesses the biggest challenge to the church today. Not to political or economic systems but to the church. Why? It's simple. Because the Western church doesn't come close to matching the level of commitment, determination, and strength of many Muslim groups. Christ and the Bible certainly call us to radical commitment, but we don't show it in the way we live. Until we do, Islam will continue to be the world's fastest growing religion—not because of its strength but because of our weakness."[4]

Exactly, Andrew. C'mon, church—wake up! We have the words of life. We must not only match Islam's commitment level; we must exceed it!

Andrew went on to talk about the neediest areas throughout the Muslim world. He mentioned that the church in the Gaza Strip had been without a pastor for many years. I was surprised to hear of a church in the Gaza Strip. I'd been going to Israel for some time and had no idea there was a church in Gaza. How *could* there be? Radical terrorist groups roam freely there. Islamic Jihad, Hamas, and the Al-Aksa Martyrs Brigade all have home bases there. Jewish settlements have been dismantled, and the people have been evacuated. As a result, there is no longer an Israeli army protecting 6,000 Jews that used to live there. Since the Israeli military left, the Philadelphia Corridor between Gaza and Egypt has become an easy entrance for terrorists and weapons. Al-Qaeda and Hezbollah from Iran have also come to Gaza. The Gaza Strip has become an arsenal of weapons and the haven of world terrorism.

The Gaza Strip is seven miles wide and twenty-six miles long. It is one of the most densely populated areas in the world, home to about 1.5 million people. And 99.9 percent of these are Muslims. Hardly a night goes by that Gaza is not in the news. When you enter Gaza, you are officially in the trenches.

About ten years ago, the only evangelical church in the Gaza Strip got a pastor. Hanna Massad is God's man for Gaza. This church has grown from a handful of members to about 300 since Hanna arrived. He now disciples a group of young men who will be future leaders of the Gaza church. The believers of the church are fearless, empowered by the Holy Spirit. They distribute food in the refugee camps. They give Bibles to all who are interested. They reach out to Muslims. This church is alive!

What impresses me about Gaza believers is that they show no traces of bitterness despite their impossible political situation. In Gaza, believers are under constant scrutiny, and on the street they choose their words carefully. One brother recently had his apartment ransacked by Islamic spies, stirring up such a commotion that other neighbors were peeking in the window, one of his friends said. They spotted an Islamic cleric watching the television as his assistants tore the place apart!

Hanna's beautiful wife, Suhad, leads the Bible Society in Gaza. She faithfully runs the staff that reaches out to anyone, whether Christian or Muslim. In the Gaza Baptist Church this year alone:

- The bus driver for the Awana club was killed.
- The guard for the church was wounded and hospitalized.
- The church was taken over twice by the Palestinian Authority in their fight against Hamas.
- The Bible Society, an extension of the church, was firebombed.
- The Bible Society was later blown up.
- Several times the church was riddled with bullets, which flew through the windows during services and during Awana.
- Several leaders were threatened and told they were being "watched" by various terrorist groups.
- A leader of the Bible Society of Gaza was martyred for his faith.

Can you imagine living like that? But such is the life of the Bible-believing, Jesus-loving Palestinians in Israel. They are caught between the proverbial rock and a hard place.

In Arab culture, there is a strong Christian tradition that pre-dates the birth of Islam by seven centuries. The Coptic Church, for example, has a long history and is accepted in Egypt despite Islam's overall control of the nation. "Christian" as I've said before, doesn't necessarily mean born-again believer. It's often used as a designation for a non-Muslim born in an Arab family. All of this is accepted within the Arab world.

In the former Iraqi government, Tariq Aziz claimed to be a Christian. Yasser Arafat's widow Suhad claims to be one, too. Does this mean they are born-again believers? Probably not. What separates nominal Christians from believers in the Middle East are two fundamental distinctions. Believers:

1. Have a born-again experience with Jesus.

2. Have a desire to convert anyone who has not had a born-again conversion. This includes Muslims, as well.

Gaza has a long and unsettling history. This was Philistine country in the Old Testament, home to one of Israel's archenemies. This spiritual stronghold is permeated with oppression. When conflict breaks out, the Erez Crossing closes, and Palestinians are kept from their jobs in Israel due to security breaches. All of this contributes to an oppressive feeling always present in Gaza. Gunfire is heard daily. There is violence in the air.

Yet Christ is being lifted up in the Gaza Strip and, one by one, Muslims are being reached for Jesus. What attracts them to Christ is the fruit of the Spirit on display through the believers' lives. The church's abundant joy is infectious. Muslims and nominal Christians notice a difference. Jesus is alive in Gaza. Signs of war are all around, but you would never know it when you enter the believers' homes. The difference is truly night from day.

A few years ago, Gaza was hit by several missile strikes after a terrorist bus bombing in Jerusalem. The news showed it live, and it was relatively close to the church. I called Pastor Hanna to check and see if everyone was all right. Unbelievably, he was unaware of the missiles because about a hundred kids were inside the church, hooting and hollering during Awana game time, oblivious to the danger all around them. Gaza outside was rioting. But inside the church, the children were completely sheltered and memorizing their Bible verses for the week.

The gospel is truly liberating people from their chains in the Gaza Strip. The church, although harassed, persecuted, and in constant danger, is unmoved by the overwhelming odds against them. The believers' vision to reach the Strip and their passion for souls are going to be rewarded at the judgment seat of Christ one day. Unless you go to Gaza, you will be unfamiliar with their names until heaven. They are warriors for Christ. Their rewards await them, and their crowns are ready.

Jordan—Launching Pad for Arab Outreach

Pastor Aziz had a startling experience. A Muslim man who lived across the street was on to the pastor. The ornery neighbor informed the seasoned man of God that if he talked to him about Jesus, he would order his murder.

Since the pastor had been arrested several times, this was nothing new to him. He was quite used to persecution by now. His wife summarized their existence with words I will remember for life: "Most of the leaders of our church have been arrested by the authorities at least once. But I think every Christian should be arrested for their faith at least once in their life because after being arrested your fear leaves you." What penetrating words those were to my soul! Would I be willing to be arrested for Christ?

After September 11, 2001, Pastor Aziz was in an Amman, Jordan, outdoor market. The man who had threatened him earlier called out to him loudly across from the fruit stand. The pastor was surprised to hear the formerly surly acquaintance tell him of his new spiritual search. "I'm sick of Islam," he blurted out. "It is consumed with violence and world domination, and I've had it!"

Aziz asked the man if he could visit with him about Jesus. He answered, "Yes, let's talk soon. But until then, when your church sings, please leave your windows open, because those songs speak to my heart."

This man's about-face is a window into the religion of Islam today. Many followers of Muhammad are privately questioning their religion and its real motives. Missionaries in the Middle East are saying that Muslims have not been this open to the saving grace of Jesus Christ for thirteen centuries.

The Jordanian pastor explained in this way: "September 11 was a terrible tragedy not just for America but for the world. If you track Islam worldwide, you will be able to find it quickly because it leaves a trace of blood in its path. But the lives that were lost on September 11 were not lost in vain because it triggered a revival among Muslims. Their religion has been exposed, and they have many questions to be answered. We believe Jesus has the answers to their questions."

The Amman church began an Internet chat room outreach program nightly. The hits were so numerous that the church had to go from one computer to three, then to five. Next, it moved up to nine computers. The volume continued to rise. The church has just purchased its fifteenth computer. Every night trained leaders from the church engage Muslims in chat rooms, answering their questions about Jesus in a safe atmosphere. Lives are rescued every night from the darkness of Islam and delivered safely into the loving arms of Jesus. Through Internet evangelism, people are having an online born-again experience in closed Islamic countries—Libya, Saudi Arabia, Iran, Egypt, Syria, and many more. The church then follows up by supplying these babes in Christ with solid discipleship materials. When someone places his trust in Christ and forsakes Islam, a thumb goes up from the happy gospel sharer. Every night, several thumbs-up are seen.

Yes, the holy fire is spreading throughout Jordan. *Jesus* films and thousands of EvangeCubes are now in the country. Believers are serious about sharing Christ and being His Jordanian ambassadors. The Jordan Evangelical Theological Seminary trains more than a hundred students per year. The Middle East's only evangelical seminary cannot enroll all the students interested. The ministries are well connected and focused on the vast needs of the region. The believers planted ten Iraqi churches throughout Jordan after the first Gulf War because many Iraqi refugees came into the Hashemite king-

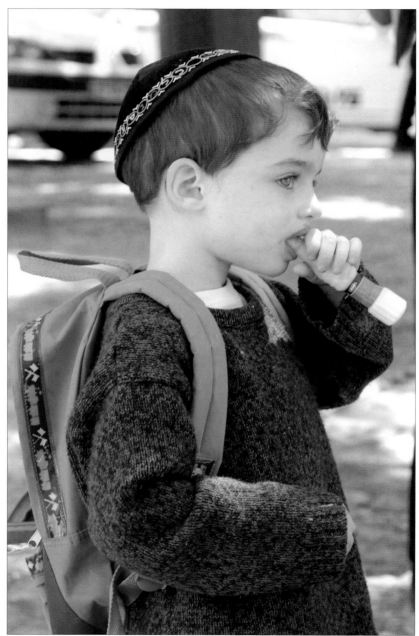

Orthodox Jewish boy enjoys a snack in the Old City of Jerusalem.

Del Tackett and author in prayer at the Roman theatre in Beit Shean, Israel.

Iranian beauty in Shiraz, Iran.

Sweet sisters in a Gaza refugee camp.

Two Moroccan Jewish buddies at Abraham's Tomb in Hebron. The boys are from Sderot which has been hit by Palestinian missile attacks from Gaza since September of 2005.

JoAnn Doyle teaching at a Women's Conference in the Middle East.

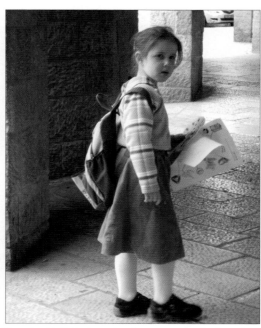

Young Jewish Orthodox girl on her way to school in Jerusalem.

Brother Andrew and author meet in Gaza.

Jewish Orthodox man reads Scripture at Israel's Western Wall. The Western Wall is the retaining wall under Israel's holiest site-the Temple Mount.

New friends in Iran.

Baptism at the Jordan River.

Image of Satan on the Dome of the Rock. Over the centuries this doubled sided picture on marble has emerged right next to the front entrance.

The first glimpse of the Treasury in Petra. This hidden city was built by the Nabateans in the Second century B.C. in the biblical area known as Edom.

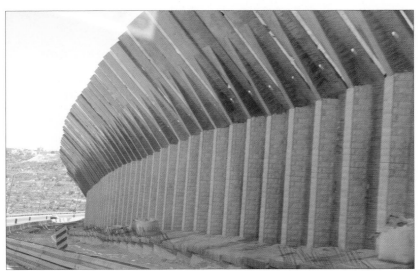

A section of the wall between Israel and the West Bank.

Israeli Soldiers.

Palestinian refugee camp family and author.

The Selah Women's Team in the Middle East.

JoAnn Doyle leads Middle East
Women's Conference.

Rami Ayyad and nephew. Rami a Palestinian brother,
was martyred for his faith in the Gaza Strip in 2007.

Kathleen Flynn worships with Arab believers.

Palestinian refugee children in Gaza.

Israeli Archaeologist near
Beit Shemesh, Israel.

Connie Prince finds a clay pot
on an archaeological dig in Israel.

Dan Hizhusen prays for the
city of Baghdad while in Iraq.

Jordanian woman with her baby.

Happy couples renew their marriage vows
in Cana, where Jesus attended
the wedding in John 2.

Hassan Nasrallah billboard in Tehran.
Nasrallah is the leader of the Iranian backed
terrorist group in Syria named Hezbollah. This
enormous poster covers one side of an entire
building and calls Iranians to help annihilate
Israel along with Hezbollah.

Recent Archaeological find of King David's Palace in Jerusalem.

Palace ruins of Darius the Great in Persopolis, Iran.

An evangelistic conversation with Iraqi students on the campus of the University Of Baghdad.

Curtis Hail President of e3 Partners and Jordanian man in traditional Jordanian kafiyya.

Poster in Tehran of Ayatollah Khameini the present day dictator of Iran, and Ayatollah Khomeini, the dictator that came into power after the Islamic Revolution of 1979.

Jordanian Muslim women at Petra.

Cheri Fitzsimmons worships
in Amman, Jordan.

David Shepherd - B&H Publishing Group
Publisher, wife Cherie, and the Doyle's
on the Sea of Galilee.

Jason Elam of the Atlanta Falcons, author,
and Nawaz Lalani on the Mt. of Olives.

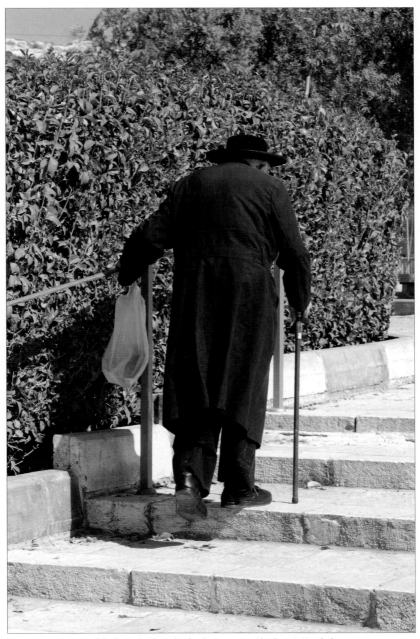

Elderly Orthodox climbs the stairs at Abraham's Tomb for morning prayers.

Jewish synagogue in Iran. There has been a Jewish population in Iran since it was part of the Persian Empire during Israel's captivity of the Old Testament.

The Cave of Machpelah in Hebron is Israel's second Holiest site. The cave is where Abraham, Isaac, Jacob, Sarah, Leah, and Rebekah are buried. The enormous stone edifice over it was probably built by Herod the Great.

The probable tomb of King Xerxes near Persopolis, Iran. Xerxes was the King of the Persian Empire and married Esther of the Bible.

Former Ambassador to Iraq L. Paul Bremer and author meet in Sadaam's palace in Baghdad.

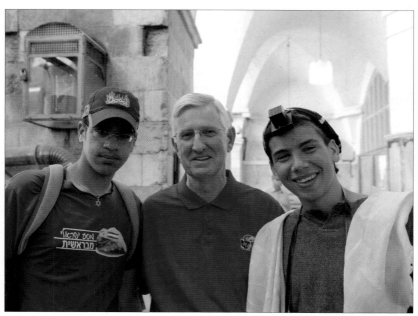

Russell Brown with young Israelis at Hebron.

Jordanian women and American women at Petra.

Lindsay Doyle with Israeli soldiers.

Orthodox Synagogue at Abraham's Tomb.

dom (Jordan) as a result of Desert Storm. The churches sensed a big open door and led many to Christ.

The Iraqis continued to hope for a return to their country one day. That day has now arrived, and believers have returned to Iraq to help stabilize the church there and begin a countrywide church-planting initiative. Pastor Aziz recently called me to say that he was in Baghdad, helping to equip the church. An American soldier preached the sermon in the worship service, and Aziz trained believers to share their faith with the EvangeCube.

It doesn't get any better than this.

The Jordanian church and its dynamic pastor are the influencers of the region. They train, shepherd, and help resource pastors in Gaza, the West Bank, and in all Arab countries. One believer is a teacher in a private Christian school. Since public schools are often lacking, many Muslim families go to private schools even if they are Christian-based. The teacher shared the EvangeCube with one class and led forty young people to the Lord! He is systematically working his way through the school.

And Their Young Men Will Dream Dreams

The prophet Joel talked about a prophetic outpouring that would bless the nation of Israel during the coming of the Lord. Visions, dreams, and a spectacular display of God's power would accompany this golden age. In the past ten years, missionaries have continually heard of a similar phenomenon in the Muslim world. People began having dreams. Others started seeing visions. Jesus was manifesting Himself to devout Muslims with overwhelming power.

I have personally met several of these people. Their stories amaze me as I see the depth of God's pursuing love. Paul said to Timothy in his pastoral Epistle to the young leader that God "wants everyone to be saved and to come to the knowledge of the truth" (1 Tim. 2:4). In other words, the heart of God cries out for a full house in heaven. Yet in many areas, the gospel is not available for all who hunger. Nowhere is this seen more than behind the spiritual iron curtain of Islam. What's a fair God to do? God often does the unexpected. The spectacular. He sends visions and dreams. God goes extreme.

We've met them. A man who saw Jesus calling him and saying, "Forsake Allah and come to Me." A woman praying to Allah, and when she opened her eyes a vision of Jesus was unfolding before her. Since Muslims have Jesus in their "system" and are familiar with Him, this helps break down any barriers that they might have with Christians in general. True, Islam teaches that Jesus is only a prophet; but when He appears with such power, they are convinced. Jesus has revealed Himself in Mecca, Baghdad, Damascus, Tehran—some of the most restricted Islamic cities. Because of His wonderful, long-suffering patience with this sin-infested world, He is not willing to give up on the people who follow Muhammad. He wants to reach them like anyone else.

And He is.

The Arab church is advancing God's kingdom into the inner recesses of Islam. The messianic church is clearly on the move, too. God is supplying His power abundantly. Pastors like Avi, Hanna, and Aziz are filled to overflowing with the Holy Spirit, and the church is on a roll. Jews are converting; Muslims are, too. Is there any hope of seeing genuine reconciliation between the two sons of Abraham? We'll cover the answer to that question in chapter 7, "The Mission Heart of God."

Dvat and Eyal—Modern-Day Ruth and Boaz

The couple is stunning. In their early twenties, Eyal and Dvat are an Israeli version of Ken and Barbie. These lovers, however, are much more than a couple of sharp-looking Jewish youth. Their depth of life experiences rivals those of people twice their age. Their journey took an unexpected turn on August 4, 2002. The devastation the two of them have had to deal with at such a young age reeks of injustice.

But they do not complain.

In the summer of 2002, Eyal and Dvat "had life by the tail." Dvat was studying to be a lawyer. She is Jewish, but her family roots are from Iraq. Before 1948, many Jews lived in Baghdad and the surrounding Iraqi communities. After Israel became a nation again, most Muslim-led nations forced Jews to leave. The refugee problem for Jews led families to Israel from all Middle East countries. Jews from Africa and Europe were also displaced and arrived steadily. Dvat loves life, and her smile lights up the room. She is focused and well disciplined. She has maintained this even in the midst of the ongoing war in her homeland.

Eyal is strong and taller than most Israeli young men. He is handsome and well spoken. Since Israel's population is so small, every young person is required to serve in the military. Both men and women serve unless there are religious objections. (The ultra-Orthodox who are so often seen at the Western Wall praying and wearing black hats and side curls traditionally do not allow their children to enter the military.) Men serve an average of two years, and women serve at least six months. The system works because it gives Israelis a vested interest in the country. Antiwar demonstrations are almost nonexistent here.

Eyal was in the midst of fulfilling his obligation to his country. He was moving up in the military, and his options were many because of his fine service within the Israeli Defense Forces (IDF). Going to his military assignment on that hot August day, traveling on bus number 361 from the coastal city of Haifa to the Galilean city of Safed, a suicide bomber under the direction of the Hamas terrorist group detonated his hidden weapon of destruction at the Meron junction.

The bus exploded instantly. Nine people were killed, and fifty were wounded. To many Americans, it was only another lead news story from the turbulent Middle East. In Colorado Springs, I watched it and turned away in disgust.

Months later while in Tel Aviv, we were introduced to Eyal, who had numerous physical problems. He recounted what it was like to be on that bus. Eyal had been visiting with others on the bus when the killer hopped on board, grabbed a soldier around the waist, and blew himself up in Allah's name. Among terrorists, the more IDF one kills or maims, the better. This bus was loaded with soldiers. Three sergeants were killed in the heinous attack.

Eyal was one meter away when the terrorist pushed the button and exploded the moving vehicle. Immediately, Eyal could not see. He felt enormous pain in one of his legs and pulled something out that had impaled it. Only when he felt a shoe on the end did he realize it was another soldier's leg that had been blown off.

The scene, of course, was mass chaos. Rushed to the hospital, the wounded were taken to surrounding area trauma centers. There were too many to handle in one hospital. Some of the dead had been twenty feet away from the scene, waiting to catch another bus. Eyal was within four feet and lived.

Dvat has supported Eyal through numerous surgeries. He was told that he would never walk again. He walks. He was told that his brain could not function properly and that they should just pull the plug on life support. His long-term and short-term memory has returned. He has hearing aids to amplify sounds. He needs an eye transplant someday when it becomes available.

He is a miracle several times over.

Eyal and Dvat have a true love story. It would have been easier for Dvat to move on and end their relationship. The road ahead is very long. Eyal does not look much like the man she fell in love with a few years ago. But love won. Through their uphill existence and their daily struggles, God has strengthened their resolve and bonded them together for life.

They married on August 4, 2004, the second anniversary of the bus bombing. This was their way of redeeming the day for good by not letting evil win. They have hope. They smile. They walk confidently toward the future hand in hand. Radical Islam lost on August 4, 2002.

Dvat gives endless attention to her fallen soldier. Like Ruth in the Old Testament, her steady attitude and loyalty to Eyal are part of a real-life Hebrew romance. They are helplessly in love, committed together for life, and unshakable in their confidence that one day Eyal will be able to see again.

For wherever you go, I will go, and wherever you live, I will live; your people will be my people, and your God will be my God. Where you die, I will die, and there I will be buried. May the LORD do this to me, and even more, if anything but death separates you and me. (Ruth 1:16b–17)

Chapter 6
The Believer, The American

The complex struggle between religion and politics is divisive even among American Christians. Lines are drawn in Jesus' family, and unfair labels are often attached. Can a believer be pro-Israel, pro-Palestinian, and in favor of the war on terrorism all at the same time?

Check the Label

Labels are dangerous. They are the ultimate way to dismiss someone you don't agree with. If I oppose your view on, let's say, theology, then by labeling you as something, I reduce you to irrelevance. "Oh, he's just a fundamentalist." "She's a little charismatic, you know." "That church is legalistic." We've all heard them.

I confess I've used labels. Lots of them. So did the people around Jesus, and He always put them in their place for stooping to that level. Whether it was egotistical Pharisees or wayward disciples, labeling was out. Jesus wouldn't stand for it. The Savior of the world often spent time with questionable people. And to the religious elite, His people-judging skills were suspect for certain. Look at a few of the people Jesus considered important:

- a blind beggar
- a leper
- a Samaritan woman

- an adulterous woman
- a demonized maniac
- a tax extortionist
- a Roman occupying soldier
- a demonized girl from Tyre, the "sin city" of the day

But in all His dealings with people, Jesus never "labeled" them. Each person was valued. Jesus went out of His way to reach those who already had been labeled.

When it comes to Israel and the Middle East, people quickly choose sides and start throwing around labels. I'm talking about Christians here! The intensity of the conflict causes people to formulate opinions regardless of whether they've ever been to the region. It seems so easy—"Can't we all just get along?"

The answer of course is a resounding no!

First, it would appear on the surface that born-again Christians are heavily weighted toward Israel's side. Perhaps many Christians see John Hagee, Pat Robertson, and Jack Hayford as high-profile American Christian leaders and assume that their stance is reflective of the majority. Although many pro-Israel American leaders such as these are well known and have national platforms, Christianity appears to be fairly split. What is it that determines a person's stance? To answer this, we must examine some of the labels that are (as usual) unfair in nature.

- *Pro-Israel.* Conservative, Bible-believing Christians often are thrown into this catchall category. If they interpret prophecy as largely unfulfilled using a literal hermeneutic (interpretation), then they will be immediately placed in this category.
- *Pro-Palestinian.* Christians who do not see the regathering of Israel as a fulfillment of prophecy or who react strongly to the enormous humanitarian needs of the Palestinian people often are tagged and put here.

Exposure to the territory is often the ultimate deciding factor. On my first visit to Israel, I had a rude awakening to this fact. While staying in

Jerusalem with my church's first tour group, I met some West Bank missionaries. They updated us on the challenging ministry in the Palestinian city of Ramallah. These people lived eight miles from Jerusalem, but it was worlds away in living conditions. The Palestinian believers were crushed between rival radical Muslim groups, yet the church was experiencing growth and blessing.

As the conversation turned toward the conflict with Israel, it was easy to detect a bias against the Jews. I expected some of this but was shocked to hear how far the missionaries went. They actually *liked* Yasser Arafat and thought he was good for the Palestinian people. How could they have an ounce of respect for the Palestinian Authority chairman? I thought he was the top terrorist of all time when considering his malicious accomplishments of the last three decades.

Likewise, I have met missionaries and other leaders who sincerely believe that Israel can do no wrong. This is amazing in light of the fact that their leadership is largely secular with strong anti-Christian leanings.

Labels. You have to be careful.

Keep Both Eyes Open

Our primary objective as followers of Jesus Christ is to reach the lost for Him from all nations. Our hope is the salvation plan available for all people, whether Jew or Arab. When going to Israel or ministering there, keeping both eyes open is essential. Jews need Jesus. Arabs need Jesus. This is obvious. The two people groups are completely different in worldview, outlook on life, and goals, yet the bottom line is that they are sinners in need of the Lamb of God's sacrifice.

There is no question that Israel is God's chosen people. The plan of God has not been ditched in order to "ace" Israel out of a meaningful future. The Abrahamic covenant still has future remaining dividends for Israel. But when it comes to salvation, God's love is for all people. This must be at the core of our passion for Israel and the Middle East.

Jewish Roots, Compassionate Heart

I love my Jewish roots! No, I wasn't born into a Jewish family, but my spiritual roots are thoroughly Jewish. All Christians have Hebraic spiritual roots. Paul says that we are "wild olive shoots" grafted into Israel, the "natural branches." We are to respect them and honor them. In Romans 11:11–21, Paul laid it out for us:

> I ask, then, have they stumbled so as to fall? Absolutely not! On the contrary, by their stumbling, salvation has come to the Gentiles to make Israel jealous. Now if their stumbling brings riches for the world, and their failure riches for the Gentiles, how much more will their full number bring!
>
> Now I am speaking to you Gentiles. In view of the fact that I am an apostle to the Gentiles, I magnify my ministry, if I can somehow make my own people jealous and save some of them. For if their being rejected is world reconciliation, what will their acceptance mean but life from the dead? Now if the firstfruits offered up are holy, so is the whole batch. And if the root is holy, so are the branches.
>
> Now if some of the branches were broken off, and you, though a wild olive branch, were grafted in among them, and have come to share in the rich root of the cultivated olive tree, do not brag that you are better than those branches. But if you do brag—you do not sustain the root, but the root sustains you. Then you will say, "Branches were broken off so that I might be grafted in." True enough; they were broken off by unbelief, but you stand by faith. Do not be arrogant, but be afraid. For if God did not spare the natural branches, He will not spare you either.

In Scripture, God's emotions are often spent over the children of Israel. God's love for them has known no limits. The prophets also pursued them with the same kind of intensity; so did the apostles. Do I have the same kind of love for Jews? I think, rather, that we Christians *use* Jewish people. We manipulate them. We hustle them like a shady used-car dealer does a first-time buyer. They know it. They have to. After all, Israel is the built-in barometer when it comes to eschatology, the study of future things. We know this since we can compare both Testaments in Scripture and trace their logical end. I confess that I, too, have had a severe case of "end-time fever" at the expense of God's revered covenant people, the Jews.

When I fell in love with Israel, I couldn't get enough of the people. The Bible came alive in a new way for me. Going to the Mount of Olives to see where Jesus ascended and will one day return shows you how real our faith is. Jerusalem is the place where the armies of the world will descend in a final attempt to eradicate the "Zionist entity" forever. Revelation 19 and Zechariah 14 record that the nations of the world will commit the fatal mistake of underestimating their opponent. The rider on the white horse is none other than the King of kings and the Lord of lords. Big mistake. While standing on the Mount of Olives, your mind's eye can see it unfold before you. One day it will happen, and then—eternity!

How can we as Christians not get caught up in all this cool stuff? The amazing centuries-old predictions continue to come into sharper focus all within our lifetime. The Temple Institute in the Old City of Jerusalem is filled with articles that its sponsors plan to use in the coming third temple. The Temple Mount Faithful are considered by the Israeli government as a fringe wacko group. They are committed to building a temple for Yahweh on Mount Moriah some time in the future. It seems hard to believe that a temple could ever be erected in Jerusalem without catapulting all of Islam into World War III. But the group continues with its enthusiasm unabated. They host tour groups that marvel at the exact replicas of the utensils used within Solomon's Temple. The candle stands, the high priests' clothes, the incense holders, and the bronze lavers have been redone with the highest attention to detail. Each year, the Temple Mount Faithful attempt to bring the uncut cornerstone on an oxcart through the Dung Gate of the Old City and place it on the temple platform. There is only one problem that occurs annually with the parade—the Muslims strongly object. The event is so explosive that the Israeli government tries to shut it down before it reaches the gate and sets off another round of rioting. The Muslims wait for the Temple Mount Faithful and unload on them with rocks if they make it through Israeli security.

How will a temple ever be built again? We know from Scripture that the Antichrist will call a halt to temple sacrifice, ordering that all fire offerings be made to him. Daniel tells us about this future abomination that takes place in the coming next house of God. The temple will be built one way or another. A plausible theory is that an outside group will do the construction, perhaps bypassing an Arab-Israeli showdown in Jerusalem.

(I love this stuff! I overdose on it. Did you know that the priests, who have to be descendants of the biblical Kohathites, have already been selected? Two hundred of them, in fact. The Jewish name Cohen is the modern family name for the Old Testament Kohathite priesthood.)

What about the centerpiece of the temple itself? What about the Ark of the Covenant? The very meeting place of God and high priest? After Israel was safely out of Egypt and Pharaoh's army had become the first sunken navy, God met with Moses to establish this visible point of contact. God would reside over the Ark of the Covenant, and the coming high priests of Israel would meet Him there face-to-face once every twelve months with fear and trepidation. God's man for the year would enter the Holy of Holies on the Day of Atonement and stand before the presence. "I will meet with you there above the mercy seat, between the two cherubim that are over the ark of the testimony; I will speak with you from there about all that I command you regarding the Israelites" (Exod. 25:22). This was the holy place and the true inner sanctum of Israel's existence for 900 years, and then the Ark of the Covenant vanished.

Where did it go? In his book *In Search of Temple Treasures*, Randall Price quotes Richard Elliot Friedman on the mysterious missing centerpiece: "There is no report that the Ark was carried away, or destroyed, or hidden.

There is not even any comment such as, 'And then the Ark disappeared, and we do not know what happened to it' or 'And no one knows where it is to this day.' The most important object in the world, in the biblical view, simply ceases to be in the story!"[1] Of course, there are a variety of theories about what happened to the ark. Here are four views:

1. Destroyed in Babylonian captivity after being transported there.
2. Transported to Ethiopia after the supposed affair between King Solomon and the Queen of Sheba.
3. Hidden in the Dead Sea cave region. In the 1990s, expeditions were led by Vendyl Jones, a former Texas pastor, who is the basis for the character of Steven Spielberg's Indiana Jones.
4. Under the Temple Mount. After the Six-Day War of 1967, Israel had control of the Temple Mount. Two prominent rabbis claimed to have found the Ark of the Covenant in a tunnel under the present-day Dome of the Rock. Israel cemented the entrance to the tunnel, fearing a major Muslim attack.

There are other theories, too, and nearly every year a new treasure hunter claims to be closing in on finding the elusive Ark of the Covenant. All of this is fascinating. Third-temple enthusiasts claim that when they are given the okay, they can have a new temple standing in about nine months. The temple instruments are prepared for usage. From reading our Bibles, we know where all of this is heading. The Antichrist is coming. A temple will be built. The final conflict is in the wings waiting to be played out.

When we examine the news and compare it with Scripture, we see the chess pieces moving into place. Brothers and sisters in Christ, this ought to motivate us into accelerated, all-out service for Jesus. Unfortunately, it usually doesn't.

For some reason, prophecy often has a paralytic effect on us. It did on me. Oh, yes, I could watch the news and quickly establish a "hot link" to Scripture. Yet I was completely unmoved with compassion for Jews. I was not overwhelmed with pity concerning their coming judgment. I did not seek out Jews with whom to share the Messiah. I did not pray for them. I did not change my lifestyle whatsoever as a result of my keen biblical insight. I say this to my shame.

Maybe you are somewhat like I was. But I have changed. I have been renewed to an active faith. I will no longer sit by and just let it all happen. I will not be a Christian who just uses the Jews.

We don't say it, of course, but it's easy to think, "The Jews are back in the land. Israel is a nation again. Jesus is coming back soon." All of these are, I believe, true statements; yet do our hearts not break for the awful road ahead for the Jews themselves? We must have compassion for God's people. We must desire the best for them. We must have our hearts broken for these people who face a coming onslaught that will pale by comparison to anything they have ever experienced in their history.

What's Best for Israel?

First, every Christian should pray for Israel on an ongoing basis. God commands us to do so, and there should be no question as to the urgency and necessity of our continual intercession for Israel. "Pray for the peace of Jerusalem: 'May those who love you prosper; may there be peace within your walls, prosperity within your fortresses'" (Ps. 122:6–7). I will cover this passage in greater detail in chapter 9.

What else can America do for Israel? I believe we need to quit forcing Israel into peace treaties that are destined to fail. Israel has had a "go-it-alone" mentality to survive its wars and crucible existence since 1948. Since we in America have been the Israelis' only true friend for decades, we certainly have Israel's ear.

I realize that I will be treading on some difficult terrain as I answer my own question here. President Bush has led our nation through one of the most difficult periods in American history. Our historic efforts in Afghanistan and in Iraq have made the world a safer place regardless of how the media tries to spin it. That is my view. When our president declared a war on terrorism, I remember thinking, *Are we in for a long war?* It will be. Make no mistake about it—we are in a twenty-first-century holy war.

That is why many American evangelicals were shocked when President Bush promoted the "Road Map for Peace." How could our president call for Israel to give up land that is rightfully hers? After all, should Israel give in to the demands of Palestinian terrorists? Are they any different than the band of thugs that we were at war with in Afghanistan or Iraq?

Today as I am writing this, Secretary of State Condoleezza Rice told Congress that "Israel and the Palestinians must push toward a final peace deal before the opportunity is lost."[2] She proposed a meeting of Israeli and Palestinian leaderships, which was held at the United States Naval Academy in Annapolis, Maryland, in November 2007. Peace *would* be great, wouldn't it? The problem is what the Bush administration is proposing in order to bring peace. This plan would be a disaster and leave Israel incapable of protecting itself.

On top of security issues, Palestinians are now saying that before they even come to a peace summit, a pre-condition for Arab control of the Temple Mount must be on the table. This is no good for Israel and no good for the United States. It's not the first time the Temple Mount has been up for grabs. It's hard to believe this is an option for Israel, considering how long they waited to reclaim Jerusalem as their capital.

In June 1967, after a shocking victory in the Six Day War, Israel claimed that Jerusalem was its eternal capital, never to be divided again. Previously, when the city was under Jordanian control, Jews were not allowed to pray on the Temple Mount or even go near it. But all of that changed in the first week of June 1967. In about sixty hours, Israel fought off the surrounding Arab nations that had vowed to exterminate it. Both rabbis and Jewish soldiers wept openly in front of the Wailing Wall. Israel's homecoming was now complete. After 1967, Jerusalem remained intact and wasn't ever on a negotiating table until the waning days of President Bill Clinton.

As the building rubble was still smoldering in New York City after September 11, 2001, Israelis were seen weeping openly for Americans who lost their lives in the attack. The sentiments shown toward us as we were suffering from national shock will always be remembered. A magazine cover from

Israel read "America and Israel, Fighting Terrorism Together." It seemed we Americans could finally relate to what it is like to live in Israel—in constant danger of fanatical Muslims attempting to blow us all up. What an existence!

Over time, however, our press appeared to employ a double standard when dealing with our enemies and then Israel's. It seems perfectly all right for us to retaliate against our enemies, but not so for Israel. I truly am amazed at how our news perceives all of this. Even the normally conservative Fox News often gets it dead wrong. Israel's army is often equated with Palestinian terrorist organizations.

Some of the worst offenders I have seen are those who provide international reporting and commentary on media outlets such as CNN. Although there are certainly some fine, fair-minded individuals who work for these networks, there are many others who are part of the moral equivalence movement. In other words, they see no difference between an Israeli Defense Force's soldier and a terrorist. They consider both of them to be mere soldiers. But this is simply not true. The IDF seeks to protect its people while the terrorists seek to use its people in any way necessary to kill Israelis (meaning, as suicide bombers). Although Israel's army does seek to root out cold-blooded killers, they are often portrayed as the true culprits themselves. In other words, the mind-set becomes "they deserve it."

Doing ministry in the Gaza Strip is a real eye-opener. We have seen Hamas, Islamic Jihad, and the Al-Aksa Martyrs Brigade "up close and personal," as they say. These terrorist organizations have no regard for life whatsoever. Not even their own. Did you know that among the Israeli fatalities in the current intifada, 75 percent have been civilians? Women and children are specifically targeted. The most vulnerable are taken out without a second thought.

While I was in Israel during the siege of Jenin, it was reported over the news worldwide that Israel had massacred more than 500 people. Of course, there were no news people present to verify these findings, but this was the story that was spread from supposed eyewitnesses. As it turned out, about fifty were killed, and the terrorist block of the fanatical West Bank city was eliminated. When the numbers were finally verified, no retractions (naturally) were issued from news organizations.

I certainly cannot vouch for every Israel Defense Force soldier, but I have met many of them, and I do know that it is not their goal to kill the innocent. Sometimes it does happen accidently, as we have seen before, but Israel apologizes and shows compassion. Its goal is to target the dangerous while protecting the innocent. There is no comparison between Israeli soldiers and Palestinian terrorist organizations, and shame on our news agencies for assuming this.

Okay, here's where I may lose some of you. But hang on if you dare. I believe that the Oslo Accords were a big mistake. President Bill Clinton put pressure on Israel, and the message was clear for them: "Give in or pay for it." It's called "sanctions." They work because they affect the economy. Without a healthy dose of American aid and business partnering, Israel's economy could be devastated quickly. Yitzak Rabin was pressured into the Oslo Accords. Benjamin Netanyahu was pressured into the Wye River Accords. Ariel Sharon's successors are being pressured into the Road Map for Peace. No other country could have this sort of sway over Israel. In short, as my friend and writer David Dolan says, "When America speaks, Israel listens." Do they ever!

Of course I want peace. I love the Palestinians who are stuck in a virtual no-man's land. I feel for them. But we have no right to pressure Israel into giving away more land. Can you imagine what we Americans would have thought if after September 11 the majority of the world's nations had unilaterally called for us to forget about the whole thing and concede to the terrorists' wishes? I don't think so! Why should we make Israel do something equally absurd?

Let's allow Israel to handle its own war. It's not ours to decide, and we could pay a big price for tying Israeli hands behind their backs and forcing another land-for-peace fiasco.

Perhaps we already have paid a big price . . .

Is America under a Curse?

The Clinton administration pushed Israel into the Oslo Accords, which ultimately fell apart. This agreement was generally applauded by the world and hailed as a great achievement for an American president. Many thought that this would surely deliver a comprehensive peace to the region. It did not, of course, and the ill-fated Oslo agreement disintegrated before our eyes. Palestinian terror groups stepped up their hate campaign and have not backed down since.

Was this a great achievement for America? I believe not. I also believe that the penalty for twisting Israel's arm into giving away yet another chunk of land is directly linked to many of our national tragedies. Look at the past decade. Is there a correlation between the 1993 peace treaty and ten years of bloodshed for us in America? You decide. Look what has happened since the 1993 Oslo Accords:

Feb. 26, 1993:   World Trade Center attacked—bomb exploded in parking garage; 6 persons killed.

Apr. 19, 1995:   Oklahoma City federal building attacked—bomb exploded outside the Alfred P. Murrah Building; 168 killed.

Nov. 13, 1995:   U.S. military camp attacked—5 killed in Riyadh, Saudi Arabia.

June 25, 1996:   U.S. military installation attacked—19 American soldiers killed in Dhabran, Saudi Arabia.

July 17, 1996:   TWA Flight 800 crashed after leaving New York City—several witnesses reported seeing a surface-to-air missile hit the aircraft; 230 died.

Aug. 7, 1998:   Two American embassies simultaneously attacked in Kenya and Tanzania (both in Africa); 224 killed.

Sept. 11, 2001:   America attacked in New York City and Washington, D.C.—World Trade Center death toll: 2,795; Pentagon death toll: 125; hijacked Flight 93 death toll: 64.

With the exception of the Oklahoma City bombings and TWA Flight 800, all of these attacks against the United States of America are from the very groups we are pressuring Israel to forgive, forget, and give land to. The Oklahoma City bombing, though not carried out by Muslim extremists, has their footprints all over the heinous crime. Timothy McVeigh did meet with Muslim terrorists possibly the day of the attack, according to Joseph Farah, who in an early 2002 *WorldNetDaily* article, delineated the alliance that Muslim terrorists and neo-Nazi groups formed in the early 1990s. The TWA Flight 800 probe has been accused of covering up information that suggested a surface-to-air missile shot by a terrorist brought the plane down.

We are in the midst of a long, sustained attack on America by Islamic groups that hate us. Not until September 11, 2001, did America realize the problems we face from inside our own country. Our borders have been easy to cross. Undesirables have had almost unlimited access to our nation, all in the name of freedom.

I was able to see this firsthand myself in August 2002 on a flight back from the Middle East. Our flight schedule was from Abu Dhabi, United Arab Emirates, to Amman, Jordan, on to Frankfort, Germany, then to Chicago, and finally to Denver. The flying marathon takes a toll. While on the third leg of the flight just after takeoff from Germany, I was hoping to get some badly needed sleep. I noticed that the flight attendant crew was huddled in the middle of the 747 and obviously disturbed about something, looking nervous and very concerned. I got out of my seat and asked if everything was okay. They assured me that it was and to please return to my seat. I tried to probe a little further, so I put the question this way: "Look, I work in the Middle East, and my dad is also an FBI agent. You people look very scared. Are you worried about a passenger on this plane?"

They immediately opened up. There was a passenger in 29G who looked Middle Eastern and was staring at the flight attendants with anger on his face. He also was opening up all the compartments in the bathroom as if he was trying to hide something. One of the young ladies remarked that because the cockpit was now locked for the flight, the attendants were on their own. No wonder they were panicking.

A call was placed to the pilots, who in turn called the FAA to check on the suspicious passenger. The FAA notified the FBI to do a quick background check, and they found out the news everyone dreaded. He was from Iraq and single. Not good! Somehow he had made it through security and was on his way to the United States. So much for my nap.

The plot started to thicken. A man in first class started to look back at the man in 29G and make eye contact with him continually. He appeared to be communicating with him. The passengers in first class were now starting to get nervous, because this second man was also Middle Eastern and was not only rude to everyone around him but appeared hostile.

Another background check uncovered another single man from Iraq. This was not looking good.

The flight was a long one, and nothing ended up happening other than the two Iraqis exchanging looks and nods. When we landed, we noticed the two men walk right through passport control and security with ease. *What in the world is going on?* we thought. Later, we saw the relieved flight attendants, who told us that the FBI were tailing the two Iraqis to see where they were going and whom they were seeing. So let me see if I get this—the plan was to let them through and see if they could find some bigger fish from the terrorist underworld.

We live in a dangerous time as Americans.

Could this perhaps be a judgment of God on us for our involvement in the ill-fated Oslo agreement? After all, who are we to give away God's land anyway? I guess if I didn't believe this, I would be guilty of a very proud heart. If I didn't believe this, I would be thinking that we in America received some sort of special exemption from the Abrahamic covenant. God is faithful and consistent in His dealings with mankind. How can we curse Israel and reap no fallout? Nobody else has escaped it throughout history. I can't help believing that the ice we're currently walking on is getting awfully thin.

What's the Answer?

Here's my take: we should just support Israel and let the Israelis handle their own security issues. They certainly don't tell us what to do or try to sanction us. They've shown in the past that they are completely capable. It's as simple as that. America is right to fight the war on terrorism for as long as it takes. But when it comes to Israel, let them work out their terrorist problems, and we'll work on ours—because the solution that is always proposed to Israel is for them to give up more land.

Any plan that calls for Israel to give up land for peace will fail. And any current or upcoming peace talks will likely be no different. It will be tried and tried again, but it will not work. The reason it will fail is because God will not endorse it. And it will never appease the Islamic leadership who desperately want all of Israel—without Jews, of course. Like his predecessors, Ehud Olmert may be pushed to sign a peace treaty he knows is doomed. At one point, sanctions were discussed with them. If America plays hardball with Israel, a few things might just happen:

- *Arms supply reductions.* Israel might no longer be able to use American military hardware in their conflict against terrorism. Last night, I watched an Apache helicopter fire at a Muslim bomb-making factory. This would be illegal if the road map is adopted.
- *Economic sanctions.* Israel might be severely penalized economically if they refuse the peace plan. Israeli businessmen know this and have begun to put their own pressure on Prime Minister Olmert.
- *American condemnation.* Secretary of State Rice vowed to blame Israel if all demands of the Palestinians are not granted by Israel.

I pray to God Almighty that we never do this to His chosen people. We should not treat Israel this way; they don't deserve it. The future health of our nation is at stake. Will we bless them or curse them?

What's Best for Palestinians?

I'm sure at this point, some readers might think that I don't have a heart for Palestinians. That couldn't be further from the truth. Their situation is so difficult that while visiting wonderful Palestinian believers, I am in anguish. Yes, I believe this is Israel's land—all of it—but that doesn't mean I don't care for the Palestinians. I do.

They have been manipulated and used for decades. Their own leadership has abused them for unattainable religious goals to prove Islam is the superpower of the world. It has failed on all fronts. The Palestinian people who suffer needlessly are no better off now than they were in 1948. Their leadership has failed, wouldn't you agree?

Let's Start Over

In the twentieth century, the physical landscape of the world changed dramatically. As the Turkish Ottoman Empire collapsed in 1917, the area went from being a vast empire spanning an entire region to several smaller national entities. In the West, we merely viewed these changes on our maps like a big jigsaw puzzle coming together. But millions of people were affected, and their lives changed forever.

This massive people-shifting became one great big migration perhaps never before seen in history. From the former Turkish Ottoman Empire, France and Britain designed new states that included Syria, Lebanon, Iraq, and Jordan. The process began to take shape in the 1920s. The British had thought long and hard about placing Jews within the region. A national home for them had been promised, but as the nations came into existence, the Jews' piece of the pie continued to shrink.

The Palestine mandate had included present-day Jordan. This would have made Israel comparable to the other nations in size. But all of that changed in 1921, when the entire area of Jordan, called Transjordan, was taken out of the equation for the Jews. Eighty percent of the land previously drawn up as a future home for them was gone.

In the Arab world, tribal battles were common before the Middle East countries were established. *Lawrence of Arabia* was the movie that brought Arab tribal wars to the big screen. Although the film was exaggerated to some degree, it depicted the strife rampant throughout the Arabian Peninsula in that time period. One ruler caught up in the conflict was King Abdullah, who was defeated in one of the wars. He was literally a king without a kingdom. In an effort to resolve this, Abdullah was given the Transjordan. His kingdom became the home for his Hashemite tribe, who believe they are descendants of Muhammad. The country reflected this as it became off-limits for Jews to live in Jordan. It was predominantly filled with Palestinian Arabs rather than Hashemites. Even today, Jordan is about 70 percent Palestinian.

When the partition plan went to the United Nations for a vote, the proposed land size for Israel was one-tenth of what had been originally promised to them. The desperate, homeless Jews took what they were given, but it was a great injustice.

Israel's future was then sifted through a complex political system. In 1948, more land was taken from them. Arabs were also given biblical Judea and Samaria, and Jordan incorrectly claimed the West Bank. The Gaza Strip was also given to Arabs. (The land is actually Israel's and should be called the "East Bank" to be geographically correct. The very fact that the territory was named the West Bank uncovers Jordan's intent to seize the land from the beginning.) What remained for Jews were three strips of land. The land was not even connected. As for Jerusalem, Jews were merely given *access* to their most prized possession. Israel was clearly cheated in the whole process.

To make matters even worse, Jordan incorporated the West Bank in 1950. Egypt took the Gaza Strip. When the two territories were run by Jordan and Egypt, respectively, they were never called "occupied." There was also no talk of a Palestinian state at that time. When this land was taken from Israel, there was not a flicker of interest within the Arab world. Only when Israel won back the land in the Six-Day War of 1967 did the outcries began.

What about Refugees?

With all of that said about Israel receiving such an unfair deal, what about refugees? I must confess I was very unsympathetic to the needs of the Palestinians until I visited their refugee camps. Regardless of how they got there, the conditions are some of the worst anywhere. In our ministry at e3 Partners, we try to help the Palestinians in the camps with food distribution, and we have plans to organize a mission trip where young people can repair the shanties that are barely standing.

I asked myself several questions as the shock of their five decades of history sunk in:

- How would I like to live this way?
- Would I be able to fight off the bitterness so many of them exhibit?
- How would I get my family out of there for good?
- What would it be like to live in a tent for sixty years?

In February 2003, the *Jerusalem Post* published an excellent section within the paper titled "Refugees Forever?" It began this way: "Unique about the Palestinian refugee problem is that it has been allowed—even forced—to continue and to grow. Every other major refugee group has been resettled within a generation. Of the approximately 135 million refugees created over the last century, only the Palestinians have retained this dismal, nationless status."[3]

Estimated Figures
- 1.25 million Greeks and 500,000 Turkish refugees resettled
- 13 million Germans ejected from their ancestral homeland in East Prussia, Silesia, and the Sudetenland by the Advancing Russian forces in World War II, resettled
- 440,000 Finns reabsorbed
- 9 million Hindus and Sikhs left Pakistan for India and 6.5 million Muslims fled India for Pakistan
- 9 million Koreans fled Communist rule to South Korea

- 4.5 million Poles resettled
- 2 million Jews fled Europe and Arab states
- 900,000 Vietnamese took to the sea in order to avoid Communist rule
- 700,000 Chinese fled to Hong Kong
- 2,000,000 Hutus and Tutsis fled ethnic massacres in Rwanda for Zaire
- Untold masses were forced from their homes in ethnically torn former Yugoslavia
- 2 million Afghans fled Taliban rule en masse, most taking shelter in Pakistan

Refugees Created by Conflicts
- 1917–1933: 8,500,000
- 1933–1945: 73,200,000
- 1945–1957: 53,650,000

The Sad Paradox

In 1947, while Britain was disengaging from Palestine, it was also withdrawing from India, leading to the birth of independent Pakistani and Indian states. Whereas the Arab-Israeli conflict created hundreds of thousands of refugees, the Indians and Pakistanis wisely agreed to transfer millions of their people across the border in order to diffuse ethnic and religious tensions. India sent Muslims to Pakistan, which in turn sent Hindus to India. Both states granted citizenship to these refugees. The much smaller—and perhaps even more solvable—problem of Arab refugees is a sad paradox, in that it has cost the Western world so many billions of dollars in humanitarian aid that only perpetuates the refugees' plight, and has monopolized its media attention for over half a century, when alternatives in refugee transfers such as the one between India and Pakistan have proven effective.*

That's what makes the situation so difficult. I minister among Palestinians and consider them some of my closest friends. I can assure you, their situation is miserable. These believers conduct meaningful, vital, life-transforming ministry in the lives of countless people. Many of the Muslims I have met in Palestinian areas are far from what I would expect them to be. Yes, Gaza is home to some of the world's most dangerous terrorist groups, but it is also home to many kindhearted Arab families. Their culture is one of the most beautiful anywhere. If you knock on an Arab door, they will invite you into their house no matter who you are. They have to; it's a core virtue for them to be hospitable to all people.

Here is the problem. The Palestinian people are being duped by their leaders, who cannot come up with an agenda that doesn't have outrageous Islamic goals. Only God can pull Arab culture out of the smothering grasp of Islam, which has shaped an Arab culture for thirteen centuries that was fragmented into tribes. Islam has successfully kept the Palestinians from moving one inch forward by turning hatred for Israel into the main issue. Privately, many Palestinians—whether Christian or Muslim—are frightened about what the future holds in a Palestinian state. They could not discuss this openly without being considered traitors or Jew-lovers.

The corruption of the Palestinian Authority is legendary. For years, billions of dollars went straight into Yasser Arafat's bank accounts, doing nothing to help feed and clothe the Palestinians. When he died, Palestinians believed that some of the wealth he had amassed would finally be shared with the Palestinian people. No dice! It seems the Palestinians are the ultimate pawns in the chess game Islam continues to play with Israel. There is no reason that homes couldn't have been built with all the money that has vanished from the people and gone into the pockets of the Palestinian Authority and now Hamas.

A startling example of the vast corruption was uncovered a few years ago when a Palestinian broke into Arafat's compound and was able to prove

*Information on previous page excerpted from *The Arabs in History* (Oxford University Press) by Prof. Bernard Lewis, leading expert on Islamic and Middle Eastern history where billions of dollars had been stashed. The man had bucks! He was loaded with stolen funds taken from the people over decades. No wonder Saddam Hussein sent suicide bomber reward money directly to the parents' home. If it went through the Palestinian Authority offices, it wouldn't have made it to the people.

Israel will always be the ultimate bulls-eye on the Islamic dartboard, blamed for every problem the Palestinians experience. It is the only explanation that Islam can come up with. I remember saying many times to people I was counseling, "The only person you cannot help is the one who doesn't have a problem." The refusal to see this reality perpetuates the cycle of Palestinian misery. But could we possibly expect Palestinians to stand up and overthrow their leadership? They are controlled without any resources to do such a thing. Refugees need so much in the way of basic necessities. The needs are enormous.

And that's where I believe we can help.

What an obvious contrast there is between light and darkness as seen in people's lives. I want Palestinians to have a better life. I want them to enjoy freedom and to have their children educated to ensure a good future! I want the best for them. Here are two Palestinian reforms that are badly needed:

1. *Give the Palestinian leadership a major overhaul.* How sad to see the dismal living conditions the Palestinians endure year after year compared to the Israeli standard of living. Arab Israelis and Jewish Israelis enjoy their health care system, the right to vote, and government assistance that they receive for each child in their family. Palestinians would flourish in a system like that! Yet they will never have these things in a Palestinian state. A dictator will run it unless the people demand something better. Many Palestinians live in tents and shacks while their leaders live in lavish mansions off of the foreign aid that was supposed to improve the living conditions for the people. Unless the people rise up and say "no more," Islamic extremism will continue to be the machine that runs their culture, and the Palestinians will pay dearly for it.

Palestinian Christians are already suffering under Hamas rule. And if a Palestinian State becomes a reality, it will only get worse. Religious freedom will be nonexistent. This is vastly different than what the Palestinians have experienced with Israel's government. The Israelis have destroyed no mosques since 1948. Not one. In wars and all conflicts, they go out of their way to protect Islamic places of prayer and worship.

My eyes were opened to this fact on my first visit to the Gaza Strip. The Israelis had bombed Chairman Arafat's compound after the P.A. had launched several suicide attacks. The compound was a mess. It looked like a tornado scene in Kansas. The buildings were flattened and destroyed. But there was no one killed in the bombing, as the chairman was in Ramallah at the time. One building stood in perfect shape among the rubble: Yasser Arafat's personal mosque. The golden dome on it made it is a mini-version of Jerusalem's Dome of the Rock. It was not even nicked. Even in the midst of the intifada that had cost Israel hundreds of innocent lives, Muslim religious buildings were still respected. Israel used pinpoint bombing techniques to ensure that.

What frightens so many Palestinian believers is what they will face when they are under a government that has absolutely no regard for religious freedom. Since the Hamas takeover of Gaza, terrorist groups have begun persecution of believers. The Hamas government has done nothing to stop this. Religious freedom is not on the radar screen of the Islamic-led Palestinian leadership.

The time is now for moderate Palestinian Muslims and Christians to overhaul the P.A. and its corrupt leadership that will control their lives with an iron fist once in power. It's still not too late. Privately, Palestinians talk about the scores of people who are fed up and ready to pay the price for a "regime change." I pray that they follow through.

2. *Start over—minus the terrorist groups.* So much would change if the unrealistic, radical Islamic goals were dropped for the good of the Palestinian people. In short, the Palestinians want a place to live, but their leadership has tweaked this and turned it into a campaign to eradicate Israel. If terrorist groups were booted out of Palestinian areas and if the Palestinian Author-

ity came up with reasonable goals, much could be achieved. Here are a few givens:

- *Israel isn't going away.* Why should the Palestinians waste effort in trying to accomplish the impossible? It's only a twisted dream.
- *Palestinians need viable representation.* Most of them do not have a latent loathing of Jews. Many Palestinians have worked with Jews before. Many have benefited personally from them. It has been done.
- *Islam's outrageous goals are put ahead of human needs.* That's just the truth. Palestinians need to do a "root canal" on their leadership and drive out fanatical Muslim extremists. If not, they could stay in tents forever. It's time to wake up and smell the hummus!
- *Israel is willing to share the land.* It has proven this over and over for decades.

To some, my conclusions will offend. Palestinians become like the Israeli Arabs? Right! Many have and live the life they always dreamed. But I say this with all seriousness. A democratic, Jewish-led government will beat an Islamic dictatorship any day of the week. My heart breaks for the Palestinian people each time I enter the West Bank or the Gaza Strip.

Something must be done, and something can. If they absorb into Israel and drop the Islamically driven refugee project, they will realize their dream finally. If not Israeli Arabs, why not erase the blackboard and begin afresh with new leadership that will put the people first and put aside unattainable goals derived from irrational fundamental Islam?

Love a Palestinian—Give 'Em Jesus

Jesus is the answer. In Palestinian areas it's no different. My desire is to see every Palestinian in Israel and throughout the Middle East hear a clear presentation of the gospel. They are responding when given Jesus in a loving, non-confrontational manner.

Palestinians typically feel that because America often sides with Israel, the implication is that Palestinians are hated. But I believe this to be an unfair charge. I do believe that the bulk of Christian ministry efforts have benefited Jewish believers at the expense of Palestinian believers. It is quite noticeable just how few ministries work with the Palestinians. This is a sad fact.

But as an American, I can be pro-Israel, which means that I believe the Jews have a biblical right to the land that God gave them and a political right to the land that the United Nations gave them. I can also be pro-Palestinian, which means that I believe Palestinians can benefit greatly from a shared existence with Israel. As much as I want Israelis to be protected and preserved, I want Palestinians to be prosperous and provided for.

That's why I am strongly behind our President's initiative that declared war on terrorism. This part is essential. As Palestinians extract this element from their society, they will see light at the end of the tunnel.

Pro-Israel, pro-Palestinian. We can be both at the same time, while ever declaring: "The answer is Jesus."

Cynical Jewish agnostics have been delivered into His awaiting arms of grace. Angry Palestinians have escaped swimming in a sea of bitterness and now are celebrating in living water instead. Christians, please don't ever sit at home, watch the news, and think the whole mess can be solved politically. If so, it would have been ironed out decades ago.

As American believers, we cannot continue to show a widespread lack of concern for the suffering Palestinian population. Biblical solutions are available. Through compassionate acts, we can meet their needs and still honor Israel. We believe Israel is to be supported. We believe this pleases the heart of God. We also should believe that we must act like the followers of Jesus no matter how the Palestinian quagmire has developed. Jesus honored Israel and still loved some of their enemies at the same time. Why can't we?

The Vise Grip Tightens—The Revival Begins

Jews are reachable. Palestinians are reachable. The church is the strongest and healthiest when it is persecuted. The worst places in the world to be a believer are really the best places to see the church in action. Our spiritual vitality blooms in treacherous places.

The *Voice of the Martyrs* (May 2003 edition) detailed the awful persecution that Palestinians endure if they convert from Islam to Christianity. "When Ali was a young boy, he listened to Palestine Liberation Organization radio broadcasts that taught him to hate Christians and Jews. He would often pray in the mosque and ask Allah to destroy Jews, Americans, and non-Muslims. When Ali first visited a church in 1997, he was shocked to hear the pastor talk about loving one's enemies. The pastor preached about how God loves all people but hates our sins. 'That touched my heart.' In the Islamic faith, there is no love for non-Muslims or our enemies like in Christianity. Ali started to attend church regularly, because for the first time in his life, he felt love, joy, and peace."[4]

But this decision definitely came at a cost. Ali was interrogated, beaten, and ordered to stop attending church. He was even shown the letter that the Mufti of Jerusalem signed ordering a *fatwa*—a call for his death sentence. The article went on to say: "About three years later, Ali was blindfolded and kidnapped by the Palestinian Security Police. His hands and feet were tied together, and he was hung from the rafters with his feet dangling just about the ground. He was beaten with sticks and electric cables."[5] Miraculously, he survived.

For Palestinians, conversion calls for persecution. No questions asked.

Abigail Lytle was not a typical fourteen-year-old living on the coast of the Mediterranean city of Haifa just below Mount Carmel. Her father distributed the *Jesus* film in the area, and the family had made a conscious effort to live in Israel despite the risks they face.

In the spring of 2003, the intifada was escalating, and the father decided to have a family meeting. He talked to his children about the situation, saying they probably should begin plans for a move back to America. It was too unsafe, especially in a Jewish community. The children prayed about it for a few days and then came back to their mom and dad with their advice. The five children all agreed that God had them there for a reason. They had been called as a family to reach the lost sheep of Israel, and they believed God would use their lives in a great way if they were obedient to His call.

Young Abigail had become involved in a children's teaching program that brought Jewish and Arabic children together in an effort to encourage successful coexistence. The class was preparing for an upcoming encounter with Arab youth in a few days. Abigail was bright and full of joy and optimism about her future in Israel. She had been raised in Israel because her father came to the land to work in the technological field. He later was on staff at a Baptist church. Abigail loved life and was a creative young lady. Her family remembers her all-out trust in God and her fearlessness despite living in a land continually at war.

On March 5, 2003, Abigail was traveling on a city bus near the Carmel center, moving toward Haifa University. In an instant, a suicide bomber pulled on the trigger and exploded the bus. The bomb devastated the bus—seventeen people killed, fifty-three injured. The scene was a usual one in Israel because the murderer had strapped the explosives to his own body and placed metal shrapnel within the device to maximize the number of injuries. Abigail was only a few rows away from the man and was killed instantly. Her parents' worst fears were realized as they arrived at the charred bus.

Abigail was gone from them.

What happened afterwards, however, was from the realm of the miraculous. Abigail's death attracted widespread attention. Her story of deciding to stay and help Israeli Jews was all over the news, since she was an American born in New Hampshire—someone who was not Jewish, yet who blended so well into Jewish culture. The press coverage was magnified and went global.

Young Abigail reminded me of Cassie Bernall at Colorado's Columbine High School. Her unshakable faith in the midst of a life-threatening situation was used by God to reach people across the world.

Abigail's funeral was broadcast in Israel on live TV. The Israeli government sent a senior official to attend the service. Her pastor talked about Abigail's life in depth. He also shared how Abigail's confidence in God came from her loving relationship with Jesus Christ.

This was a first in Israel. The gospel was being heard all over the country. It was also being beamed across the world simultaneously. I watched it myself in Colorado.

In Israel, funerals are often gloomy and despairing. This one was not. Abigail's parents made a conscious effort to express their grief and to lay it all on Jesus. The ceremony was marked by hope and faith in the One who said, "I am the resurrection and the life. The one who believes in Me, even if he dies, will live" (John 11:25).

Senior Knesset member Yuval Stenitz represented the government at the funeral. He remarked later that he had witnessed more than the power of religion at the service. "He had seen the vigor of faith. A TV reporter, hardened after having been assigned to many a funeral (and Israel has many such these days) confessed that he was deeply moved, even to tears, by what he had seen. A week later, the Haifa municipality was still astir as officials spoke of the amazing funeral. The sense of communal affection was also outstandingly uncommon to the average Israeli mind."[6]

Truly, Abigail's life and death touched more people at once than her family's ministry could in their whole lifetimes. The next meeting of the Arab Jewish youth was dedicated to Abigail and her friend Yuoal, who also gave her life up that day. Abigail's father, Phillip, could never have shown the *Jesus* film to that many people in decades of faithful service.

Jesus took young Abigail home, and her departure brought Him glory all over the land He loves. Jesus was exalted and seen in Israel as the real answer to life's deepest problems in this hurting region. The irony of the situation is that Abigail's pastor, Samuel, is Arab—preaching at a predominantly Jewish funeral. Only Jesus could orchestrate all of that. Samuel pastors a Jewish congregation. How's that for reconciliation? A non-Jewish American girl gave her life for Jews. An Arab pastor serves Jews. All of it was wrapped up together neatly by God Himself. The result? The majority of Israel was given the privilege of hearing and seeing what Jesus is really about.

Ali, the Ramallah believer, is now free of all of the hatred stewing around him. So are Abigail's parents, even though the loss of their precious daughter remains devastating. Remarkably, they plan to stay in Israel. Pastor Samuel is also free from the bitterness between Arabs and Jews. Abigail is free and home enjoying the presence of Jesus Himself. In all cases, Satan lost. Jesus won.

As Americans, when we truly want the best for people, our attitudes and actions may not fit nicely in a category. Labels won't fit either. I am pro-Israel. I want the best for the Israelis, and that includes keeping the land that is rightfully theirs. I am pro-Arab. I want the best for the Arabs, and that includes overcoming radical Islam, the religion that makes killing the ultimate answer for everything. I am in favor of the war on terrorism; it is a just war.

More important than being an American today is obviously being a believer in Jesus Christ. We possess the key that unlocks the spiritual stronghold chains that are squeezing Israel. In the end, Jesus is the only One who can make a difference. Only He can transform the hearts of those in conflict. Without Him, it will never end.

Abdul—He Smiles for Jesus

Before Abdul met Jesus, he had every reason to frown. Growing up in the West Bank, Abdul was sure of one thing—he hated Israelis. They were the reason for everything that was wrong in his life. He was often subjected to searches at border crossings, and the daily clashes with Israel made life in the West Bank miserable. Abdul wanted to kill as many Jews in life as he could. This would please Allah. Soon Islam would win and the Jews would be exterminated from Israel. At least that's what Yasser Arafat, Mahmoud Abbas, and other Palestinian leaders promised.

Abdul was on the path to becoming an Islamic terrorist. What else was he going to do with his life? He had no idea another invasion was coming. And this time it wouldn't be the Israelis coming to fight against him. This time it would be Jesus coming to free him.

One night Abdul dreamed about a man in a white robe walking on water, saying, "Come follow Me." Abdul had never experienced anything like it. The next day he arose from bed and could not keep from smiling. "Who was that in the dream?" he wondered. Abdul thought about the dream all day. He had felt so peaceful during it. How could it be that today he didn't have a care in the world—even in the midst of his city Jenin getting bombed all day?

That night the man in the white robe came to Abdul again. This time he introduced himself to Abdul: "I am Jesus, and I want to take your sins away. I want to give you eternal life." In the morning, Abdul woke up and knew he had to find Kamal, his best friend while growing up. Kamal had recently told Abdul that he, too, had experienced a dream that had changed his life, though he wouldn't actually tell Abdul what it was. But Kamal had been different ever since. His usual grumpy demeanor had been replaced with a smile.

Abdul made a beeline for Kamal's home.

"Was your dream about Jesus?" Abdul blurted out to Kamal, immediately as he entered his house.

"Yes, but how did you know?" Kamal seemed startled.

Abdul went on, "I had a dream, too. Jesus was in a white robe and told me He would forgive me of my sins and give me eternal life. I will never forget the way I felt when He was near."

"Neither will I!" Kamal added. He then began going through the gospel with Abdul, sharing verses from the Bible that was hidden under his bed. They talked for hours about Jesus. Finally he was ready. Abdul and Kamal knelt together, and Abdul received Jesus as his Lord and Savior. Peace filled the room. The guns and the bombs exploding in the background went unnoticed. They were in the presence of God.

Abdul and Kamal began to share their faith all over Jenin. People seemed interested, but both of them were warned about persecution if Hamas and Islamic Jihad heard about their conversion.

Soon they did. Within days, the two found themselves in jail. Hamas was threatening death to both of them.

The days were grueling. But after numerous beatings and a month in prison, Israel invaded Jenin to root out terrorist groups. The Israeli Defense Forces came in full force. Tanks, missile launchers, and hundreds of soldiers were positioned throughout Jenin.

In the prison cell, Abdul feared for his life. "Why are you so frightened, Abdul?" Kamal said. "Jesus will protect us, and the Israelis will probably let us out of jail when they get here. They don't have anything against us believers. They know we're safe."

Within minutes, the Jewish soldiers were calling at the prisoners in Arabic to stand back from the cell doors. One by one, the locks were shot off by the Israelis. Abdul could hardly believe his eyes. He was free! He ran for an Israeli tank, jumped on the gun barrel, and kissed it.

"God bless Israel!" Abdul shouted.

Today, the smile never leaves his face. He cannot contain his joy. Jesus gave him a new heart and a new nature. Abdul lives somewhere in Israel and attends a messianic congregation. What a turnaround! At one time he wanted to kill Jews, and now he worships with them. Abdul loves Jesus, and he loves Israel, too. He works with Arabs and Jews and is part of the reconciliation movement in Israel.

He was destined to be a terrorist and eventually a suicide bomber, but Jesus set him free—freed him from his sin, freed him from a terrorist jail, freed him from the hate and bitterness that ruled his life.

And now he smiles.

You will know the truth, and the truth will set you free.
(John 8:32)

SECTION THREE

MAXIMIZING THE MOMENT

The American church is at a critical juncture. God wants to use us to influence the nation of Israel on its journey back to God. He also wants us to participate in the Middle East revival that has already begun with Arabs and Jews. This is the mission heart of God. We must pray like never before. We must also wake up the sleeping giant of our day—the Western church. America has sent the gospel around the world. Now we need for the power of the gospel to return to our shores.

Chapter 7
The Mission Heart of God

God intends to use the church to bring Israel to its senses and Arab nations to repentance in the future. More Jews and Muslims have converted to Christianity in the past few years than in the last several centuries. It is time to hear the good news from the Middle East.

Mission Central

The greatest enterprise in all of history is the New Testament church. Listen for what God is accomplishing by His awesome power through Christ and His beloved church:

> Remember that at one time you were Gentiles in the flesh—called "the uncircumcised," by those called "the circumcised," done by hand in the flesh. At that time you were without the Messiah, excluded from the citizenship of Israel, and foreigners to the covenants of the promise, with no hope and without God in the world. But now in Christ Jesus, you who were far away have been brought near by the blood of the Messiah. For He is our peace, who made both groups one and tore down the dividing wall of hostility.
>
> In His flesh, He did away with the law of the commandments in regulations, so that He might create in Himself one new man from

the two, resulting in peace. He did this so that He might reconcile both to God in one body through the cross and put the hostility to death by it. When Christ came, He proclaimed the good news of peace to you who were far away and peace to those who were near. For through Him we both have access by one Spirit to the Father. So then you are no longer foreigners and strangers, but fellow citizens with the saints, and members of God's household, built on the foundation of the apostles and prophets, with Christ Jesus Himself as the cornerstone. The whole building is being fitted together in Him and is growing into a holy sanctuary in the LORD, in whom you also are being built together for God's dwelling in the Spirit. (Eph. 2:11-22)

Several phrases have special application to Jews and Arabs today:
- "For He is our peace"
- "tore down the dividing wall of hostility"
- "one new man from the two, resulting in peace"
- "that He might reconcile both to God in one body through the cross"
- "For through Him we both have access by one Spirit to the Father."
- "growing into a holy sanctuary in the Lord"
- "being built together for God's dwelling in the Spirit"

This passage that God inspired Paul to write is about Jewish-Gentile barriers that have been collapsed all at once through the power of His cross. I don't mean to toss the context in the trash can, but look at these phrases and think about Jewish-Arabic barriers instead. Imagine the joy in Yahweh's heart when the sons of Abraham, Isaac, and Ishmael reconcile—when Jew and Arab forgive each other. Ah, the beauty of it. The holiness of the moment covers over the centuries of rooted bitterness and washes it clean. It is one of the most noticeable reconciliation miracles among all people groups.

The world's attention is continually captured by the strife and acidic hate of the Middle East. How many times is the lead news story direct from

Israel, with another up-close picture of more bloody violence? But the power of the cross of Christ and the cleansing effect of His blood is the only blood that's needed to end this conflict.

During the Gulf War of the 1990s, evidence of wall crumbling began to circulate throughout churches in Israel. As in America, many churches in Israel seem to be separated along ethnic lines—Arab churches in one section of the city, Jewish messianic churches in another. I believe this grieves our Father's heart. The biggest praise session of all time is going to be the one in heaven in which people from every tribe and tongue worship our holy God together. And during the 1990s war, we got a glimpse of it—Arab believers reaching out to Jewish believers in the midst of Saddam's barrage of Scud missiles landing in Israel.

His target city was Tel Aviv for three reasons:

1. *Israel has a nuclear reactor in the Tel Aviv area.* Saddam tried to bait the Israelis, knowing that if they jumped into the fray, other Arab nations would join his cause.

2. *Tel Aviv is free of Muslim holy sites.* So if Saddam had fired away at Jerusalem and happened to accidentally stick a missile through the Dome of the Rock or Al-Aqsa Mosque, the entire Muslim world would have descended on Baghdad to take out the Iraqi dictator.

3. *Tel Aviv has the largest population in Israel,* and thus the Butcher of Baghdad could have gotten more bang out of his bombs by aiming at this coastal city.

Jewish people were understandably frightened and on edge as soon as American troops entered Iraq. Saddam had promised to strike Israel if the United States struck Iraq. He made good on his promise, and Israelis hid nightly in their sealed rooms in anticipation of the next missile barrage. Some of the Jewish people who panicked the most were survivors of Nazi concentration camps. They were reminded of the painful past they had survived and now faced again.

This is when Arab believers went into action, reaching out to comfort their hurting Israeli brothers and sisters. In doing so, they put their own lives in danger because Saddam was catapulted to number-one hero status among Palestinians and even some Arab Israelis.

In one instance, an Arab pastor living in the Arab section of East Jerusalem offered a Jewish family refuge in his own home. He called a Tel Aviv pastor and asked the pastor, his wife, and three daughters to come stay with him and his family. As the messianic pastor told me the story, I had tears in my eyes. If the Arab pastor had been caught with Jews in his house in the midst of Iraq's attack on Israel, who knows what would have happened?

"One new man from the two, resulting in peace."

The Arab Mind-Set Tethered to Islam

In his book *Circle of Fear*, Hussein Sumaida tells his story as an Israeli spy in Iraq. The cloak-and-dagger real-life thriller uncovers the thinking that oozes out the Muslim world today:

In spite of the concentrated effort to turn everyone into America-haters, everyone continued to love American clothes, hamburgers, blue jeans, music, and the rest of the outer shell of American culture. At the same time, deep down, many had a genuine hatred of American global power. The reason for this can be explained in one word: Israel. It is a measure of the depth of the Arab's hatred for Israel that, even though they loved so much about American pop culture, when it came down to brass tacks, they viewed America as the enemy. America meant Israel. Anyone who fails to understand this will not understand why "the situation in the Middle East" cannot be solved. Because America is so intimately allied with Israel, and Israel is seen as the root of all evil in the Arab world, then whenever anything bad happens in the Arab world, it is the fault of the Americans. I don't say this as theory but as a fact. There is no intermediary analytical thought. My theory is my belief, therefore a fact.[1]

Only the power of Almighty God can give a new mind to a person who thinks like this. Only Jesus Christ can release a person from generational sin entrenchment that runs this deep. Arab people need release from thirteen centuries of Islamic enslavement.

The Jewish Mind-Set Still Searching

At a 2003 Billy Graham crusade in Dallas, Texas, this preacher of the ages said that the last time he was in Jerusalem, he enjoyed a visit with the chief rabbi of the Holy City. The rabbi remarked to Graham that Judaism and Christianity had much in common. Where the two parted company was over the person of the Messiah. "You believe the Messiah is Jesus and we're just not sure," the rabbi said.

To which I would love to ask the rabbi if I ever meet him, "Well, how long is it going to take for you to make up your mind?"

Actually, this is a major step forward for the leading Jewish rabbi to admit his searching with such candor. Jesus is often dismissed altogether. But God must be working in his heart to bring him to this point of openness.

Why is it so hard for the Jews to receive their spiritual laser treatment and correct their eyesight once and for all? Because the time has not been right. The evidence has been written down in their own words. Jewish commentaries paint a picture of the Messiah that can only be Jesus. In the Talmud and the Midrash—the rabbinical interpretations of the Law, prophets, and writings—their own pens led them on a trail through the centuries straight to Christ. Listen to the learned rabbis:

THE CONCEPT OF THE MESSIAH

"And as for the wonders that are not the work of Adonai, when he, that is the Messiah, comes then he will heal the sick, resurrect the dead, and to the poor announce glad tidings" (4Q521, Dead Sea Scrolls at Qumran).

"It was taught in the School of Elijah, the world will endure 6,000 years—2,000 years in chaos, 2,000 with Torah, and 2,000 years will be the days of the Messiah" (Babylonian Talmud, Sanhedrin 97a).

THE MESSIAH TO APPEAR IN ISRAEL

"The King Messiah . . . from where does he come forth? From the royal city of Bethlehem in Judah" (Jerusalem Talmud, Berakoth 5a).

"The Messiah . . . will arise in the land of Galilee . . . the Messiah shall reveal himself in the land of Galilee because in this part of the Holy Land the desolation [Babylonian exile] first began, therefore he will manifest himself there first" (Zohar III, Shemoth 7b, 8b, 220a; Otzar Midrashim, 466).

THE MESSIAH TO PROVIDE ATONEMENT

"Rabbi Yochanan said, 'The Messiah—what is his name?'. . . And our Rabbis said, 'The pale one . . . is his name,' as it is written 'Surely he took up our infirmities and carried our sorrows—yet we considered him stricken by G-d, smitten by him and afflicted'" (Babylonian Talmud, Sanhedrin 98, p.2).

"The Messiah our righteousness has turned from us. We are alarmed, we have no one to justify us. Our sins and the yoke of our transgressions he bore. He was bruised for our iniquities. He carried on his shoulders our sins. With his stripes we are healed (Isa. 53). Almighty G-d, hasten the day that he might come to us anew; that we may hear from Mt. Lebanon [a figurative reference to the Temple] a second time through the Messiah" (Ancient hymn-prayer by Eliezer Hakkallir sung during the Musaf Service on Yom Kippur; included in some *Siddurs*, which are prayer and hymnbooks Jews use on Friday evening).

RECOGNIZING THE MESSIAH

"Prepare the way! The King Messiah comes . . . may the mountains abase themselves, may the valleys be filled, may the cedars incline to render him homage. Prostrate yourselves all of you before the Messiah King, and bend your knees before him who is seated at the right hand of the Holy One" (Zohar I.4b).

"Now there was about this time, Yeshua (Eaysoos in Greek), a wise man, if it be lawful to call him a man, for he was a doer of wonderful works, a teacher of such men as receive the truth with pleasure. He drew over to him both many of the Jews and many of the Gentiles. He was Mashiach (Christos in Greek); and when Pilate, at the suggestion of the principal men amongst us, had condemned him to the cross, those that loved him at the first did not forsake him, for he appeared to them alive again the third day, as the divine prophets had foretold these and ten thousand other wonderful things concerning him; and the tribe of Christians (followers of Messiah), so named from him, are not extinct at this day" (*Antiquities of the Jews*, book 18, chapter 3, paragraph 3; Yosef ben Mattityahu, aka Josephus).

"Our Rabbis taught: during the last forty years before the destruction of the Temple, the lot for the L-rd (on Yom Kippur) did not come up in the right hand; nor did the crimson-colored strap become white (on the neck of the scapegoat); not did the western-most light shine; and the doors of the Hekal (temple) would open by themselves" (Babylonian Talmud, Yoma, 39b).

The Hebrew expression *la chaim* means "to life." Steve Herzog explained its meaning this way: "Jewish people frequently wear gold charms depicting this Hebrew character on chains around their necks, emphasizing the fact that life is Judaism's most precious and cherished commodity."[2] Life is precious to Jews worldwide. They have experienced death so often; living the day to its fullest is the objective, but a tall order at that.

How ironic that life is what every Jew desires to live to the hilt. "I have come that they might have life and have it in abundance" (John 10:10). Jesus knew that locked in every Jewish heart was this innermost desire.

No civilization of people has been more threatened throughout their history than the Jews. Nations have turned on them. Kings have attacked them. They have been the human punching bag of the ages. Satan has deceived even himself into thinking he could slaughter them for good. World rulers have made it their main objective and continue to do so today.

In junior high, upper-class bullies picked on me. I was so ridiculed at one point that I decided to fight back. I wasn't going to take it anymore! My

Irish blood was boiling—watch it, buddy! Unfortunately, the day I got guts was the day that Steven Custer picked on me. He was roughly two and a half times my size. I was losing until my older sister, Terry, intervened. I hated being picked on. But Israel has experienced this from day one. Its birth as a nation came at the end of 400 years of slavery in Egypt. Oppression? The Israelis have had it! Genocide? Attempted first on them. Ruled over in their own country? Let's see: the Romans, the Mamluks, the Turks, the . . . oh, that's enough. Israel has been the continual victim of the world's bullies. Everyone has gone after them. It's almost as if a nation can't be on the who's-who list unless somewhere on its agenda is the liquidation of Israel. Does anybody out there not find this a little over the top?

That's why we, the church, must bring life to Israel. That's a powerful message for the Jews. When so many would like to bring death to them, we offer life. Any Jewish person values life.

Just Do It!

What is Israel's future as far as God's plan goes? Robert Thomas answers this beautifully.

Old Testament Messianic prophecies begin as early as Genesis 3:15, a verse that depicts the Messiah's mission of bruising the serpent's head. It was some time before the revelation of the mission of Israel, however. That awaited the call of Abraham (Genesis 12:1–3). From that point on, the mission of Israel paralleled that of the Messiah in many ways. Why did God single out Abraham and his descendants from the rest of mankind? It was His chosen method of dealing with humans as a whole to limit His special attention to one segment of them. He gave this segment of people a mission to the rest of the world so that He could fulfill through them His ultimate mission for all people. In light of Israel's failings along the way, the Messiah has filled and will fill the gap in redeeming Israel so that Israel can eventually fulfill her responsibility to the rest of the world.[3]

Thomas went on to say that the ultimate goal of the Messiah and Israel is to bring glory to God. I would add that this is the ultimate goal of the church, as well. The God of Israel displays His concise, consistently planned outcomes in Scripture this way:

- *The Messiah*: "Glorify Your Son so that the Son may glorify You" (John 17:1b).
- *Israel*: "Rejoice, heavens, for the LORD has acted; shout, depths of the earth. Break out into singing, mountains, forest, and every tree in it. For the LORD has redeemed Jacob, and glorifies Himself through" (Isa. 44:23).
- *The church*: "In Him we were also made His inheritance, predestined according to the purpose of the One who works out everything in agreement with the decision of His will, so that we who had already put our hope in the Messiah might bring praise to His glory" (Eph. 1:11–12).

Okay, it's a clean sweep. The Messiah, the nation of Israel, and the church are God's primary vehicles to bring Him glory. The apostle Paul said that because this is spiritual priority-one, it ought to permeate every phase of our living no matter how big or small. "Therefore, whether you eat or drink, or whatever you do, do everything for God's glory" (1 Cor. 10:31).

The Messiah, Israel, and the church have all been called to glorify. The pursuit of this is much like climbing a large mountain. Jesus, of course, was the first to arrive at the summit. The church is in the midst of its climb. Israel got lost along the way. How can Israel bring glory to Almighty God in its present state of rejecting the Messiah? They cannot. The question is: Can we, the church, do anything about it? Can we give a hand to God's chosen people who collectively have made the biggest mistake in all of history and have gone the wrong direction? Can we expect a spiritual U-turn?

I believe so. And here's how we, the church, can help Israel "for the praise of His glory."

Get Out the Sackcloth and Ashes

Thomas Cahill, writer of *How the Irish Saved Civilization*, also penned another best-seller entitled *The Gifts of the Jews: How a Tribe of Desert Nomads Changed the Way Everyone Thinks and Feels*. Cahill flatly rejects biblical inspiration. In his eyes, anyone who upholds this belief is delusional. Nevertheless, he surprisingly makes some insightful deductions about Jews worldwide:

> "Our history is replete with examples of those who have refused to see what the Jews are really about, who—through intellectual blindness, racial chauvinism, xenophobia, or just plain evil—have been able to give this oddball tribe, this raggle-taggle band, this race of wanderers who are the progenitors of the Western world, their due. Indeed, at the end of the bloodiest of centuries, we can all too easily look back on scenes of unthinkable horror perpetrated by those who would do anything rather than give the Jews their due."[4]

I agree. Unfortunately, our entire church history has been caught up in this type of thinking, too. Jews have been misunderstood by us Christians. We still see deep pockets of anti-Semitism within the church.

In John Hagee's book *Final Dawn over Jerusalem*, he grimly recounts how the Nazi agenda was extracted from the church's treatment of the Jews throughout history. Buckle your seat belts; the ride is rough.

Roman Church Policy

1. Prohibition of intermarriage and of sexual intercourse between Christians and Jews, Synod of Elvira, AD 306.
2. Jews and Christians not permitted to eat together, Synod of Elvira, AD 306.
3. Jews not allowed to hold public office, Synod of Clermont, AD 535. Also Fourth Lateran Council, 1215.
4. Jews not allowed to employ Christian servants or possess Christian slaves, Third Synod of Orleans, AD 538.
5. Jews not permitted to show themselves in the streets during Passion Week, Third Synod of Orleans, AD 538.
6. Burning of the Talmud and other books, Twelfth Synod of Toledo, AD 681.
7. Christians not permitted to patronize Jewish doctors, Trulanic Synod, AD 692.
8. Jews obligated to pay taxes for support of the church to the same extent as Christians, Fourth Lateran Council, 1215.
9. Jews not permitted to be plaintiffs or witnesses against Christians in the courts, Third Lateran Council, 1179.
10. Jews not permitted to withhold inheritance from descendants who had accepted Christianity, Third Lateran Council, 1179.
11. Jews must wear a distinctive badge, Fourth Lateran Council, 1215.
12. Construction of new synagogues prohibited, Council of Oxford, 1222.
13. Christians not permitted to attend Jewish ceremonies, Synod of Vienna, 1267.
14. Jews forced to live in ghettos away from Christians, Synod of Breslau, 1267.
15. Jews not permitted to obtain academic degrees, Council of Basel, 1434.
16. Mass extermination of the Jews in the Crusades. Fourth Lateran Council called upon secular powers to "exterminate all heretics," 1215. The Inquisition burned Jews at the stake while confiscating their property, 1478.

Nazi Policy

1. Law for the Protection of German Blood and Honor, September 15, 1935.
2. Jews barred from dining cars, December 30, 1939.
3. Law for Re-Establishment of the Professional Civil Service, April 7, 1935, by which Jews were expelled from office and civil service jobs.
4. Law for the Protection of German Blood and Honor, September 15, 1935, forbade Germans from hiring Jews.
5. Decree authorizing local authorities to bar Jews from the streets on certain days (Nazi holidays), December 3, 1938.
6. Nazi book burnings in Germany.
7. Decree of July 25, 1938, forbidding Germans from patronizing Jewish doctors.
8. Jews to pay a special tax in lieu of donations for party purposes imposed on Nazis, December 24, 1940.
9. Jews not permitted to institute civil suits.
10. Decree empowering the Justice Ministry to void wills offending the "sound judgment of the people," July 31, 1938.
11. Decree forcing all Jews to wear the yellow Star of David, September 1, 1941.
12. Destruction of synagogues in entire Reich, November 10, 1938. The Jews refer to this night as Kristalnacht.
13. Friendly relations with Jews prohibited, October 24, 1941.
14. Jews forced to live in ghettos, order of Heydrich, September 21, 1939.
15. All Jews expelled from schools and universities throughout the Third Reich with the Law against Overcrowding of German Schools and Universities, April 25, 1933.
16. Hitler's Final Solution called for the systematic slaughter of every Jew in Europe. He took their homes, their jobs, their possessions (even the gold fillings in their teeth), and finally their lives. His justification? "It's the will of God and the work of the Church."[5]

How could this have taken place? The early church fathers clearly got us off to a terrible start in our treatment of Jews. As the leaders go, so goes the church.

If I had to single out the worst example of anti-Semitism within the church, it would be John Chrysostom. He was born in the place believers were first called Christians about AD 350. He became a bishop of Constantinople and a major church influencer regarding Jewish treatment. He was the prince of preachers of the fourth century and wrote extensively, being hailed as a church hero for his unwavering commitment to Christ. His legacy is one of excellence in application of the Scriptures from the Greek Bible. His sermons have survived and are still read 1,600 years later. Known as the "golden mouth," he was the first in a long line of gifted communicators of the Word of God. But his views on the Jewish people need to be repudiated once and for all.

David Dolan records these incriminating words:

Father Flannery cites many other instances of growing hostility toward the Jews by early church fathers. This hostility reached its height in the sermons and writings of John Chrysostom (AD 344-407). According to Flannery, Chrysostom "stands without peer or parallel in the virulence of his attack." He quotes from eight sermons by Chrysostom—the most popular preacher of the fourth century—in which this preacher called the Jews "lustful, rapacious, greedy, perfidious bandits, inveterate murderers, destroyers, men possessed by the devil" with the "manners of the pig and the lusty goat." Jews "worship the devil," and their religion is "a disease." They have fallen into such a state because of their "odious assassination of Christ." Therefore, God hates the Jews, who will always remain without the temple or a sovereign nation. If all of this did not lead to obvious conclusions among his Christian audience, Chrysostom spelled it out even more explicitly for them, calling for a perpetual Christian "holy war" against the Jews: "He who can never love Christ enough will never have done with fighting against those who hate Him."[6]

As the church continued to walk in this error, only a few reasons can explain this position:

- *Racism.* Hatred of Jews because of their religion. This doesn't wash, however, since Jesus, the prophets, the apostles, and first church leaders were all Jewish.
- *Ignorance.* Could the church have been only moderately guilty because we were in the dark about God's plan for His chosen people? No excuses; it's throughout the Bible. The New Testament clearly presents the fact that God is not finished with the Jews.
- *Jealousy.* Are Christians guilty of being jealous of God's relationship with Isaac's descendants? This doesn't square either, as Romans 10:19 tells us God will make Israel jealous of the Gentiles, not vice versa.
- *Replacement.* This view is akin to theological suicide for it falsely asserts that God is done with Israel. In this view, the church takes the Jew's place and even receive their promises now. It is not only arrogant but throws a literal interpretation of God's Word out the window.
- *Deception.* Satan has a personal agenda to convince the world that Jews are to be blamed for every problem known to humanity. The father of lies has done a superb job of this; apparently he has even convinced some believers, too.

It's time to conduct the funeral and to pronounce that Christian anti-Semitism is dead and will not be resurrected. Anytime we take the same stand on an issue as the world does, that ought to tell us something.

We must repent of this ongoing evil and seek God's forgiveness. We must be moved with compassion as Jesus was. He wept for Jerusalem as He was overlooking the city. Pray that God opens your spirit to have the same heart for Jews as He does. The church is held back in its mission as a result of this evil heresy.

Yes, I have strong feelings about this. I am guilty, too. I have judged, condemned, and laughed at Jewish people myself. I'm sure this broke God's heart. Would you join me, though, in praying for forgiveness?

> Holy God, the God of Israel, I ask You to forgive me when it comes to my thoughts, actions, and words against the people You chose to bring glory to Your name. I have been unfair to Jewish people, and I repent. I commit to turn away from this evil. I pray Your Holy Spirit will convict me if I fall for this trap of Satan again. I love Your people. Please give me Your love for them. I also ask that You place in me a passion to reach them for Jesus. I want them to be saved. Apart from Christ, I know they have no chance. Break my heart over this, Lord. Use me to reach Jewish people, I ask. Send me, Lord.

Let's be honest. We have blown it, believers. And it is time to admit the truth. I dare you to ask a Jewish person for forgiveness. You will not believe what that does to your Spirit. I know. I've done it. It is healing. We need it and so do they.

My wife, JoAnn, and a few of our kids were once at a movie called *Remember the Titans*. The movie was a favorite for jocks, but it carried a strong message of racial reconciliation. My wife was constantly reminded of the tension between blacks and whites in America throughout the movie since she was sitting next to a woman who was black. After the credits rolled by, JoAnn couldn't stand the conviction any longer. She said to the woman, "I am so sorry for what you and your family have probably experienced as far as racism in your lives. I just want to ask you if you would please forgive me for all the discrimination and grief you've gone through as a result of bigotry shown to you by white people." The woman hugged my wife and said, "First of all, thank you!" And then she went on to say "I do forgive you."

I know, some of you will no doubt be saying that when it comes to Jewish people, "I've never uttered an anti-Semitic remark in my life." Well, then, when others have, did you stand up and defend God's covenant people? Neither have I. That's why I have asked them to forgive me. I want them to know that I recognize how wrong this is. I tell them that Christians are changing, and we do want to be their friends.

In Israel recently, an Arab-Israeli pastors' meeting in Jerusalem was visited by the presence of God. As the clergymen were discussing how they could better coordinate and be more effective, the God who dwelled on the Temple Mount for centuries descended in power. An Arab pastor "broke the ice" by getting on his knees before the Jewish pastors. He asked them to forgive him and his people. He told the messianic pastors that his people had been guilty of bitterness and hatred of Jews for centuries. "Forgive us for all of the things we've done to you and for how much you have suffered on account of us, the Arab people." In a moment of holy conviction, all of the Arab pastors were on their knees seeking forgiveness also. The Jewish pastors fell to their knees and likewise asked for forgiveness. "We have hated your people, too; we are just as guilty." No one wanted to go home. Yahweh was there, and His presence was sweet. Isaac and Ishmael embraced each other that day in Jerusalem. Ah yes, after 4,100 years of conflict, it was about time, don't you think?

The conflict between Christians and Jews has been in full swing for over 1,970 years. It's about time to end this thing. Let's ask God's forgiveness. Let's ask *their* forgiveness. Let's go on.

Until we face the truth and do something about it, we have little chance of befriending Jews and leading them to their awaiting Jewish Messiah. This will bring our Father much glory. When we reach out to the lost sheep of Israel, we truly are following Jesus.

What about Ishmael's Descendants?

I hope by now you have a new sense of passion for Jews. What about Arabs, though? Are you moved with passion for them? I wasn't for a long time. When one goes to Israel, it's easy to relate to the Jews because of our common roots. It's also easy to forget about Arabs altogether.

Abraham, of course, had Ishmael before he had Isaac. Ishmael was thirteen years old, in fact, before Isaac arrived. The story is probably quite familiar to you. Abraham's wife, Sarah, had started to panic because she was now old and still not pregnant. So she tried to fulfill God's promise of a descendant her own way. When the slave woman Hagar slept with Abraham at Sarah's request, she became pregnant. Sarah then had second thoughts. In the midst of an emotional overflow, Sarah cruelly sent Hagar away. But in amazing irony, the angel of the Lord is the one who reached out to Hagar.

Why do I find this ironic? Because Muslims today believe they are descendants of Ishmael. This admittedly is debatable. Yet they believe it strongly. Who was the one who reached out to Hagar with compassion and "found" her? It was Jesus. Jesus is the Angel of the Lord of the Old Testament. We know this because characteristics of God's nature are seen in the Angel of the Lord. They are not seen in other angels of the Lord. Only the capital-A "Angel of the Lord." In Genesis 16:9, The Angel of the Lord promised that He would increase Hagar's descendants, making them too numerous to count. A mere angel would not make this promise because he would be incapable of delivering on it. Only God could do this. This was a pre-New Testament encounter with Christ.

Therefore, it was Jesus who showed the first act of compassion and kindness for the mother of Ishmael. Muslims believe they are directly linked to this son of Abraham, but if it hadn't been for Jesus, he probably wouldn't have made it to birth. His mother would have had great difficulty surviving and giving birth in the desert between Israel and Egypt. Jesus Himself told Hagar to go back to Abraham. She bore Ishmael, which in Hebrew means "God hears." The Lord had heard a desperate mother's cry, searched for her, made her a promise of many descendants, and brought her back to safety.

But the happy home was soon in chaos again. Hagar foolishly mocked Sarah at a feast in honor of Isaac. Hagar was again banished to the desert, this time with Ishmael, now a teenager. But the water was soon gone, and Hagar began to sob. This time her son joined her. The Angel of the Lord came to the rescue again, calling to Hagar from heaven. He said that Ishmael had called out His name, and God had heard him crying. God was moved. He promised Hager that not only would Ishmael survive but would flourish into a great nation. He next met their obvious physical needs and opened her eyes to show her a well of water for her thirsty boy.

Take all of this in. Jesus:

- heard Hagar crying and responded in love.
- brought her out of the harsh desert back to Abraham to have a safe birth.
- was not finished with her, even though Hagar brought on her second banishment from Abraham.
- again heard her cries and her son's also, and was moved.
- promised to make Ishmael into a great nation, which must have been a little hard to comprehend for Hagar, who believed Ishmael was close to death.
- met their needs with the water.

Genesis 21 goes on to say that God was "with" Ishmael. He was raised in the desert and later united with his half-brother Isaac to bury their father Abraham in Hebron. Abraham did leave everything he owned to Isaac. Make no mistake about it, the Abrahamic blessing was transferable through Isaac, not Ishmael. Yet none other than Jesus Christ Himself intervened on behalf of the future great nation.

This is amazing to me. If Muslims are descendants of Ishmael, then they have Jesus to thank for it. Without Jesus, they wouldn't be here. Arabs who are Ishmael's offspring would be gone also. But the Muslims have never thanked Jesus. Instead, they have tried to destroy His church.

The Angel of the Lord—Jesus—had compassion on Ishmael. And we should have compassion on them also since the Arab people are enveloped in the false religion of Islam. I believe we should start there. We must bring them Jesus. They are reachable. That seems like a good place to begin. When President Bush said that terrorists had hijacked the religion of Islam, I thought about those words for a while. I think it's truer to say that Islam has hijacked the entire Arab culture!

The Angel of the Lord prophetically laid out the "way of Ishmael" in Genesis 16:11–12, when He said to Hagar: "You have conceived and will have a son. You will name him Ishmael, for the Lord has heard your cry of affliction. This man will be like a wild ass. His hand will be against everyone, and everyone's hand will be against him; he will live at odds with all his brothers."

Whoa, was Jesus ever right! Arabs are famous for the conflict within their enormous family ranks. People often ask me, "How have the Jews survived living among Arabs that outnumber them ten to one?" I say two things:

1. The Abrahamic Covenant was given to Israel from God.

2. The Arabs fight with each other as much as they do with Jews. Their hostility toward each other has kept them from solidarity.

One of the gems I remember from a seminary professor was: "It's not hard to find what Satan's up to; just look at what God's doing, and Satan's trying to undo it." Simple but true. God said that Ishmael's descendants would be a fractured family, but Satan has tried to bring them together. The vehicle he has used is the religion of Islam.

Muhammad, I believe, fell under demonic influence. His visions of "Allah" threw him into seizures that certainly didn't originate in heaven. They were bizarre, to say the least. In the classic work *The Story of Islam*, Theodore Lunt writes, "The visitations occurred several times, and each time they were accompanied by violent physical effects upon Muhammad. He was angry if anyone looked at him: his face was covered with foam, his eyes were closed, and sometimes he roared like a camel."[7]

He murdered. He had numerous wives, his last one being just nine years old. He controlled women. Islam allows four wives; Muhammad had as many as he wanted. Of course, this was his privilege since he was a prophet of God. How convenient! And how a woman can ever remain Muslim after she has read the Koran is beyond me. Muhammad made the following prophetic declarations about women:[8]

- They are the majority of the people in hell.
- They lack intelligence.
- They lack faith.
- They possess sinister characters.

- They can only have one-half of the man's rightful inheritance.
- If a woman walks in front of a man while he is praying, the prayer is no good and has to be said over. (This is also true if a donkey or a dog does the same thing. This declaration really amazes me.)

Don McCurry in his fine work titled *Healing the Broken Family of Abraham* compared Muhammad with Jesus. It is illuminating.

MUHAMMAD	CHRIST
• Reflected the qualities of a seventh-century Arab man	• Reflected the image of God
• Instituted holy war in God's name	• Taught disciples not to fight
• Institutionalized looting of war victims	• Warned against covetousness
• Taught vengeance	• Taught forgiveness
• Legalized polygamy and concubinage	• Upheld the ideal of monogamy
• Demeaned the role of women	• Honored women
• Made divorce easy for men, but not for women	• Spoke against divorce
• Taught a sensuous view of paradise	• Indicated an afterlife on a higher plane in the presence of the Father
• Institutionalized Arabic Middle Eastern rituals of religious duties	• Taught that true worship was in spirit and truth
• Advocated once-in-a lifetime pilgrimage to Mecca	• Taught that we are lifelong pilgrims in this world
• Substituted his law for Mosaic Law	• Fulfilled Mosaic Law in love
• Ignored the need for blood sacrifice for sins	• Came to give His life, shed His blood for the sins of others
• Maintained that atonement for sins was not possible	• Came to make atonement for our sins
• Denied the Crucifixion	• His life culminated in crucifixion, resurrection, and ascension
• Had no power over Satan or demons	• Broke Satan's power in life and at the cross
• Had no power to give his disciples	• Gave his disciples power and authority over demons
• Assumed Islam was the expression of the kingdom of God	• Introduced the kingdom of God and Himself as King
• Reduced Jesus to being a prophet for his age only	• Was the culmination of offices of Prophet, Priest, and King for all time
• Cursed those who thought Jesus was the Son of God	• Said that he who honors the Son honors the Father
• Had no concept of God as our Father	• Came to bring us back to our heavenly Father
• Confessed he could do no miracles	• Attested to the presence of the kingdom with His miracles
• Died	• Died and then rose from the dead[9]

But Satan's blinding of Muslims is powerful. Only Jesus can open their eyes. And He is doing that as a tidal wave of conversions to Christ is sweeping across the Muslim world.

Muslims have a new openness to Jesus. The growing negatives emanating from their religion have catapulted even devout Muslims into a spiritual quest. We have found this to be true in all of our mission activities throughout the Muslim world. Today in Iran, for instance, 70 percent of the population claims to be atheist. Islam has wrecked their country and isolated Iran from the West. But Iranians in general love the West. They probably have cousins living in Europe or the United States. Two million Iranians now live in America, a quarter of a million in Los Angeles alone.

This new openness can only be explained this way: God has orchestrated a major revival among Muslims. They are giving Jesus a second, third, and fourth look. The gospel is hitting home with them since they have no sacrifice to pay for their sins in their system. They are beginning to understand the need for a Savior.

McCurry continued in his book with a salute to the first Protestant missionary to Muslims, Henry Martyn, known for having said he wanted "to burn out for God." A learned man, he could speak Urdu, Persian, Arabic, and Sanskrit. He was trained at Cambridge University. Although he died at thirty-two, he became the "fireball for God" he hoped to be. He was not only a missionary. He translated the New Testament in three languages, one of which was Arabic. He wrote tracts. He debated Muslims. He developed seven principles for working with Muslims. And 200 years later, they are still effective:

1. *Share your own personal experience.* Your testimony of how you experienced the forgiveness of sins and peace with God through Jesus Christ.

2. *Appreciate the best in your Muslim friend* and ascribe such qualities to God working in his life. The same could go for those elements in Muslim culture that are genuinely approved by God.

3. *Keep your message Christ-centered,* as you talk about the grace of God and how it is mediated through Christ and carried forward by the sanctifying work of God's Spirit.

4. *Draw your Muslim friend into the study of the Scriptures* so that he can discover these new truths for himself.

5. *Play the role of a supporting friend* as your Muslim friend goes through this time of critical investigation and decision-making.

6. *Create a favorable atmosphere in society* by ministering to human needs.

7. *Trust the Holy Spirit* to work in your Muslim friend as he seeks his place as a believer in his Muslim context.[10]

Whether Muslims are descendants of Ishmael is not all that important. We must reach out to them as the Angel of the Lord did to Ishmael when he was near death in the desert. Jesus' perfect love for people demands that we pursue them just as He does. No one is outside the far-reaching hand of God. No one. This is the time, believers. The harvest is ripe.

Expect a Miracle Today

At e3 Partners, "expect a miracle today" is a ministry phrase we try to live by. It was coined by our ministry president Curtis Hail, but it's not just a cute phrase from the head man. It's what Curtis lives by, and it has become a rallying cry for ministry. I believe that bringing the gospel to the world today is the ultimate challenge. It takes every ounce of devotion to God. It takes your passion, energy, creativity, and every bit of drive the Holy Spirit places you. And then it takes some more.

Nowhere have I seen those words realized more than in Israel and the Middle East. "Expect a miracle today" is written in the heart of every Middle East believer. They expect miracles and they see miracles! Wouldn't it be great if the American church lived like this? God is so vigorously pursuing Jews and Muslims today that seeing the miraculous is normal here.

We've seen in this chapter that even though Jewish unbelief and Arabic ties to Islam are formidable foes, they can be overcome. Jesus has awakened His bride to intercession, fasting, prayer walking, and prayer for the nations. Christians from various parts of the world travel thousands of miles to Israel for the sole purpose of "praying on location." Healing between Arabs and Jews is happening within the body of Christ. Both groups are burdened for each other. God is replacing the enmity between the descendants of Abraham with genuine affection and biblical reconciliation. Not only are Arab and messianic pastors praying together; they are exchanging pulpits. Walls of separation are falling. Centuries of mistrust are evaporating. The church is triumphing again in the land in which it was born:

- In Jerusalem, a messianic church prays for the Arab church in the Gaza Strip.
- A prayer meeting in the Holy City meets weekly now with hundreds of Arab and Jewish believers praying as one.
- A messianic congregation supports a Jerusalem Palestinian church financially.
- A wounded Palestinian from Bethlehem was given an Israeli soldier's identification card so he could travel to Jerusalem for an operation that saved his life.
- In a Tel Aviv rehabilitation center, Jewish believers wheelchair-danced with an Arab soldier from Lebanon who lost both of his legs in a war with Israel. His Jewish friends are family now.
- In Ramallah, a desperate Palestinian woman pleaded with Israeli soldiers to let her through closed checkpoints and into a Jerusalem hospital. Her son was dying. He not only lives, but the woman received no bill for the expensive surgery and hospital stay.
- Life-giving churches in Israel, Jordan, Egypt, Syria, Iraq, Iran and other Middle East countries are experiencing significant growth in the midst of unstable times.
- A saint of God smuggles Bibles into Saudi Arabia by packing them in the tires of his car.

- An American soldier preaches at a local Baghdad church after the Iraq war. The Iraqis welcome him with open arms. He is followed by an Arab believer from Jordan who trains the Iraqis in the EvangeCube so they can begin an outreach campaign in Saddam's former capital city.

Traveling the United Arab Emirates, our mission team was warned that if we were caught with EvangeCubes, they would be confiscated and we would be sent out of the country immediately. Peter Pintus, Allen Reedall, Jay Straub, and I entered with more than a thousand of them in our suitcases. The churches of the United Arab Emirates prayed and fasted the whole day and pleaded for a miracle. They got one. We were there to see it.

The EvangeCube, if you don't know, is a visual presentation of the gospel and an excellent cross-cultural tool because it is all pictures and is told as a story. It has six pictures that vividly communicate Christ's death, burial, and resurrection. It truly is anointed by God.

We were told ahead of our arrival that picture 2 would be the big problem to the Muslim guards at the airport—the one of Jesus dying on the cross, a definite no-no in the world of Islam. Muslims believe Jesus existed and even was a prophet, but they stop there. Jesus as an atoning Savior and Lamb of God who died for our sins is to Muslims a figment of our Christian imaginations. A picture of Jesus on the cross can send an observant Muslim "into orbit."

Within minutes, four guards were taking EvangeCubes out of the boxes as fast as they could.

Then God did a miracle before our eyes. He kept the guards from ever seeing Jesus on the cross. For twenty minutes they turned the cubes every which way. And every time, they missed seeing Jesus on the cross! Every time! As a result, about 1,000 believers were trained how to effectively share their faith and are evangelizing this Muslim country. Jesus, who made the blind man see, did just the reverse on the guards. He made the seeing men blind. Hallelujah!

I close with this. Serving Christ in Israel or in the Middle East is not for the faint of heart. It is dangerous because Satan is losing ground fast, and he is on the prowl trying to devour the church. He will lose, of course, but he will attempt to intimidate the church through persecution and even martyrdom.

Yet Arabs and Jews are experiencing *musahala*, Arabic for "reconciliation." Satan cannot explain this since Islam says it is impossible. Our holy God is pulling the church together, strengthening it, and sealing the evil one's fate all at once. Would we expect the deceiver of nations to go down without a fight? I don't think so. That's why serving Christ in the Middle East is so dynamic and thrilling. These are the front lines of God's kingdom advancing into darkness and shining God's light.

For us believers, it doesn't get any better than this. How privileged we are to live in this generation! Since the first century, there has not been a revival in Jerusalem or Israel or the entire Middle East like this.

This is classic spiritual warfare. And your help is needed. Even though we are winning, the battle rages. In chapter 8 we will find out where you fit into all of this. You have an assignment. Lives are hanging in the balance. All hands on deck, believer.

Rima—The Life-Giver

The spiritual barometric pressure is rising in the Gaza Strip. A string of suicide bombings and border conflicts have resulted in closing all entrances into Israel. No one goes in; no one goes out. The Palestinian workforce is grounded for the week. There will be no one bringing in extra food, supplies, or paychecks. Lockdown is here again.

It's hard to sleep at night with the drone planes patrolling and watching. Because Gaza City is home to some of the worst terrorist groups in the Middle East, this is where Israel makes lightning-fast strikes to settle the score. Once the terrorists strike the Jewish innocents, the Israeli Defense Forces almost always make a move into Gaza. After the drone planes locate the guilty, Apache helicopters arrive to dispense retaliation. With precision accuracy, they fire and take out another terrorist mastermind. There are many more within the city's confines.

The believers want the terrorists gone also. Their lives are being controlled by them. This is no way to live. How do people keep from losing their minds here? Missiles, machine-gun fire, and mass demonstrations occur on a daily basis. Children are raised in Gaza. Can you imagine a childhood in this pressure cooker?

Rima's home seems to be in another hemisphere. Or at least another time zone. It is completely detached from the rage in the street below. There is life here. With death and suicide all around, this is a spiritual oasis. Rima and her husband minister in the name of Jesus and in the power of the Spirit in this place. She is a true life-giver. Her spiritual gifts are hospitality, encouragement, and teaching. She is a discipler of women. They are drawn to her. What wisdom she passes on to the young married women and the engaged.

Rima is one of the best cooks anywhere. Believers enjoy delicious meals daily from her kitchen, as if there's an unlimited food supply in the Gaza

Strip. When you're served at Rima's, the food keeps coming. Fresh fish, chicken tabouli, baba ganoush, hummus, and endless pita bread for Arabia-style dining.

When I first met Rima, she cooked for about thirty people. Yet the apartment is very small, and her kitchen has a tiny electric stove with only two burners. Rima often cooks the night before and all day to have enough to serve her guests. I believe she feeds more people of Gaza than the United Nations does. She is one amazing woman.

But with Rima, the food is just another creative vehicle for ministry. What happens around the table for hours at a time is what it's all about. Gaza is a dangerous place, but somehow it all goes away at Rima's. In the Old Testament, the Lord established cities of refuge for criminals to find safety. In Gaza, it's just the opposite. Rima's home is a place to which the innocent flee. Jesus is lifted up here. Prayer meetings last into the early hours of the morning. The praise sessions are beautiful and impacting. Jesus is so real here. Believers often arrive tired, frustrated, and on edge due to the conflict everywhere they look. If they are from Muslim families and have escaped to become followers of Jesus, they find safe passage here. If they are unable to feed themselves due to the latest city lockdown, they are fed until stuffed here. The believers of the area receive a spiritual booster shot at Rima's.

Amazingly, Rima and her husband did not have a passion in their hearts to reach Muslims for Christ until just a few years ago. They previously avoided Muhammad's followers, preferring to labor in Christian areas. But God performed a double bypass operation on this couple, bypassing both of their hearts and giving them His heart for Muslims. They now overflow with passion to reach them with Christ. Their church has experienced steady growth each year since they arrived. Many of the women Rima disciples will be pastors' wives someday. With church planting on the horizon, these women will be the Rimas of tomorrow, the next life-givers.

When you enter the Gaza Strip for the first time, you are immediately struck by the hordes of people. They are packed into a small space for such a large city. This contributes to the oppressive feel of the area. The spiritual warfare is so intense here, it is not uncommon for believers to get sick shortly after they arrive in Gaza.

But the fruit of the Spirit is on display in Rima's home. It is a magnet to Gazans. There is only one evangelical church in Gaza City—one church for 1.5 million people. Yet Rima serves them, combining a Martha work ethic with a Mary heart for God. She is making a difference for Jesus Christ in the place where suicide bombers grab the headlines. But Rima wields more influence, and hers will last all the way into eternity.

"Many women are capable, but you surpass them all!" Charm is deceptive and beauty is fleeting, but a woman who fears the LORD will be praised. Give her the reward of her labor, and let her works praise her at the city gates. (Prov. 31:29–31)

Chapter 8
Global Praying That Is Truly Biblical

What's needed in a hurry is a strategy for intercession to maximize the moment in Israel and in the Middle East. Intensive prayer movements are fueling the revival that the region is now enjoying. Want to sign up?

Smoking for Jesus

It was surprisingly hot for January in Israel. Our day as a mission team had been filled with ministry in Nazareth, and we were due in Amman, Jordan, in a few hours to train a Nazarene Church in how to share its faith using the EvangeCube. We were running late. Going into Jordan through the Sheik Hussein bridge is normally an easy route into the Hashemite kingdom, but today it was backed up. Would we arrive for the church service on time? Jordanians and Iraqis were waiting for us.

After long waits, our group of fourteen was almost through until we hit security. That's where the trouble all began. Carrying about 1,200 Evange-Cubes, we prayed that the guards would scan the first few bags and then send us through. We were told to proceed and were out of the doors when one of the guards looking through the last bag spotted something.

"Wait a minute!" he said.

Since I was the leader of the mission group, I was escorted alone by one of the guards into a room for some questions. I walked into a small office, where six Jordanian men were also sitting and waiting. All six were smoking.

The leader of security was sitting behind the desk, and he was angry. They had seen the picture on the cube of Jesus on the cross, and he held it up to me. He slapped the picture with the back of his hand, and we held this conversation:

Guard: "We don't want these in Jordan! These are not allowed here!"

Tom: "I've been to Jordan before, and we were able to bring Evange-Cubes in. Did the rules change?"

Guard: "We don't want these in Jordan!"

Tom: "This is my fifth time to Jordan, and I love your country!" (Feeble attempt at schmoozing!)

Guard: "We don't like your president either! George Bush should not start a war with Iraq. If he wants to fight someone, why doesn't he go after North Korea?"

Tom: (I wanted to say, "Actually, I think they're next in line," but I figured that would score zero points, so I just said . . .) "I'm sorry you feel that way!"

There was an awkward silence. All six men were looking at me. I guess it was still my move. At that moment, the interrogator lit up a cigarette and handed it to me. I took it. I'm not sure why; I was never a smoker. Yeah, I tried a cigar in junior high but got real sick. Hadn't touched tobacco since. Until now. I sat there with the cigarette ash getting longer and longer, not puffing it. Finally, the ashes were falling off, and the angry questioner asked me one more question.

Guard: "Do you smoke?"

Tom: "No, I don't."

He started to laugh at me, that I had taken the cigarette but didn't smoke. All six men were laughing, and in an instant all the tension was out of the air. I felt like I could breathe in there again, even with all the smoke!

Guard: "Okay, we will let you in with these this time. It will cost you 400 dollars."

Tom: "That's a little steep. How about 200?"

Guard: "How about 400 dollars?"

Tom: "Okay."

It was worth a try, right? Praise God, we were through and on our way to the church in Amman, arriving just after the service had begun.

That night the worship was passionate and sweet. I didn't see any dry eyes in the house as Jordanians, Iraqis, and Americans lifted Jesus up high over Jordan. We arrived in time, so did the cubes, and approximately 190 people were sent on their way to share their faith throughout Jordan and Iraq. God turned a tense situation into one filled with laughter. As I left the border, in fact, one of those six guards asked for an EvangeCube. Who knows how God will use that one?

Someone has said that taking the gospel into a foreign country is an act of spiritual warfare. Satan will retaliate when we advance into one of his strongholds. Therefore, it's very common at country borders to encounter resistance. We have often found that team members may suddenly get sick or may get agitated with each other. All of this can happen upon entrance to a nation where there is a strong aversion to the gospel. This is understandable in Muslim-dominated countries. Satan has strong-armed them and controlled them for several centuries.

Prayer—The Slender Vein
That Moves the Hand of God

Prayer is of utmost importance for missions advancement worldwide. The area from ten to forty degrees north of the equator, called the 10/40 window, is home to the least evangelized people globally. But spiritual breakthroughs are starting to occur as a result of intensive prayer strategies in this area. The chains are stronger and tighter there. Historical footholds must be broken. But prayer is the precursor to God's hand moving.

I believe that the church took a turn for the better in the 1990s. Prayer groups for Israel began springing up in various places, and they all had one thing in common—fervency. The God of Israel began to burden His church for Jews, Arabs, and their tenuous situation. Up until then, gains for Christ had been very modest. I believe this was a turn for the better since we, the body of Christ, began to fall on our knees in anguish over Israel's present plight and the difficult days ahead.

In many churches, Israel is merely a major point in the overall study of eschatology. The Jews are back in the land, so Jesus' return must be around the corner. But to put it bluntly, there should be more prayer going on for Israel and less prophecy. Prophecy is great to study, but we need action, folks.

One of my heroes is Joel Rosenberg. He has written three best-selling novels and most recently a best-selling nonfiction book called *Epicenter*. Joel is an expert on biblical prophecy. He is not only a gifted communicator and writer, but he has mobilized scores of people to action through the Joshua Fund. This nonprofit organization has a goal of generating 125 million dollars of relief and aid into the Middle East where it is most needed. This fund will help Jews and Arabs all through the region.

Now *that* is motivating believers into action! We can no longer merely sit by and put check marks by our "prophesies fulfilled" lists. We cannot remain idle. If we do, we run the risk of repeating the mistake the church in Nazi Germany made. The evangelical church for the most part was complacent during Israel's darkest hour. Due to a superiority attitude that was the logical result of replacement theology, the church turned a deaf ear to the Jews. What had happened to Jesus' words during this period in history: "Blessed are those who hunger and thirst for righteousness"?

Great, Jesus is coming back! Great, Jewish people are back in the land! Great, Arabs are coming to Christ! But the real question is, "How can believers help?" The key to opening the door to the Middle East revival is prayer. We need you to pray. So let's start with what we're up against, and then we'll cover how to pray.

What We're Up Against with Palestinians

Palestinians have a major uphill battle! Their culture is riddled with Islamic fanaticism. It will be a miracle of God to see this type of leadership passed over in favor of moderate, peace-promoting leadership. But it has to be done. This will allow the church's expansion to occur, and terrorist groups will be out of a job. They will be forced to move on. Can that really happen? I believe it can. The forces of God's heavenly army cannot be matched by the powers of evil. Starting now, a new chapter in Palestinian history needs to be written.

Pastor and author John Hagee in his book *The Battle for Jerusalem* gave the following insightful views concerning some true lowlights from the past. The PLO, he delineated, holds several records of dubious distinction:

- *Greatest variety of targets*. Between 1968 and 1980, the PLO committed more than 200 major terrorist acts in or against countries other than Israel. Their targets included forty civilian passenger planes, five passenger ships, thirty embassies, and economic targets such as fuel depots and factories.
- *The worst midair explosion*. February 21, 1970. The Popular Front for the Liberation of Palestine (PFLP) blew up a Swiss airliner, killing thirty-eight passengers and nine crew members.
- *The most sustained terrorist campaign*. Between September 1967 and December 1980, the PLO carried out at least three hundred attacks in twenty-six countries. Total casualties: 813 killed, 1,013 injured.
- *The largest number of hostages held at one time*. Three hundred passengers were held hostage on four hijacked jets. The PLO demanded the release of terrorists held by Britain, Switzerland, and Germany. The plan worked.
- *The largest number of people killed and wounded by a single booby-trap bomb*. July 4, 1975. Fifteen Israelis were killed and eighty-seven

wounded by a PLO bomb planted in Zion Square, Jerusalem.

- *The wealthiest terrorist organization.* Although it is impossible to determine how wealthy the PLO is, in the early 1980s it was known that the PLO had an annual income of at least 800 million pounds sterling."[1]

Palestinians finally had enough of the Palestinian Authority. The Palestinians were used to corruption, greed, and continual lying from their leadership. But after two decades of this, they rejected it. In January 2006, the Palestinians had an election, and with great optimism they booted out the P.A. Unfortunately, they voted in Hamas, which brought on a new set of problems. Hamas has made no bones about the fact they will be bringing Sharia Law to Gaza. The Gaza Strip may get the nickname "little Iran" soon.

This kind of terrorism has grown to become a part of the Palestinian landscape. It has been ongoing for so long that it is routine. While I was counseling as a pastor once, a woman from a particularly disturbing family life and painful past said to me, "When all you've seen your whole life is abnormal, then that becomes normal to you." How true. How descriptive of the Palestinian state of affairs. The rank-and-file Palestinian is frustrated and tired of empty promises, tired of being used politically as the focal point of desperation while their leaders live in lavish homes and spend the money intended for the people.

While on my first trip into the Gaza Strip, I had the joy of staying with a wonderful Palestinian family. Their home was very modest with no hot water or other kinds of "luxuries." As we ate a very small breakfast of cucumbers, hummus, and rice, I thanked the mom of the house. She was not a believer but a very good moral woman nonetheless. After I thanked her for breakfast, she said it was her pleasure and that "President Arafat has authorized an extra pound of rice this month for Palestinian families." Her comment was meant to be a compliment to her leader. To me it wasn't. I smiled politely, but I was finished with my breakfast! How long will they stand for this meaningless game that's being played out with their lives? I guarantee you, the

Palestinian Authority isn't stuck with rice and cucumbers for breakfast!

Yet this existence is considered normal and will not change with a Palestinian state. Refugees will be declared "free," yet they will remain in tents. Terrorism will not cease because Israel will not be giving Hamas, Islamic Jihad, and the other terrorist groups what they want—Israel's annihilation. Living conditions and health conditions will remain the same. Endless bundles of money will be given to the leadership to distribute among the Palestinians, and it just won't make it there. I don't believe the peace treaties will work either. There may be some temporary reprieves in the parade of violence, but peace won't last. It can't. Not while Islam is being interpreted literally from the Koran, the way it is in most places. Why should it be any different in Israel or in the Middle East?

Islam vs. the World

In *Secrets of the Koran*, Don Richardson laid out the overall Islamic strategy for world domination. Here are the general points of their plan: legal and illegal immigration of Muslims into Western nations, a "behind-the-scenes" takeover, widening Islamic influence, a multibillion dollar international mosque construction and Koran translation program, and infiltration of Christian colleges and churches to seduce Christian women."[2]

The best place to see this happening is in England and other European countries. Since the church in Western Europe has been dead for years, Islam has gained a major foothold (although in the last few years the church is showing signs of awakening in Europe). Islam is way in front of evangelicals as far as influence is concerned. Richardson went on: "Naive Europeans who think they are showing tolerance to a mere religion are actually inviting a very potent political invader into their societies."[3]

In one instance, Prince Charles was invited to join a prestigious Muslim gentlemen's club. After joining, he soon learned he was expected to show support to the club by helping the Islamic men's group accomplish something. It seems the influential Muslims of Britain coveted a piece of property owned by Oxford University. Oxford was not selling until Prince Charles pressured the academic institution to give in and sell the chunk of land to the Muslims for a new Islamic studies center.

This is what we're up against, Christians. Islam is wealthy, expanding, and becoming more persuasive within Western democracies. On American university campuses it is becoming more active. Since most colleges in America are bastions of liberalism, they become a vast moral vacuum. In Berkeley, for example, a man sued the university because he wanted to attend school naked—and won. Islam sees the crumbling of U.S. values and attempts to take advantage of that. If a man can go to school naked for four years in the name of freedom of speech, how will we ever stop Islam? Its goal is to appear harmless at first, gain acceptance, and then plant expanding roots. To Islam, American campuses are ripe for the picking. Islam has found a base of operations on the university scene. They offer an alternative in the place where right and wrong have been dismissed altogether.

In another realm, Islam has spread like wildfire in American prisons among young black men. The latest figures show that 77 percent of young black American men grow up in fatherless homes. The dad's obligation to role model and be the primary moral influencer in the black home is at best happening only 23 percent of the time. Many young black men end up in prison with the lack of any parameters of virtue in their lives. When they do, Islam is there waiting for them.

Charles Colson of Prison Fellowship has noticed the alarming trend of black conversions to Islam in prisons and penitentiaries. With chaos in the inner city, Islam provides a different way. Muslim clerics promise that black inmates will not be raped if they convert and become followers of Muhammad. Also, as a black pastor friend of mine once said, "When it comes to religions, young black men desire one that has plans to take over the world, rather than one that calls for 'turning the other cheek.'" How sad that Islam is being perceived as the religion of power and Christianity of weakness. Now that's deception. Islam is on the move in prisons and in black communities across America.

What We're Up Against with Jews

I remember someone asking Billy Graham what he thought was the most common sin worldwide. Greed? Lust? Covetousness? Dr. Graham said that the worst and most potent sin force in the world was racism. I did not hold the same view as the esteemed evangelist until I became a missionary, but I have seen the effects of it now on four continents. He is right. It is a pervasive force in any culture.

More than any people in history, Israel has been a victim of racism. In chapter 11 of Genesis, God decided to separate the nations because of the rank disobedience of the people. After the Flood, God specifically commanded the survivors to "be fruitful and multiply and fill the earth" (Gen. 9:1). But the people didn't want to fill the earth. They wanted to stay right where they were. They liked it there. So the Tower of Babel became their symbol of spiritual rebellion. The Mesopotamian ziggurat became a massive idol to self. The first skyscraper was built in an effort to get to heaven and have a showdown with God. And Babylon, in present-day Iraq, is the location of the group's rebellious act. God put an end to it quickly. The area of Babylon has been a breeding ground for evil ever since.

In Genesis 12, God plucked Abram out of this culture fraught with iniquity. He told him to take a journey but didn't tell him where he was going. No exact coordinates were given, but Abram left and followed God anyway. What a contrast between Abram and the people of Babel. The people of Babel were told to leave and didn't, even though God had created the nations in their midst. Abram was told to leave and did, without knowing where he was going. The contrast between Abram as the forefather of the Hebrews and the Babylonian gang is clear. God drew Abram away from the pagan people. It became Abram versus them. Even though Abram was steeped in paganism, Yahweh pulled him out of it and took him to another region. He had His chosen people. It was God and the Hebrews against the world.

It still is.

No, not much has changed since then. God chose the people who would later become known as Israel as His people in an eternal covenant, loving them above all other peoples of the earth. Satan, on the other hand, chose to hate them above all peoples of the earth. This is how it's been from the first book of the Bible until today: God and Israel against the world.

Over time, the Jewish people developed a tough outer shell because of the opposition they encountered wherever they lived. A callousness has resulted, a toughness that is hard to break. If the Arabic generational sin is hatred toward Jews, then the Jewish generational sin is pride. In the Old Testament, God termed this as being "stiff-necked." They were proud, self-sufficient, and assumed they had a built-in invincibility.

Let's face it—Israelis are a nation of overachievers. They excel in just about everything they put their minds to. And they are often quick to remind everyone of this, what with their God-given prosperity from generation to generation. Don't get me wrong—they are some of the hardest workers I have ever seen, but they have taken a certain pride in their achievements also.

When I first arrived in the Holy Land, our guide told us what the difference was between American mothers and Jewish mothers. When a child goes to school in America, his mom says, "Don't forget your lunch." When a child goes to school in Israel, his mom says, "Don't forget your books." (By the way, the moms on our trip agreed that he was right.) So with five major wars in sixty years under their belts, continual terrorism, and hostility all around them, many Israelis believe they merely have outsmarted everyone. If they fail to see the powerful hand of God sustaining them, there is only one other option: take credit for it. Their sheer will to survive is intense. Since they are surrounded by Muslims everywhere, they must always maintain a national sense of alert. They are under constant threat. People turn on them quickly. And as Europe is being infiltrated with Muslims, even the distance between Israel and European nations is widening. As the current intifada enters its fourth year, a European boycott has hurt Israel's already sagging economy. But they will survive and flourish again.

I would say, though, that some of the bravado normally on display in Israel is fading because this situation shows no signs of letting up and no real hope is on the horizon. This has hit the average Jewish person living in the land of Israel awfully hard. Some have even begun to talk about the death of Zionism. Despair is plentiful.

With the intifada continuing to take innocent Israeli lives regularly, many consider a new proposal as the answer—a wall. When Israel originally entered the land of milk and honey, of course, the walls came tumbling down around Jericho. Today, they're going back up. But again, the answer is flawed; it has only opened up another new set of problems.

Recently on the Trans-Israel Highway, an eight-meter-high wall was built around the green line in order to keep Israeli citizens safe and terrorists out. The Watchman's Prayer Letter details yet another sad story for an Israeli family:

> The fact that the much touted eight-meter-high wall that is being built along the green line could not save seven-year-old Noam Lei-bowitz is a tragedy that should have been foreseen. As the family was driving in their car on the Trans-Israel Highway, terrorists got to the Israeli side of the wall by going through the water system (the draining ditch under the wall). A few bursts from a Kalashnikov rifle penetrated the car, killing the one child and injuring her sister and grandfather. The gunmen got through the drainage pipe by cutting through steel grating inside the tunnel; then they returned the same way. The failure of the wall should say something loud and clear to everyone, and it is simply this: "Horses and chariots, only the God of Israel can save His people."[4]

How defeating all of this must be to the average Jewish man or woman who has sacrificed so much to answer the call deep within their nature to re-turn and reside within their homeland. Another security measure. Another way around it.

That is precisely the point. No amount of man-made devices can stop the hatred of the human heart. Racism runs deep in the Middle East soul.

It has been the cultural driving force ever since God chose Abram and re-named him Abraham. Satan has seen to it. Israel is neck-deep in a swirling cesspool of racism. It is satanically inspired, and it is spreading. Israelis can-not "think" their way out of this one. Only the God of Israel can fix it.

The word *Hamas* is synonymous with everything that is wrong in Is-rael. Less than fifteen years ago, Hamas was a splinter group considered in-capable of accomplishing anything more than occasional, random acts of violence. Today it is the top threat within the borders of Israel. In recent days Egypt, the grandfather figure of Islam, has negotiated with Hamas in order to achieve a cease-fire. Abdul Ranusi, a movement leader, remarked that "cease-fire" was not in the Hamas vocabulary. Now that they have taken over Gaza, they have dug themselves in for a long war with Israel. The for-mer "club" has become a movement, and its ranks are swelling. Every single peace proposal that Israel signs promises a reduction in terrorism. They all sound similar—same song, second verse. But it never pans out. It never quite materializes. Terrorism groups are getting what they demand and then are expected to go away quietly. But more than ever, terrorist groups are feeling empowered, and their growth is exponential.

Israel has wiped out buildings that produce bombs for Muslim kamikazes. It has waged a war on Hamas, Islamic Jihad, Al-Aksa Martyr's Brigade, and others. Israel has unleashed modern technology to root out terrorists, and its results have ended up offending a majority of the world. One Palestinian friend from Gaza told me how Israeli Defense Forces soldiers find a terrorist in the midst of the 1.5 million people in the Gaza Strip. When they locate a Palestinian willing to be an informant, they pay him maybe $250 to take a bottle of liquid and spray the top of a terrorist's car or home, if possible. The spray contains strong infrared chemicals. At night, the soldiers fly over in a helicopter and perform the precision missile strike on the car or house they spot with their infrared glasses that the crew wears onboard the chopper. We have been in Gaza during the strikes. The Israeli Defense Forces usually get their man.

Herein lies the problem. There is an unlimited supply of Palestinian men and women willing to die for the cause. Israel will be shooting missiles at infrared marked cars for years. Hamas and other terrorist groups are growing faster than the Israelis can kill them.

Israel also fights tremendous battles from within. In June 2003, Jerusalem held its second annual gay parade through the streets of Jerusalem. Since Israel is very secular, things like this are becoming normal. The nation has become a carbon copy of American culture. In 2007, the gay-pride organization tried to host its first event within the Old City walls of Jerusalem. Its goal was to walk through the city gates and announce their presence in the Holy City. With strong opposition from the ultra-Orthodox and Orthodox Jews plus messianics, the parade was diverted to the more secular downtown area.

The ultra-Orthodox Jerusalem, called Mea Shearim, segregate themselves from society. The community in West Jerusalem is strident in keeping the laws of the Tanach or Old Testament. Sabbath violations are considered one of the greatest offenses. This is the place where driving a car through the community on the Sabbath will result in your car being pelted with rocks. So on one hand, a gay parade tries to enter into the Old City and have free expression at Israel's holiest sites. On the other hand, the ultra-Orthodox have built their community to resemble an Eastern European Jewish ghetto that vigorously keeps the law. The diversity of the country has shattered the unity Jews experienced in the early years of their national existence. Politically, there are about twenty parties now. The country has just about everything America has as far as racial problems. With immigration streaming in from Russia, Ethiopia, and even America, ethnic tension is often high. Within Judaism, Jews from Europe known as Ashkenazics notoriously struggle with Sephardics from Spain and Arab countries, and vice versa.

Are you getting the picture? It is not only a few in the land who fear that Zionism is experiencing an implosion.

The Prayer Force

That's where we come in. Every Christian needs to be a praying Christian. If you're like me, this spiritual essential needs work in your life. It does in mine. What has given me new motivation, though, has been traveling to the Middle East. Walking the streets of Jerusalem. Visiting the refugee camps in Gaza. Feeling the desperation. That is critical for prayer. We know this about Christians and prayer—we will pray if we're desperate enough. Desperation combined with faith is powerful in the life of any believer. Because Arabs and Jews are now open to the gospel, now is the time to pray. Here is how you can help.

Ticker-Tape Prayers

On September 11, 2001, America was hit by an Islamic death squad. Since the situation was so fluid and several things were developing in several locations, massive amounts of information needed to get to the American public at once. Announcers didn't have time to read every story, so the solution was the ticker tape. CNN, FOX, MSNBC, and other stations began using a running recap band on the bottom of the screen. It kept the public abreast of the changing situation and condensed the lead news stories of the day.

The first time I remember seeing this was when our president was being flown around the country to safety. I remember being angry that the networks might actually be exposing his whereabouts. If terrorists could get the CNN feed—and they certainly could—they might be able to track down the commander-in-chief and others. Of course, the White House was in a declared state of war, and to protect our president, reports deliberately listed several places he might have been.

I believe George W. Bush was God's man to guide America through the worst national tragedy our country has ever undergone. He stood tall. As a believer, he also sought the face of God for help in the midst of the chaos. It was evident the power that resonated from our president was a result of God's working in him through the prayer that was directed toward heaven on his behalf.

According to the World Prayer Center in Colorado Springs, our president now has an official prayer team of well more than two million intercessors. This is the official list, yet perhaps millions more pray for him daily. Since then, the prayer team for the president and the ticker tape have stayed. In November 2008 we will elect a new U.S. President. This President will have to make critical decisions on issues of major importance. What to do with Iran's growing nuclear arsenal and the future of a possible Palestinian State are just a few of the pressing questions. The President needs daily prayer, no matter how we voted in the general election. Here's how we can combine them both.

The ticker tape is a built-in emergency prayer alert for Christians. It is something we can utilize on a daily basis as an up-to-date prayer mobilizer. If you're like me and you overdose on news, you have to guard against two things:

1. *Avoid becoming a fear-based Christian.* The news is depressing! If you're not careful, it will wrap you up in overwhelming anxiety. In Israel, many Palestinians and Jews don't watch the news. I asked a Jewish woman in Jerusalem why no one seemed to watch the news in Israel. She said, "Because the news makes us go crazy!" Good point! If you exist on a steady stream of news and fail to take "every thought captive to the obedience of Christ" as Paul told us to in 2 Corinthians 10:5, you'll probably struggle with cynicism or depression. Wait a minute, Christian; we win this thing in the end, remember?

2. *Make the news a spiritual experience.* Make it a time to pray. I'm serious. The ticker tape highlights the hottest spots of conflict worldwide. The latest stories from spiritual warfare front lines are linked with the majority of the unrest and evil around the globe. The two are connected.

Here's an example: No matter how you may feel about it, the war in Iraq was really an effort to keep under control an Islamically controlled state that had designs on Israel and an emerging and advanced weapons program. True, there are many other things involved, yet at the core was fundamentalist Islam that with its sights set on Israel and the West. Also, it did help that Saddam Hussein believed he was Nebuchadnezzar in a reincarnated state. Nebuchadnezzar was the only Arab leader to ever defeat Israel and control their land. In 586 BC, Babylonian captivity removed the Jews from their beloved land and returned them to the place Abram started from. God wanted the nation to start over, and he took them back to their roots in Mesopotamia. True, Nebuchadnezzar did defeat Israel, but only because God let him. This is often overlooked, of course, but in Jeremiah 34:2, Yahweh told the prophet what was coming: "I am about to hand this city over to the king of Babylon, and he will burn it down." Amazingly, an event that occurred in 586 BC became added motivation for Saddam's preparation to strike Israel. The conflict was motivated by religion. As far as the Middle East goes, that is usually the root of the problem.

Praying with the Ticker Tape

Seeing Gaza in the news is a regular occurrence. Let that set off an alarm in you to pray! As I said before, there is one evangelical church in the Gaza Strip. One! So when you see the latest border clash with Israel, try not to get sidetracked—prayer is what is needed. The church of dynamic believers in the Gaza Strip needs your fervent intercession.

Jerusalem, Tel Aviv, the West Bank, Haifa, the Galilee, Gaza—all of these places have a vibrant church with the extremely difficult task of doing ministry within the war. They are strategic placements of the church within the spiritual war zone. They need your prayers daily.

Throughout the Middle East in radical Islamic pockets, there is a vibrant church present and serving Jesus with united hearts. Did you know there are brothers and sisters in Saudi Arabia and an underground church in Mecca? When you see a story on Saudi oil, terrorism, or the Muslim annual pilgrimage—the *hajj*—pray for the church there. It is illegal to be a Christian in Mecca, Saudi Arabia. Christians are killed there. The house church movement needs your prayers.

In Tel Aviv, the messianic congregations need your continual prayers. The congregations need prayers in Jerusalem. When you see Jewish cities or settlements in the news on the ticker tape, let it be like a shofar blowing to beckon the chosen people to a biblical feast. It is a call to prayer. These

Christians are doing front-line ministry. They are at the bomb blasts. They are attending funerals. They are trying to bring the light of Jesus Christ into the darkness. They need spiritual reinforcements. They get tired and frustrated like we do. Prayer is what keeps them going.

In a June 2003 bus blast, Ron Cantrell, an American believer who lives in Jerusalem, was on the bus and miraculously survived. He was dazed and wandered home. His family gave praises to God that he lived, then were horrified to find pieces of flesh all over his back from the deadly explosion. This is life in the land of the Bible these days. No one should have to live like this! Prayer is their lifeblood. We must lift them up in prayer.

After working with the underground Iranian church, I will never be the same. I fell in love with these outgoing, joy-filled believers. Do they ever know how to worship God! When you think about what is on the horizon for them, their future does not look rosy. Yet they push aside the prospects of nuclear war and make Jesus their focus. How humbling it was to hear that the Iranian believers pray for us American believers every day! The Iranians? Praying for us? Considering what they were facing, we should be on our faces daily for them.

God has sufficiently chastised me and my wife, JoAnn, in the need for prayer—especially for Israel and the Middle East. I pray He will do the same work in you.

Internet Prayers

Several Internet sites can keep you updated on the latest needs of the church worldwide. If you want your prayers to go global, get on the Net.

At e3 Partners, our ministry team has developed an excellent and practical Web site where you can link up with what God is doing around the world. We maintain an updated prayer list from front-line churches, and you can be a prayer partner with these Middle East pastors. This is real front-lines stuff. If you have a love for the Middle East, this will take you into the heart of the spiritual conflict and provide updates on the progress of this ministry as well as up-to-the-minute prayer needs. (www.e3partners.org)

Our new ministry Web site is called Good News from the Middle East, designed by our son Tommy. He has put together a great tool for anyone who wants to hear how God is powerfully moving in the Middle East. We focus on the overcoming church and provide portraits of real, faithful heroes as they live for Jesus in the most challenging circumstances. My wife, JoAnn, and her women's ministry team, Selah, give practical ways to help hurting women of the Middle East. Selah was born this year and has become a fast-growing ministry due to the enormous needs of Middle East women. I believe God's hand is in this ministry because of the godly leadership and number of hours they spend in prayer.

Joel Rosenberg, author of many best-selling books, gave us the idea to create a Web site and highlight the good news in the Middle East. One night we were having dinner, and he said, "Tom, you have got to get these stories on a Web site! Believers in America need to know how our awesome God is transforming lives in the Middle East. Why don't you see if the name Good News from the Middle East is available on the Internet as a Web site name." A few days later, my good friends Tom Lamphere and Jan Richey checked, and sure enough—it was available!

Thank you, Joel! Thank you, Tom and Jan! Thank you, Tommy, for putting it together! Yes, Mom and Dad are very proud of you. This Web site seeks to inspire and renew your passion for Christ by bringing you the good news from places like Israel, Iran, Syria, Egypt, Jordan, Afghanistan, as well as other "spiritual hotspots" in the region. Want to get to know your brothers and sisters in the Middle East? Meet them here and start praying for them today. (www.goodnewsfromthemiddleeast.com)

Joel Rosenberg has developed another wonderful resource for the Middle East. His Web site delivers up-to-the-minute news and provides opportunities to get involved and make a difference in Israel and other neighboring countries. Joel is an expert on the Middle East, and when it comes to prophecy, he is at the top of the "A" list. Joel came to faith in Jesus Christ from an Orthodox Jewish heritage. His grandparents escaped Jewish persecution in Russia during the early part of the twentieth century. Joel can get real news from the Middle East and help your prayers become more strategic and focused. You can also sign up for "Flash Traffic" and get bi-weekly email updates. This Web site is a must for anyone interested in the Middle East! (www.joelrosenberg.com)

Brother Andrew's ministry, Open Doors, has been a refuge for hurting believers worldwide for five decades. His work in the Muslim world is effective and strategic. At e3 Partners we are privileged to work with some of the same leaders who are laboring with Open Doors. Brother Andrew is dynamic and has accomplished much for believers in the Middle East. In the early years, his ministry concentrated on Russia and the Soviet empire. Later, God began to break Andrew's heart for lost Muslims. His ministry has been redirected to the Middle East. For all of us who love to smuggle Bibles and EvangeCubes into the Middle East, Brother Andrew is our hero! (www. opendoorsusa.org)

DAWN (Discipling a Whole Nation) is a Christian research and strategy ministry. It has an excellent resource called the "Friday Fax" that updates prayer needs weekly. (www.dawnministries.org)

The World Prayer Center, an Internet interactive prayer site, is a great place to pray for current needs globally. You can even listen to praise music as you have your own personal prayer session. (www.prayerteam.org)

The Voice of the Martyrs is dedicated to the persecuted church. This is one of my favorites. It will connect you to believers and their needs from hot spots of persecution worldwide. (www.persecution.com)

CFI (Christian Friends of Israel) offers the Watchman's Prayer Letter, a monthly report emailed directly to your computer. CFI has a heart for Israel and will keep you updated on the latest from Israel. (www.CFIJerusalem.org)

Mission Network News is a daily report of five to six top stories from around the globe. Some of the stories give the results of what God is doing in a particular area. Some stories give breaking prayer needs. This is another good prayer site. (www.mnnonline.org)

AD 2000 and Beyond's "Praying through the Window" program states, "The core of the unreached people of our world live in a rectangular-shaped window. Often called 'The Resistant Belt,' the window extends from West Africa to East Asia, from ten degrees north to forty degrees north of the equator." This AD 2000 ministry coordinates all kinds of prayer initiatives. This is also one of the best sites. (www.ad2000.org)

There you go. Ten ways to turn your computer into a weapon of prayer. The Internet has much evil connected to it, but we can use it as a powerful tool for God to mobilize large prayer groups. Get connected.

"With every prayer and request, pray at all times in the Spirit, and stay alert in this, with perseverance and intercession for all the saints" (Eph. 6:18).

Thirty-One-Day Prayer Journey through Israel

A good way to utilize this for devotions is to read a Proverb, then pray for the corresponding city of the day. The cities are listed below, and a prayer map at the end of the photos section will help you locate each day's prayer site.

Day	Place	Day	Place
1	Jerusalem	17	Caesarea
2	East Jerusalem	18	Tulkarm
3	Tel Aviv	19	Netanya
4	Nablus	20	Palestinian Refugee Camps
5	Haifa	21	Eilat
6	Jenin	22	Latrun
7	Tiberias	23	Hadera
8	Ramallah	24	Jewish Kibbutzim
9	Nazareth	25	Safed
10	Jericho	26	Acco
11	Jaffa	27	Kiryat Shmona
12	Bethlehem	28	Afula
13	Ashkelon	29	Ashdod
14	Hebron	30	Israeli Government Offices
15	Beersheba	31	Palestinian Authority Leadership
16	The Gaza Strip		

Pray for gospel exposure and conversions, churches to grow and plant new churches, biblical reconciliation between Jews and Arabs, revival to spread to the rest of the Middle East, and all mission groups in the area, such as the International Mission Board, Campus Crusade, Youth with a Mission, e3 Partners, and International Bible Society.

Travel to Israel

This is the best way to pray—on location. Prayer groups travel to Israel every year. They tour biblical sites and help local churches and ministries. But above all, they pray. This is done through many ministry groups. As believers saturate the area and the people with passionate prayers, Satan's strongholds will begin to loosen and salvation will occur. This is an exciting way to immerse yourself in God's work in Israel.

Many people today are afraid to go to Israel, yet Jews and Palestinians need us more than ever. As Christians, we must advance the gospel into the dark parts of the world without fear. Muslims are sending missionaries to America. Are we going to sit back and do nothing? We have the words of life. We have the solution to all the hate. We have the power of the Spirit of God within us. We have the promise that Jesus will build His church. Why not take a trip to the front lines where the action is?

People ask me all the time, "Aren't you afraid to go to Israel?" I believe in the sovereignty of God and that He alone has our days numbered. Of course, we are not to test the Lord and do something stupid. We don't live on the dangerous edge for some twisted thrill. Yet we are to take the gospel everywhere. My good friend Curtis Hail once said, "Until it is my time to go and be with Jesus, I am bulletproof." So are you!

In conclusion, global praying that is truly biblical is needed above all in Israel and the Middle East. Passionate prayer. Prayers of faith. Continual prayer. Fasting. Weeping before the Lord. All of these are needed. Both Jews and Palestinians are desperate. Will we share that desperation with them? We must.

Prayer is number one. We must advance on our knees first. Chapter 9 will tell you what else you can do.

Avi—The Reconciler

Avi has always appreciated his Jewish roots. Born into a more traditional Israeli family in Tel Aviv, he always observed the Jewish holidays. Avi was the typical young Jewish Israeli with dreams of exploring the world to see what it had to offer him. He especially had a desire to visit Las Vegas, Nevada, to get rich.

At one point in Avi's life, his sister shared with him her newfound faith in Yeshua (Jesus). Avi had no interest in religion at this time and did not seriously consider his sister's comments. Upon visiting her later in Florida, in fact, he was somewhat confused why his Jewish sister would be attending a Baptist church. But out of curiosity, he decided to attend this church at his sister's invitation.

He was shocked at what he observed and encountered there. Immediately, he was struck by the passionate worship as he entered the sanctuary. His shock turned to amazement as he realized the people, many of whom were Gentiles, were more familiar with the Scriptures than he was as a Jew. A profound joy seemed to fill the people's hearts. This provoked his heart to jealousy for what they had.

Avi was about to experience the ultimate paradigm shift. "How could all of this be real?" he thought. Yet the joy in the room intrigued him, and deep down inside he longed to be filled with it.

In Romans 11:11, Paul said that "salvation has come to the Gentiles to make Israel jealous." This is exactly what was happening in Avi's heart! He asked himself, "Why do they have such joy? Could these people possibly possess what I have always longed for—a living relationship with God?" After hearing the gospel taught at a youth group, Avi reached out to his Jewish Messiah in childlike faith. His loving Father reached out to him as Avi received Jesus, the Jewish Messiah, as his Savior. And immediately, an inner joy he had never known flooded his soul.

He now has the living relationship with God he always desired.

Today, Avi lives near Tel Aviv and reaches people of all races and religions for Messiah Yeshua through the Dugit Messianic Outreach Center (*dugit* means "small fishing boat" in Hebrew) right off Dizengoff Square in the heart of the city. He has a passion to see Jews and Arabs come to know Yeshua and be reconciled together as the "one new man." Avi has a godly wife, Chaya, and three daughters. He also pastors the Adonai Roi Messianic Congregation in Tel Aviv (*Adonai Roi* is Hebrew for "the Lord is my Shepherd"). This dynamic congregation works hand in hand with the Dugit Messianic Center to reach the lost with the gospel and disciple them as believers in their Jewish Messiah Yeshua. It has a steady stream of new believers as a result of its sensitive yet powerful outreach efforts, in which teams come from all over the world to help share the gospel of Yeshua. Russian Jews, Orthodox Jews, Palestinian Arabs, and an assortment of agnostics, atheists, and New Age followers have been rescued from the kingdom of darkness at Dugit.

Among believers, Avi is a respected and recognized leader in Israel. His congregation has multiplied and sent others to plant new congregations. He also works with other ministries. Currently, Avi and his leadership team are praying about beginning another outreach center, "Dugit 2."

The God of Abraham, Isaac, and Jacob made Avi *jealous* through the Gentiles before He made him *zealous* for Him and the lost sheep of Israel. Avi is a true hero in Israel, yet he constantly battles persecution, threats, and discrimination from some of the religious Jews and antimissionary organizations. The bulk of the persecution comes from the Orthodox Jewish leadership. During street preaching, it's not uncommon for local religious Jews to shout, blow whistles, and scream at Avi during his messages. But with patience and a big smile, his gentle answer turns away their wrath, and the joy he displays gets the attention of skeptics who also hunger as Avi once did.

Avi speaks the truth straightforwardly, and the people drink it in. Yeshua's words in John's Gospel are fitting of Avi: "Here is a true Israelite, in whom there is nothing false" (John 1:47 NIV).

So that He might create in Himself one new man from the two, resulting in peace. He did this so that He might reconcile both to God in one body through the cross. (Eph. 2:15b–16a)

Chapter 9
Waking Up the Western Church

The vast resources God has lavished on us from heaven are needed to spread the gospel, disciple new believers, and plant strong churches in the Middle East. It's time for action and strategic involvement in the biblical heartland. Every believer should help and can. Here's how.

The Responsibility of the Blessed

I am guilty. I have sinned greatly against my country America. It happens every time I return home from a mission trip. I get critical of America. I try not to, but inevitably it happens. When seeing the unmet needs of the rest of the world, it's hard not to compare it to our abundance. We have so much. God has blessed America like no other nation throughout history. This is the generation that has it all.

In the past few years, however, the United States has undergone a recession. With corporate scandals and a sagging stock market, Americans have been worried about the future. "What about my 401(k) plan?" "Will I have enough for retirement?" "Will I be able to provide for my children in the days ahead?" All of these questions are important ones. Scripture is clear about financial planning. The point is that we are privileged to be able to ask these kinds of questions. How many people around the world have no possibility of ever attaining these things, much less of asking these questions?

The answer, of course, is the majority of the world.

Is blessing bad? No. These are gifts from God's gracious hand. James reminds us that "all good gifts" come from heaven. They are ours to enjoy. But most importantly, they are ours to use. Our resources can make a major difference for the cause of Christ globally. We will give an account one day at the judgment seat of Christ for everything. The gifts that the Holy Spirit bestowed on us at His discretion will be examined. Did we use them for God? If we were given the gift of encouragement, who was encouraged? If the Spirit of God gave us the spiritual gift of evangelism, was anyone saved as a result of it?

Our resources will be examined also. Time to get the checkbook out, folks! Did we spend it all on ourselves? Could we have made a difference for Jesus with all of our stuff? Did we waste it on the superficial that burns up in the end anyway? What survived the fire and transferred into eternity? Kingdom results are what we're looking for. We are responsible.

Another question we could be asked is, "How did you treat God's chosen people?" The church in history has a notoriously bad history with Jews. If nations are judged for it, what about the church?

The church needs to be Israel's best friend. We must. But before we look at how we can do it, let's take a quick review of Israel's history for the last twenty centuries.

Whatever Happened to the Jewish Race?

The New Testament church began about AD 30 (read Acts 2). God still had an unconditional covenant with the Jews. We often lose perspective of this as we become absorbed in our own Christian history in Acts 2 through the rest of the New Testament and on to today. What happened to Israel after the church began? Get up to speed with this condensed time line:

AD 30	Jesus' death and resurrection. The church is born.
66–73	First Jewish revolt against Rome.
70	Second Jewish Temple destroyed under Roman General Titus and tenth Roman Legion, fulfilling Jesus' prophecy in Matthew 24:1–2. A majority of Jews scatter.
132–35	Second Jewish revolt against Rome called the Bar Kokhba Rebellion— 1.5 million Jews killed; 985 villages and 50 fortresses destroyed in Israel.
136	Roman Emperor Hadrian renames Jerusalem as Aelia Capitolina and builds pagan temple over site of temple. Jews banished from Jerusalem.
222–35	Roman Emperor Alexander Severus allows Jews to begin visiting Jerusalem.
306	Christian church Council of Elvira forbids marriage to Jews and bans all relationships with Jews.
415	Cyril, bishop of Alexandria, encourages violence against the city's Jews. He incites Greece to kill or expel Jews.
571	Muhammad, the founder of Islam, is born.
627	The Arabian holocaust begins. Muhammad kills thousands of Jews in Medina and surrounding villages. He takes Jewish women and children as slaves.
637	Muslims capture Caesarea and force Jews to wear yellow patches for identification.
692	Dome of the Rock built on first and second temple site by Caliph Abd el-Malik.
722	Leo III of Constantinople forces Jews to "convert" to Christianity.
1096	First Crusade; Jews massacred in European Cities.
1099	Crusaders capture Jerusalem and massacre thousands of Jews.
1227–74	Thomas Aquinas, well-known church theologian, calls for all Jews to become slaves.
1229	King Henry III of England forces all Jews to pay half the value of their property in taxes and orders Jewish worship be conducted quietly so Christians do not have to hear it while passing by synagogues.
1267	Vienna city council forces Jews to wear cone-shaped hats and badges to identify themselves.
1285	In Munich, Germans burn 180 Jews alive in city synagogue.
1321	Jews accused of poisoning France's water wells. More than 5,000 Jews killed before King Philip admits they were innocent.
1348–49	Black death (bubonic plague) blamed on Jews; 210 Jewish communities destroyed in Europe as retaliation.
1391	Archbishop Ferrand Martinez of Spain campaigns against Jews and kills 10,000.
1420	All Jews expelled from Lyon, France.
1493	Jews expelled from Spain; 200,000 leave.
1496	Portugal expels Jews.
1516	Jewish ghettos begin in Venice.
1536–41	Suleiman the Magnificent, ruler of the Turkish Ottoman Empire, rebuilds Jerusalem city walls with seven gates and Tower of David that all stand today.

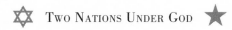

1543 — Martin Luther writes About the Jews and Their Lies, an anti-Semitic booklet. He uses the term "vermin" for Jews.

1555 — Pope Paul IV builds Jewish ghetto in Rome and forbids Jews from owning real estate. They are forced to wear caps to identify themselves.

1615 — King Louis XIII of France gives Jews one month to leave or face death.

1622–29 — Persian Jews are forced to convert to Islam.

1648 — Over 100,000 Jews massacred in Poland.

1670 — Jews expelled from Vienna.

1730 — First synagogue built in America in Manhattan.

1781 — Joseph II of Austria drops "badge law" for Jews after 513 years.

1834 — The Spanish Inquisition ends.

1840 — "To Jew" becomes a verb to describe unethical business practices.

1860 — Theodore Herzl, the father of modern Zionism, is born.

1862 — Gen. Ulysses S. Grant expels all Jews from Kentucky, Tennessee, and Mississippi.

1866 — Jews become the official majority in Jerusalem again.

1896 — Herzl publishes The Jewish State; Zionism is born.

1903 — British government proposes a home for Jews in Uganda.

1916 — Ottoman Empire of 400 years collapses. Turks no longer rule Middle East.

1917 — Russian Revolution claims 200,000 Jewish lives.

1921 — Jordan established, taking land promised to Jews for the new Israel.

1922 — Balfour Declaration of Great Britain promises future home for Jews in Eretz Israel (the land of Israel).

1925 — Hebrew University opens on Mount Scopus, Jerusalem.

1930 — British white paper stops Jewish immigration to Israel.

1932 — Saudi Arabia is established. Iraq gains independence from Great Britain.

1933 — Adolf Hitler becomes chancellor of Germany. Cardinal Pacelli, who becomes Pope Pius XII, issues Hitler Concordat and accepts Nazi socialism and anti-Semitism as core values.

1938 — Kristallnacht—Germany burns down Jewish synagogues. Charles E. Coughlin, American Catholic priest, launches media campaign against Jews. Catholic churches display Nazi flags and ring their church bells to welcome Nazi troops in Austria. Nazis begin forcing Jews to wear yellow stars to identify themselves. This is copied from the church.

1939 — S.S. St. Louis carrying more than 900 passengers is turned away from America and Cuba.

1942 — Nazi leaders adopt Final Solution for Jews at Wannsee Conference.

1943 — King Christian of Denmark stays in his Nazi-occupied country and helps 7,000 Danish Jews escape death camps. To empathize with Jewish families marked by the Magen David, the king wears one himself, though a Christian.

1945 — WWII ends and Nazism falls. Holocaust, which claimed 6 million Jewish lives, ends.

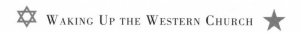

1947	U.N. proposes Jewish state. Dead Sea Scrolls found in Qumran.		1993	Oslo Agreement between Prime Minister Rabin and Chairman Arafat is signed.
1948	Israel becomes a nation, May 14. British mandate ends, May 14. Five Arab armies invade Israel, May 14. President Harry S. Truman recognizes the state of Israel in its first house of existence.		1994	Yitzhak Rabin, Yasser Arafat, and Shimon Peres are awarded Nobel Peace Prize.
1948–49	Israel's War of Independence.		1995	Rabin is assassinated. King Hussein begins Dome of the Rock restoration.
1956	Suez War.		1998	Israel has its 50th birthday. Hamas pledges to renew the intifada if Jerusalem is not the capital of a Palestinian state by 1999.
1967	Six-Day War. Israeli Air Force attacks Egyptian, Jordanian, and Syrian air bases and defeats Arab armies.			
1968	PLO calls for Israel's destruction.		2000	Israel withdraws from Lebanon. Intifada begins again. Prime Minister Ehud Barak offers the Temple Mount to Yasser Arafat for peace. He turns it down.
1968–70	War of Attrition with Egypt.			
1973	Yom Kippur War with Egypt and Syria.			
1975	U.N. equates Zionism as racism.		2003	Operation Iraq Freedom in Iraq. Road Map for Peace is adopted by U.S. calling for a Palestinian state within three years.
1981	Israeli Air Force destroys Iraq's nuclear reactor that threatens their national survival.			
1982	War in Lebanon.		2006	Israel goes to war against Hezbollah, the Iranian terrorist group in Lebanon.
1987	The Palestinian Intifada (uprising) begins in Israel.			
1991	The Gulf War begins. Israel attacked with Iraqi Scud missiles. Arafat backs Saddam Hussein.		2007	Israel bombs Syrian nuclear development facility located 50 miles from the Iraqi border, September 6.

No wonder that although historians estimate that the Jewish race should have grown to 120–130 million by now, they only number approximately 12 million people today. Yahweh's chosen people have endured a sustained assault since their very beginning. Satan has inspired a variety of people groups to become Jew-haters throughout time. "A thief comes only to steal and to kill and to destroy" (John 10:10a).

But when God rules the earth in His millennial kingdom, all opposition to the Jews will be silenced. Even Israel's longtime enemies will turn to God and give up their hatred.

On that day there will be a highway from Egypt to Assyria. Assyria will go to Egypt, Egypt to Assyria, and Egypt will worship with Assyria. On that day Israel will form a triple alliance with Egypt and Assyria—a blessing within the land. The LORD of Hosts will bless them, saying, "Blessed be Egypt My people, Assyria My handiwork, and Israel My inheritance." (Isa. 19:23–25)

Jacob will no longer be ashamed and his face will no longer be pale. For when he sees his children, the work of My hands within his nation, they will honor My name, they will honor the Holy One of Jacob and stand in awe of the God of Israel. (Isa. 29:22b–23)

This will be quite a quantum leap for Israel. The Jews will go from being the despised of the world to the favored of all.

But a critical event will happen for Israel before all of this takes place. They will repent and discover their Messiah. They will be cleansed. "On that day a fountain will be opened for the house of David and for the residents of Jerusalem, to wash away sin and impurity" (Zech. 13:1).

What a glorious turnaround for Israel! Finally, Jews will be revered and honored. They will no longer have a host of enemies trying to wipe them out. That will all be over. When Jesus rules from Jerusalem, they will be safe. Jerusalem will live up to its name—it will be the "city of peace."

Do we Christians have any input into this? Will the God of Israel use us to help restore them to Him? Will we have any influence in their eternal destiny? I believe so. I also believe that because of our Judeo-Christian roots in America, we have stayed on course in our overall support of Israel. America is the one place where the church has stood strong for Israel for the most part. As Bible-believing Christians, we may not always have had the purest motives. We may have been more excited that the end times appeared closer since the Jews were back in the land. We may also have been morally convicted about their ongoing persecution.

Now it's time to empathize with them.

Maximizing the Moment

Jewish people ought to feel that Christians are there for them no matter what. They ought to be able to sense our love and respect for them. The *Voice of the Martyrs* says that Christians are being persecuted in fifty-five nations. Almost one-fourth of the world hates the church and wants its progress slowed down or stopped altogether. Globally, Jews and Christians are the two groups of people most often persecuted and killed. The fifty-five nations that violently oppose us are for the most part Muslim. Communism is still a foe, too. Yet isn't it interesting that since September 11, 2001, Jews and Christians realize they have a common enemy—fundamental Islam? We should have realized this earlier. It is written plainly in the Koran, according to former Islamic professor Mark Gabriel:

> Take not the Jews and the Christians as auleya (friends), they are but auleya of each other. And if any amongst you takes them (as auleya), then surely he is one of them. (Surah 5:51)[1]
>
> O you who have been given the Scripture (Jews and Christians)! Believe in what we have revealed (to Muhammad) confirming what is (already) with you, before we efface faces (by making them like the back of necks; without nose, mouth, eyes) and turn them hindwards, or curse them as we cursed the Sabbath-breakers. And the commandment of Allah is always executed. (Surah 4:47)[2]

If a Muslim reads the Koran literally, he will not want to be a friend of either Jews or Christians. Not only that, he has koranic justification to kill them. Now, as I have said before, for the majority of Muslims, a literal rendering of verses such as these is untenable. They see *surahs* like these as outdated and no longer applicable. To them, this is merely history that was fulfilled at the beginning of Islam. The wars that helped establish it as the "power religion" of the day are now over and done with. The majority of Muslims have not made it their personal life goal to fulfill these verses and kill Jews and Christians. They may not especially like us, but murder is out of the question.

Yet there are Muslims who wholeheartedly support the literalness of ko-ranic interpretation. Every *surah* to them is binding for today and must be realized for Muhammad's followers.

An eighteenth-century movement within Islam started an effort to take Muslims back to this kind of literal interpretation. The Wahhabi branch of Islam grew over time. Saudi Arabia finally embraced it, and it became the underpinning of the House of Saud. Since 1932, when Saudi Arabia became a nation, the Wahhabi belief has driven the Saudis to a stricter, more tradi-tional form of Islam. Hence, that's where the majority of the September 11 terrorists were from. Their belief system took them to the logical end—the killing of Christians. The fact that we support Israel made it even more ap-pealing.

After September 11, our common enemy was identified. Jews are being killed by strict Muslims. Christians are being killed by strict Muslims. There are 109 verses in the Koran on war. This does not include verses where war is mentioned in a story. These are the verses that explicitly command or en-courage war. Muhammad himself fought in forty-seven wars. This problem is not going away very soon, folks.

There is also another group on the Islamic "hit list." It is Arab believers, whether they be Palestinians, Jordanians, or Iraqis. They are in a frightening situation that controls their lives and their existence. The believers in Gaza live in it. That's why they have given their lives to share Christ's love within the world of Islam. It is their only hope to change anything. Gabriel wrote, "The leader of Libya, Muammar Qaddafi, considers himself to be a great thinker, and he announced one day that he had a solution to the problem. His solution was for the Christians to convert to Islam, and then they would be brothers and sisters with the Muslims, and the fighting would stop. Qad-dafi said, 'I hope there is a new generation of Lebanese Christians who will wake up one day and realize Arabs cannot be Christians and Christians can-not be Arabs, so then they will convert to Islam and be true Arabs.'"[3]

The lines are drawn in the sand—Christians, Jews, and Arab believers versus the world of Islam. Over 1.3 billion Muslims are now spread out globally. If the fanatics are only 10 percent of Islam, that still is a major force. One hundred thirty million is roughly half the size of America. Fanatics could have lower numbers or higher.

Here's how to maximize the moment:

Love a Jewish person

In America, Jewish people are approachable and often open to relationships with believers. If we seek them out and really befriend them, it will be a great start.

Ask for Forgiveness

I know we had nothing to do with the anti-Semitism of the Roman Catholic Church during the Middle Ages. Certainly what happened in the Spanish Inquisition repulses us. Nazi German treatment of Jews and the Holocaust is even worse. How could the black death be blamed on the house of David? But these events did happen in supposedly Christian countries. How will Jewish people know that we detest these "false works" of our Christian faith unless we tell them? Look at some of the things that Christian leaders had to say about Jews. Martin Luther, Augustine, Origen, and Chrysostom all had strong anti-Semitic feelings. They also were in places of leadership, and thus they helped direct the Christian masses toward anti-Semitism.

After you have established a loving relationship with a Jewish person or even a family, hit the problem head-on. Here's what might be appropriate to say: "You know, with you being Jewish and me being a Christian, we both have a lot in common. We believe in and read the same prophets. We believe that the God of Israel will be the victor at the end of time. But as a Christian, I want you to know that I am aware of how the church at times has been at the forefront of Jewish persecution. It was wrong, and I ask your forgiveness. I was ignorant about the dark side of Christian history until recently, and I repent before you. Please forgive us. I believe Christians ought to be the best friends Jewish people ever have. I want you to know I will never be a part of any anti-Semitism. If I see Christians who have even a trace of this, I will correct them. You have my word."

ENCOURAGE JEWS

Wow, how's that for an icebreaker? We believers are children of the truth. We bring the good, the bad, and the ugly into the light. When we do something like that, real spiritual healing can take place.

I love the words of Isaiah when prophesying about the coming Redeemer. He said the Messiah was going "to comfort all who mourn, to provide for those who mourn in Zion; to give them a crown of beauty instead of ashes, festive oil instead of mourning, and splendid clothes instead of despair" (Isa. 61:2b-3a). Jesus' very presence brought the Jews honor, joy, and hope. As His followers, let's do the same for them today.

An Israeli government official in the Netanyahu administration named David Bar-Illan once said this to our church tour group: "Look, we Jews have so few friends in the world that we'll take them where we find them!" Doesn't that sound like people who need believers to put their arms around them and love them?

Do you know about the Steven Spielberg project? After he directed the movie *Schindler's List*, Steven Spielberg decided to film the testimony of every remaining Holocaust survivor worldwide. Quite an ambitious goal. He has labored on this project for years now. Since many survivors are older and passing away, Spielberg tried to do the personal interviews as quickly as possible. Once a person dies, if he has no remaining relatives, his story will be lost forever. One problem Spielberg encountered was surprising. It seems that the Shoah (Hebrew for Holocaust) had left some survivors in so much pain and fear that they did not want to tell their stories. Many of them feared they might suffer recriminations if they told what really happened. What depth of pain the Jews have endured!

They need us. They need our friendship, our love, our support, our understanding. Their pain is enormous. Church of Jesus, let's be the home base of Jewish blessing. Stan Kellner, a good friend of mine, is a believer who is Jewish. Stan has shared the gospel with his people for about twenty-five years. Here are some practical pointers from this experienced veteran of Jewish outreach:

- Not every Jew is an Old Testament scholar.
- Not every Jew is observant. Define scriptural terms for Jews, such as sin, salvation, and eternal life.
- Portions of church history have contributed to "gentilizing" the church. Help your Jewish friends understand that they are made complete in the Messiah.
- Use Scripture with your Jewish friends. God's Word will always make an impact on them.

Share with Sensitivity

The last thing we believers need to do is try to coerce a Jewish person with a tract containing the four spiritual laws. They don't need us to rush them. Listen to their objections. There are reasons why they haven't received Jesus as their Messiah. These reasons usually are not based on the person of Jesus but rather on the character of His followers. Here are three important hurdles for Jewish people:

1. *"If I become a Christian, then I'm no longer Jewish."* Answer: Becoming a Christian has nothing to do with being a Gentile and forsaking your Jewishness. It is all about a Jewish person embracing the Jewish Messiah.

2. *"How do I know if Jesus fulfilled the Bible's prophecies of the Messiah?"* Answer: A good question and of utmost importance to a Jew. If you are unfamiliar with the prophecies, here are a couple of great chapters loaded with future promises that Jesus fulfilled: Psalm 22, Christ on the cross; and Isaiah 53, the explanation of the cross.

Also, Jesus can be traced all the way through the Psalms. Here are a few prophetical verses in the Psalter and their corresponding verses in the New Testament indicating the prophecies' fulfillment:

Psalm	New Testament	
2:7	Hebrews 1:5–6	The Messiah would be the Son of God.
16:8-10	Luke 24:5–7	He would be resurrected from the dead.
22:1-21	Matthew 26–27	He would agonize on the cross.
34:20	John 19:36–37	His bones would not be broken.
41:9	Luke 22:48	A close friend would betray Him and reject Him thoroughly.
68:18	Ephesians 4:8–10	He would ascend to heaven.
69:21	Matthew 27:48	He would be offered vinegar on the cross.
89:3-4	Luke 1:31–33	He would be a descendant of David.
96:13	1 Thessalonians 1:10	He would return to judge the world.
110:1	Matthew 24:44	He would be the son of David, yet David's Lord.
118:22	1 Peter 2:7–8	He would be rejected by many people but not by God.

This is all good, solid evidence for a seeking Jewish person. In chapter 7 of this book, Jewish commentaries were quoted from trusted rabbinical writing. These can be helpful, too. What's important is to make the discussion into some kind of a spiritual showdown. When a Jewish person asks a question, answer it with a question as Jesus often did. If the question is, "How do I know if Jesus fulfills the Bible's prophecies of the Messiah?" a good question/answer would be, "What do you think about these Scriptures?" Invite the person to read over the verses on his or her own and get back together later.

3. *"What will my family think?"* Answer: (Truthfulness is extremely important here). If your family is the typical Jewish one, they probably won't like it at all. Remember, Jesus said this is a probability. He also said, "The person who loves father or mother more than Me is not worthy of Me" (Matt. 10:37a).

These are tough words, for sure. But in many cases, God uses the child to reach his parents and gently lead them to the Savior.

LET'S REVIEW

1. Start a friendship with a Jewish person and honor that person as Jesus did.

2. Ask forgiveness for past church sins. Assure the person of your friendship and commitment to stand with him and against anti-Semitism in the future.

3. Encourage him by appreciating his spiritual heritage.

4. Share with sensitivity. Look for common ground.

5. Answer his questions. He has good reasons for them. Scripture given to them to read on their own can be a powerful tool. Ask the Holy Spirit to illuminate the Word of Yahweh and open his heart to these words in a new way.

6. At the proper time, give her a chance to receive Yeshua as her personal Savior. When the Holy Spirit convicts her, she will be ready. I have seen this over and over.

Love a Muslim

The majority of Muslims are God-fearing, zealous, committed, and humble and don't hate Americans. I feel as comfortable in the West Bank or the Gaza Strip as I do in Jerusalem. I love these people, and I want you to love them also.

Believers, these people are open to Jesus. We cannot let this moment pass without swift action. But before we talk strategy, let's take a crash course in Islam. Don McCurry is an expert on the subject and has labored in Muslim outreach for more than forty years. His booklet *Now You Can Know What Muslims Believe: A Muslim World Overview* is an excellent primer on Islam. Here are some background essentials to help you deal with Muslims:

Muslim Beliefs and Practices

From Muhammad's teaching and life, a double-edged movement was born: the religious and the political. (Islam makes no distinction between the two.) Religiously, the essence of Islam can be broken into two categories: the beliefs (Iman) and the duties (Din). In reality, there are hundreds of items in the area of beliefs and thousands in the area of practices; but for practical purposes, they are summarized under six articles in each category. These are the distinctives of Islam.

THE BELIEF SYSTEM OF ISLAM (IMAN)

1. *There is one God.* He has no partners (no Trinity). He does not beget (like humans; therefore, God could not have a Son). He is absolutely sovereign, responsible for all that happens (thus making Him the author of evil).

2. *God created angels.* These angels are everywhere. One sits on one's right shoulder recording one's good deeds; another sits on one's left shoulder recording the bad deeds. On judgment day these records are opened and on the basis of them the person is rewarded or punished. Satan was formerly an angel. He was turned into a jinn because he disobeyed God in refusing to worship Adam. Jinn are another order of supernatural beings, supposedly created from fire. They can possess humans.

3. *God appointed prophets for every age.* This line starts with Adam, includes many biblical characters, such as Noah, Abraham, Ishmael, Isaac, Jacob, Joseph, and others like David, Solomon, Jonah, Zechariah (the father of John the Baptist), John the Baptist, Jesus, then a couple of nonbiblical prophets from Arabia, and finally, Muhammad. In this schema, Jesus is only a prophet, and Muhammad is the last and greatest of the prophets, the "Seal of the Prophets."

4. *Holy Books.* Every prophet was given a Holy Book by God. Supposedly there were as many as 124,000 prophets from Adam to Muhammad. Muslims believe that all of these holy books have been lost except the Torah (Law) given to Moses, the Zabur (Psalms) given to David, the Injil (Gospel) given

to Jesus, and of course, the Quran, or Koran (Recitation) given to Muhammad. Muhammad believed each book was preexistent and was sent down to each prophet as needed. Muslims believe the same thing today.

5. *The Day of Judgment.* God will judge the world on the "Day of Doom." Everyone's good deeds will be weighed in a balance scale against his bad deeds. A wonderful, sensuous paradise of gardens, fruit trees, streams, rivers of wine, and black-eyed virgins will be awarded to every man whose good deeds outweigh his bad deeds. A fiery hell is the reward of those whose bad deeds outweigh their good deeds.

6. *The Decrees of God.* Everything is determined by a Sovereign God. He is responsible for everything, including evil. He chooses to lead astray whom He will and to guide aright whom He will. No one can withstand His decree on any point.

THE DUTIES OF ISLAM (DIN)

1. *The Confession of the Creed (Shahadah).* "There is no God but God and Muhammad is the Messenger of God." To say this and mean it makes you a Muslim. If you renounce this faith after once you have made this profession, you are to be put to death.

2. *Ritual Prayer (Salat).* The good Muslim is to say his prayers five times a day: 1) just before daybreak, 2) at noontime, 3) in mid-afternoon, 4) at sunset, and 5) anytime after sunset before going to sleep. This has to be done in Arabic exactly the way Muhammad did it and taught it.

3. *Giving of Alms (Zakat).* Giving one fortieth of your income to the poor or religious causes is mandatory. Voluntary giving (*Sadaqat*) is also encouraged.

4. *Keeping the Thirty-Day Fast (Sawm).* This is done during the lunar month of Ramadan. It comes eleven days earlier every year. It is not a complete fast. You may not eat from just before daybreak until sunset every day. You may eat as much as you want between sunset and sunrise. You are supposed to study the Quran, or Koran, during this month, reading one thirtieth each night.

5. *Going on the Pilgrimage (Hajj)*. This is obligatory, once in a lifetime for all healthy people who can afford it. The pilgrim is to go to Mecca, walk around the "House of God" (the Kaaba) seven times, stone the devil, say his prayers at the "Station of Abraham," drink water from the well of Zamzam (in memory of Hagar and Ishmael), and several other things.

6. *The Duty of Striving in the Way of God (Jihad, Holy War)*. A few Muslims, especially in the West, try to say that this is not a duty. But the Quran or Koran teaches it, Muhammad practiced it, and Muslims have practiced it ever since.

The overall goal of Islam is to conquer the world by any means necessary: war, preaching, economic inducement, or coercion. Since their religion is the "right" religion, and Muhammad was the "last and greatest Prophet" and he taught it, every Muslim is obligated to participate until Islam is the religion of everyone on earth.[4]

Okay, now that you are familiar with the basic beliefs and duties of the religion, let's go on. How do I love a Muslim?

CONFESS YOUR PREJUDICE

One problem we Westerners have with Muslims is that we often stereotype them. I know this from experience. I did it. After I had been to Israel for the first time, I was so Jewish-focused that I wouldn't give Muslims the time of day. I shared the bad news throughout this book about radical Islam. But as you prepare for outreach, remember that most Muslims are very nice, warm people. The chances are slim that they have a bomb under their jacket. They probably don't work for Hamas.

They do need Jesus, however. They will listen to you. If they are traditional and dress like seventh-century Arabs, don't let that throw you. Ask God to give you a love for Muslims. He can give you a passion to reach them. He will tenderize your heart for them. They are about 21 percent of the world's population. Your effort and participation in this world outreach program is vital.

At this point, I must confess the prejudice I had toward not only Muslims but Arabs at one time. Again, my love for Israel seemed to overshadow the needs of the Arab people. I was not driven to them especially. I felt in some way that if I reached out to Arabs or Muslims, I was forsaking Israel.

But you know what? God's love is for all people. Both Jew and Arab. He wants Ishmael's descendants saved too. I have learned that you can love Israel, honor and support the Jews, and still love Arabs too. That's okay with God. Just because I believe Israel has a biblical and historical right to their land doesn't mean I can't also have a desire to reach Arabs with Jesus.

I was in a Denver restaurant years ago when two Arab men walked in. They both had black leather coats on and spoke with heavy Arab accents. All of this Middle East stuff was new to me, and I immediately began to judge them in my mind. *I bet they're terrorists. Maybe they've been planted in America as spies.* (Lots of other real edifying thoughts like these.) Well, wouldn't you know that the two men came and sat right next to me at another table? I began to kind of eavesdrop like Maxwell Smart or Inspector Clouseau. I felt I surely would uncover a sinister plot already underway.

I did learn a lot about them by listening to their conversation. To my horror, I soon realized that these two men were believers! I began to hear them talk about what the Lord was doing here and what the Lord was doing there. Did I ever feel like two cents! *What a jerk you are, Tom! You judged them just because of their race.* Those thoughts ran through my mind.

Then it got worse. I said hello and asked, "Are you guys believers?"

"Yes," they said, "we're believers from Syria. Are you one too?" At that point I felt so bad, I doubted I was a believer myself! I reluctantly said, "Yes, I am." Immediately these brothers told me all about their mission trips into Syria and how dangerous it was for them to share the gospel at home. They also worked in orphanages there. They invited me to go with them next time.

Man, I was feeling worse by the minute! I had judged them. They sure didn't judge me, though. Before I knew it, one of the brothers insisted that I follow him home for coffee and to meet his wife and kids. I went. I had a blast. There is nothing like Arabic hospitality! These people were like long-lost relatives.

I went to missionary training school that afternoon. I learned that as Americans we often carry prejudice toward Arabs and Muslims in general. Get rid of it or you'll go through life and never reach one of them.

BEGIN A FRIENDSHIP

In America, we have Muslims in most major cities. The population is growing, and America has about equal numbers of Muslims as Jews. They enjoy religious freedom here, and that is new to them if they're from the Middle East. When they migrate West, Muslims tend to leave some of their tradition behind. Both women and men often drop the robes and burqas prevalent in Islam-controlled areas. If they do keep their traditional clothes, they probably are somewhat isolated in the United States. They are used to this and often crave friendships. After September 11, Muslims encountered much misunderstanding in our country and underwent public scrutiny. Muslims in traditional garb especially felt the stares of wondering people in public places.

I was shopping in a department store in Denver, and a woman waited on me as I was shopping for my wife. She was Persian and her accent had a familiar tone. I had to ask, "Are you from the Middle East by any chance?"

She said, "Why do you ask?"

I replied, "I travel there quite a bit, and I love Iranian culture. I love the people, the food, and their warmth. I was just curious."

Sensing I was accepting of her, she then answered, "I'm from Iran, but I don't like to tell people that."

I said, "I bet that's hard at times for you. I hope you feel welcome in America."

She said, "Thank you very much!"

This is typical, I think. She wasn't dressed in traditional Muslim clothes, but as we visited a while, I could tell that she was fairly open. She was approachable also after she realized that I appreciated her culture.

Get to know a Muslim family. You'll be surprised. Once you've been in their home and been blessed by their hospitality, you'll have friends for life. We must build bridges with Muslims if we expect to reach them.

ASK QUESTIONS

Muslims love to tell people about their religion. They hope to "set us straight," so they often talk freely about their faith. Dedicated to their religion, they fail to see the huge spiritual gaps that exist within Islam. They are works-motivated. They pray five times a day. They may even read their Koran.

Yet the great spiritual chasm for Muslims is in the area of atonement. Who will pay for their sins? What sacrifice will satisfy God? What happens to their sins? Muslims have no answer to these questions. With their theology of works justification, they have no certainty that they will ever make it to paradise. When it comes to terrorist acts, this is often the motivation behind the violence. The rationale for these crimes is usually to win enough points with Allah to earn salvation. In places where women have become suicide bombers like in Israel, the motivation is usually to erase a serious offense. Women who are divorced bring disgrace to their family, and this is seen as a quick fix to restore their honor.

Muslims struggle with the very same thing that all God-fearing people who don't know Christ struggle with. The question they cannot answer is whether they will have enough good works to outweigh the bad works. Will they be on the positive side of the ledger when they die? Will they build up enough equity in life to earn a place in eternity? We can show them, of course, that ultimately this system breaks down, since even one sin unpaid would exile us from heaven forever.

So after you develop a solid friendship, investigate a little. Nonthreatening questions that are asked gently and not aimed at starting an argument can make them think about things. Here's one: "As Christians, we believe Jesus paid for our sins because we are incapable of doing it ourselves. What do you as a Muslim believe?"

Since Muslims believe Jesus was a prophet, ask what your friend thinks of him. How about this question: "As a Muslim, have you ever wondered what Jesus was all about?" And later, "I'd like to tell you about Him. Would you tell me all about Muhammad?"

If you ask penetrating questions in a spirit of love, the relationship will continue even if he's not yet ready to trust Christ as his Savior. Always remember, do not be condescending. Do not argue.

POWER PRAYING

If we Christians will love Muslims and build friendships with them, the doors will fling wide open for the saving power of Christ. After we have a spiritual dialogue in a calm and affirming atmosphere, the next step is most important. Get on your knees. If we pray for the Muslims we know every day, we would start to see results. God has given the church in America a golden opportunity. Muslims live throughout our country. We can do a lot to erase their notions about Christians in general. Most of all, the Holy Spirit will use the relationship. He will begin to penetrate Muslim souls with your love and concern.

Pray with them also. Muslims usually react positively when you ask them if you can pray for them. Who doesn't need prayer? "Do you have anything I can be praying about for you?" We have tried this in refugee camps in the Gaza Strip with Muslims. They often keep their eyes open because they are curious about Christians who pray with passion. The fruit of the Spirit in our lives is so attractive to them!

Believer, you have power in Christ. Put it to work. Reach out to Muslims. The fields are ripe. Now *that's* a way to engage in missions right here in the United States while getting involved with Israel and the Middle East.

GET GLOBAL

If you've been a Christian for years and find yourself getting complacent, you probably need to be mission challenged. It's easy being a Christian in America. We don't suffer persecution, and we have every kind of Christian resource available for our use. We have more churches than ever in America. Sadly, though, our general church numbers have been stagnant for the last twenty years. We are not growing as we should be. Why is this?

I believe it's because we're not persecuted. We don't have a real possibility of going to jail for being a follower of Jesus Christ. Therefore, we lack a sense of desperation. Since we're not desperate, it affects our prayer lives, and our prayer lives affect everything else. If we're not desperate in our prayers and grappling with God over lost souls, our prayers become shallow and often self-centered. If I don't feel especially moved that my next door neighbor is going to die one day and go to hell, then the bulk of my prayers probably will be filled with "gimmies." "God, I need this." "Can I please have Your help with this one?" In other words, I become totally self-absorbed.

But believer, God expects more from you. Much more. You are a part of the single, biggest rescue project in the history of mankind. God's power is moving across the globe today. Salvations are up—way up. I know we're not seeing it here in America, but trust me, it's happening. That's why it's imperative to get globally connected. If you plug into what God is doing in the world today, you'll not only be able to help believers around the globe, you'll be more intent on it happening in America. Use the Web sites mentioned in chapter 8 to get started.

In a pastors' meeting in Colorado Springs a few years ago, the participants talked about what makes an effective church. A diverse group of Christians—Southern Baptists, Presbyterians, charismatics, and others—these preachers represented churches that were vibrant and growing. They also had at least one other thing in common: a heart for the world. God blesses churches and believers that long for Him to reach this world with His glorious gospel.

Is your church snoozing through the current revival? Here are four ways your church can wake it up.

1. *Get your pastor on a mission trip*. Believe me, he will have the time of his life. There are plenty of great mission groups to go with. At e3 Partners, we offer 200–300 mission campaigns a year. I personally lead at least five per year to Israel and the Middle East. You can get in touch with us at www.e3partners.org. If your pastor can only go once a year, your church will change. Mine did. I say this from experience since I was the senior pastor who was coaxed to go by people within the church. On my first mission trip,

I led more people to Christ in one week than I did in one year back home! That will charge up any pastor.

2. *Pray fervently.* Start a prayer group in your local church. You can do this in a home Bible study or in an adult Bible fellowship class. Use chapter 8 for resources, or if you have a group of missionaries that your church supports, pray for them. Prayer letters are revitalizing to your foreign missionary family. They often feel forgotten on the field. These are heroes of our faith. Your communication will bless them.

3. *Give generously.* After you support your local church, why not give to the local churches outside of America? Their resources are so little that often they have nothing or very little coming in financially. Giving to the work of God in the Gaza Strip, Jerusalem, or Amman, Jordan, for example, is a great investment. These believers make the most of every day and will be faithful with your gifts.

If your church is excited about missions, maybe you can adopt a church, a city, or a region. Right now, ministries are looking for that throughout Israel, Jordan, and Egypt. U.S. churches should give a minimum of 10 percent of their income to missions. Encourage your pastor to begin moving your church's percentage of giving upward toward 20 percent.

4. *Maximize your possessions.* There is no doubt that God has blessed us in the United States. We should not be ashamed of it in any way, but rather be thankful. Yet God is going to hold us believers accountable for how we use our resources. Here is the test to see if all your possessions mean too much to you, to determine if they are controlling you. Would you be willing to give them all away? (Would I?) If God said, "I want you to move to Israel and reach Jews and Arabs for My sake," would you do it?

Maybe God is calling you to downsize. My wife and I are in the process of doing just that. It's tough with six children, but we know this is what God wants for us now. Pay off those credit cards, and even if you sent a small portion of that to the front lines, it would make a huge difference.

Catch the Wave

I believe, in America, we are experiencing the second wave of missions. Initially, as God raised up America, we fulfilled a strategic role that no other country could have. We were and are today, without a doubt, the primary force behind world evangelization. We in America send more people, more money, and more resources to the mission field than any other nation. We are privileged to do so. The majority of mission agencies are from the United States. The world's two largest mission organizations are American—Campus Crusade and Southern Baptists have thousands of missionaries on the field each year.

But during world evangelization, something happened along the way with the American church. It peaked, and its growth began to slow considerably. I know many churches in the United States are reaching the lost and are in the midst of their own growth spurt. But overall, the outreach of U.S. churches has been flat for two decades now.

I believe that we now need to learn from the church in the mission field. They have only a fraction of what we have in America as far as opportunities for training, resources, and funding. Yet they are more effective than we are.

That's where the wave comes in. The first wave went out from America, and its evangelistic splash covered the world. Now the churches in the mission field are sending a wave back toward us in the United States. Their zeal and simplicity is pointing us American believers back to our spiritual roots. A much simpler church is where I believe we're headed in the West. Prayer, fasting, evangelism, discipleship, Bible study, and the spiritual disciplines are all major components of the mission field church. Those basics are what American churches need today. We must aim at excellence while staying true to the essentials of our faith. We don't have to aim at sophistication. We do have to be passionate about everything we do for Christ, though. That's what we can learn from churches in other parts of the world.

They are effective, unpretentious, focused, and have a great amount of passion. Desperation combined with all-out passion is powerful. Bring these characteristics back to America in our day, we pray, O Lord!

Two Nations under God

Why should America care about Israel? Because we have often been the sole friend of the nation of Israel. God has lavished rich blessings on our country as a result of our honoring His people Israel. His promise to bless those who bless them and to curse those who curse them still affects the destiny of nations today. America is no different and will pay a very high price if we ever turn our backs on Israel. It will be our greatest national disaster.

Judaic, Christian, and Islamic roots run centuries deep in Israel and even more so in Jerusalem, the spiritual capital of the world. Religion, politics, culture, and history have all had a head-on collision in the Holy City of God. But none of these disciplines, either individually or corporately, have any chance of solving the region's conflict. They just don't have the right solutions to defuse the powder keg that is already lit. Since the problems are spiritual in essence, sorting out the Middle East maze demands spiritual answers if anything is to be resolved.

Satan is using radical Islam to stir up as much Jewish resistance as he can worldwide. But in Exodus 34:24, the God of Israel promised, "I will drive out nations before you and enlarge your territory. No one will covet your land when you go up three times a year to appear before the LORD your God." Israel enjoyed life in the land for a time. Amazingly, there were three land components given to the nation of Israel. Satan is desperately trying to undo all three of them today.

Exodus 34:24	*Today*
I will drive out the nations from the land.	Nations are now trying to drive Israel out of the land.
I will enlarge your territory.	Israel's territory is now shrinking.
No one will covet your land.	The entire world covets the land of Israel.

The answer to the Middle East puzzle is Jesus and His church. Israel needs to turn to her Savior. The church should be Israel's best friend. Scripture promises that Israel will one day repent and embrace Jesus as Messiah. We can and should be the people who help move the Jews in that direction. The church is called to influence Israel.

Because we support Israel does not mean Palestinians are out in the cold. The church is the answer to their problems also. Radical Islam will not deliver what it promises to the Palestinian people. It will continue to make guarantees that it has no capacity to make good on. Palestinians need to dump their leadership that is driven by fanatical Islamic dreams, such as the destruction of Israel.

We must support the awesome Palestinian believers who are making a major impact in the world of Islam. They are powerhouses for God. Palestinian believers and messianic believers are experiencing true reconciliation in the midst of the volatile land of Israel. Jesus and His church are proving to be the only answer to centuries of war and conflict. God's love is for all people. Palestinians desperately need to be assured of the American church's support, too.

The moment to maximize our impact is now. The mission heart of God is bringing about a revival in Israel and in the Middle East. You are needed for strategic intercession. God is using the growing intensive prayer movement focused on Israel and also the Middle East. As followers of Jesus in the Western church, our involvement is the biblical heartland. In doing so, God also wants to wake up the church in the United States. He wants both Israel and America to have a vibrant church today. It is the real hope of both nations, America and Israel, who are called to be two nations under God.

ACKNOWLEDGMENTS

Thank you to the following people who made vital contributions to *Two Nations under God*.

MOM AND DAD DOYLE for your love, encouragement, and prayers. I am so blessed to have you as my parents. You are a gift from God to me.

MY SISTERS TERRY AND MARY for being wonderful and for being two of my most favorite people in the world.

MOM RENDA for loving me like a son and for your help with research.

THE DOYLE, RENDA, CRISPELL, BELL, AND MERRITT FAMILIES because of your continual love and encouragement.

GINGER BROMLEY for your servant's heart, joyful attitude, and lightning fast typing.

CURTIS HAIL AND THE e3 PARTNERS TEAM for your passion to reach the world for Christ.

THE B&H TEAM of David Shepherd, John Thompson, Lawrence Kimbrough, Jeff Godby, Paul Mikos, Jean Eckenrode and many others. You have been such a blessing to work with.

OUR PRAYER AND SUPPORT TEAM. Thank you for investing in God's great work in the Middle East.

We love you all, and to God be all the glory!
Tom and JoAnn Doyle

SPECIAL THANKS FOR THE GREAT PICTURES TO:

RUSSELL BROWN

ANNA BROWN

ALLEN REEDALL

JARRELL PRINCE

JAN RICHEY

TOM LAMPHERE

HELEN TONGAI

RHONDA MARTIN

ERIC AXLEY

NAWAZ LALANI

LISA LALANI

JULIA SCHATZ

DARRELL BEVELHYMER

LINDA SIMS

TOM KIRK

DAN HITZHUSEN

Notes

Chapter 1: Extreme Spirituality

1. Dore Gold, *The Fight For Jerusalem* (Washington, D.C.: Regnery Publishing, Inc., 2007), 7.

2. Ehud Avriel, *Open the Gates! A Personal Story of "Illegal" Immigration to Israel* (New York: Altheneum, 1975), vi.

Chapter 2: Endangered Species

1. F.F. Bruce, *Israel and the Nations* (Downers Grove, Ill.: InterVarsity Press, 1997), introduction.

2. Ibid.

3. H. Wayne House, *Israel: The Land and the People* (Grand Rapids, Mich.: Kregel, 1998), 27.

4. Ibid, 28.

5. Avriel, *Open the Gates!*, 190.

6. Charles Feinberg, *Israel at the Center of History and Revelation* (Portland, Ore.: Multnomah, 1964), 135.

Chapter 3: A Promise That Shaped America

1. "United States Literature," *Encyclopedia Judaica*, vol. 15 (Jerusalem: Kregel, 1971), 1571.

2. Ibid.

3. Ibid.

4. Ibid.

5. Ibid., s.v. "United States of America; Anti-Semitism, 1654."

6. Joshua Brandt, "Voices from Doomed *St. Louis* Haunt Researcher," *Jewish Bulletin of Northern California* (Oct. 8, 1999).

7. John Cornwell, *Hitler's Pope: The Secret History of Pope Pius XII* (New York: Penguin, 1999), 80.

NOTES

8. Erwin L. Lutzer, *Hitler's Cross* (Chicago: Moody, 1995), 102.

9. Ibid, 146.

10. Ibid, 147–148.

11. Ibid.

12. Ibid.

13. Larry Collins and Dominique Lapierre, *O Jerusalem* (New York: Simon and Schuster, 1972), 28.

14. Ibid., 27.

Chapter 4: Dangerous Alliances

1. Tim Dowley, *Eerdman's Handbook to the History of Christianity* (Grand Rapids, Mich.: Eerdmans, 1977), 269–270.

2. Amotz Asa-El, *Spectacular Israel*, ed. Shai Ginott (Hugh Lauter Lewin Associates, 1998), 14.

3. Mark Gabriel, *Islam and Terrorism* (Lake Mary, Fla.: Charisma House, 2002), 81–82.

4. David Dolan, *Israel in Crisis* (Grand Rapids, Mich.: Revell, 2001), 94.

5. "Arab Antisemitism Documentation Project," Middle East Media Research Institute (May 2003), Special Dispatch Series No. 446.

6. Mark Gabriel, *Islam and the Jews: The Unfinished Battle* (Lake Mary, Fla.: Charisma House, 2003), 92.

7. Dolan, *Israel in Crisis*, 96–97.

8. Don McCurry, *Now You Can Know What Muslims Believe: A Muslim World Overview* (Colorado Springs, Colo.: Ministries to Muslims, 2001), 15.

Chapter 5: Heroes of Our Faith

1. Benjamin R. Barber, *Jihad vs. McWorld: How Globalism and Tribalism Are Reshaping the World* (Great Britain: Corgi Books, 2003), xxvii.

2. Ibid., xxvviii.

3. "Why a Magazine? Why Kivun?", *Kivun*, ed. Tsvi Sadan (June, 2003), 2.

4. Brother Andrew, *The Calling* (Nashville, Tenn.: Moorings, 1996), 224.

Chapter 6: The Believer, The American

1. Randall Price, *In Search of Temple Treasures* (Eugene Ore.: Harvest House, 1994), 77.

2. "Israel Today," *Daily Headline News and Updates*, Staff Writer (Oct. 25, 2007).

3. *The Jerusalem Post*, Special Supplement (February 21, 2003), 2.

4. *Voice of the Martyrs* (Bartlesville, Okla., May 2003), 6–7.

5. Ibid.

6. Baruch Maoz, "A Faithful Witness in Israel," *Banner of Truth* (Carlisle, Pa.: Banner of Truth), June 21, 2003.

Chapter 7: The Mission Heart of God

1. Hussein Sumaida with Carole Jerome, *Circle of Fear: My Life as an Israeli and Iraqi Spy* (London and Washington, D.C.: Brassey's, 1991), 40.

2. Steve Herzog, *Jewish Culture and Customs* (Bellmawr, N.J.: Friends of Israel Gospel Ministry, 1997), 57.

3. House, *Israel the Lane and the People*, 274.

4. Thomas Cahill, *The Gifts of the Jews: How a Tribe of Desert Nomads Changed the Way Everyone Thinks and Feels* (New York: Anchor Books, 1998), 3-4.

5. John Hagee, *Final Dawn over Israel* (Nashville, Tenn.: Thomas Nelson, 1998), 3–4.

6. David Dolan, *Israel at the Crossroads* (Grand Rapids, Mich.: Revell, 1991), 34–35.

7. Theodore R. W. Lunt, *The Story of Islam* (London Church Missionary Society, 1909), 36.

8. Abd El Schafi, "Behind the Veil" (Colorado Springs, Colo.: Voice of Truth Press, 1996), 77–124.

9. Don McCurry, *Healing the Broken Family of Abraham* (Colorado Springs, Colo.: Ministries to Muslims, 2001), 277–79.

10. Ibid., 177-78.

Chapter 8: Global Praying That Is Truly Biblical

1. John Hagee, *The Battle For Jerusalem* (Nashville, Tenn.: Thomas Nelson, 2001), 55–56.
2. Don Richardson, *The Secrets of the Koran* (Ventura, Calif.: Regal Books, 2003), 162–74.
3. Ibid., 170.
4. Lonnie C. Mings, "Hamas Road Map to Violence," *Watchman's Prayer Letter* (July 2003), 1.

Chapter 9: Waking Up the Western Church

1. Gabriel, *Islam and Terrorism*, 35.
2. Ibid., 35-36.
3. Ibid, 83-84.
4. Don McCurry, *Now You Can Know What Muslims Believe*, 2–4.